DANCE
COMPOSITION
& PRODUCTION

SECOND
EDITION

Elizabeth R. Hayes

Dance

Composition

& Production

SECOND EDITION

"The woods would be very silent
if no birds sang except
those that sang the best."

Dance

Composition

& Production

SECOND EDITION

Elizabeth R. Hayes

A Dance Horizons Book
Princeton Book Company, Publishers
Pennington, NJ

A Dance Horizons Book
Princeton Book Company, Publishers
P.O. Box 57
Pennington, NJ 08534

Cover and interior design by Anne O'Donnell

Library of Congress Cataloging-in-Publication Data

Hayes, Elizabeth R., 1911–
    Dance composition and production / Elizabeth R. Hayes—2nd ed.
        p.   cm.
    Rev. ed. of: Dance composition and production for high schools and colleges. 1955.
    "A Dance Horizons book."
    Includes bibliographical references and index.
    ISBN 0-87127-188-5
    1. Dance production—Study and teaching. 2. Choreography—Study and teaching. I. Hayes, Elizabeth R., 1911– Dance composition and production for high schools and colleges. II. Title. GV1782.H39 1993
792.8'4—dc20
                                                            93-8558

Contents

Selection of Program Material
Program Arrangement
Auditions
Rehearsals and Performance
Preliminary Showings

Chapter 10
Music for Choreography 149

Collaborating with a Composer
Accompaniment Derived from the Dance Movement
Creating One's Own Score
Accompaniment Derived from Existing Musical Forms
Technical Concerns
Basic Music Resources

Chapter 11
Designing the Costumes 171

Costume Shape and Line
Costume Color
Costume Texture and Fabric
Creating the Design
Building a Basic Wardrobe
Hair Styling and Makeup
Conclusion

Chapter 12
Constructing the Costumes 187

Modifying the Basic Leotard and Tights
Pattern Making, Cutting, Fitting, and Sewing
Costume Dyeing
Making Masks and Headdresses
Foot Gear
Costume Organization and Final Check
Working with a Costumer

Chapter 13
Lighting the Dance 205

Stage Lighting Instruments
Illuminating the Dance Movement
Use of Colored Lights
Collaboration Between Chorcographer and Lighting Designer

List of Illustrations

Preface to the Second Edition

Anyone who attempts to put into writing the methods for teaching or stimulating creative activity immediately places himself in a vulnerable position.* Teaching in any field of endeavor is or should be creatively conceived even when the subject matter is factual. Therefore, it is doubly essential that methods for teaching dance composition, the substance of which is inherently creative, should not be allowed to become stereotyped. The purpose of this book is not to delineate formulas whereby successful teaching of composition will be assured to its adherents. Rather, the book is intended to help the inexperienced teacher understand his function as the catalytic agent who sets into motion the creative faculties of students. In addition, it offers suggestions to stimulate compositional endeavors that have been used successfully by teachers of contemporary dance. The beginning teacher may find it helpful to follow such procedures literally at first; however, it is hoped that as he grows in experience, these suggestions will encourage him to discover his own methods of motivating student composition.

The book is intended to be a stimulus to creative teaching rather than a crutch that might deter the development of independent thought and ingenuity. Specific examples of dance studies or of dances that have been created as a result of these various teaching procedures have, for the most part, been purposely omitted. Not only are such examples difficult to present adequately in writing, but such materials are apt to be misused by teachers who are searching for dance routines rather than for methods of stimulating student creativity.

This book has been designed primarily to help the teacher who has an understanding of and background in dance technique but who needs assistance in effecting a transition from the teaching of technique to the teaching of composition. Experienced teachers may not be in immediate need of such assistance, yet the author hopes that these materials include ideas for the teaching of composition that will be helpful to them.

---

*The terms "he," "himself," and "his" appearing throughout this book are used in a generic sense rather than as a representation of gender.

Most of this source material deals with the composition of dance studies rather than with the creation of fully developed dances. Such studies are intended especially for students who are still in the exploratory phase of their artistic development and who can profit from isolating certain elements affecting movement for compositional experimentation. Selection of the particular studies to be used in class activities must be made on the basis of individual and group needs.

The author believes that any attempt to design a specific program of guidance for students who have progressed to the art level of dance composition is inappropriate. Individuals who are naturally creative choreographically need little artificial motivation; they need merely the opportunity and the freedom to work according to their own devices. The instructor can, however, share with these students the understanding of compositional form which he has gained through added years of experience.

Although the book is intended particularly to meet the needs of teachers of dance at the high school and college levels, the basic philosophy and concept of the teaching of composition can be adapted for other age levels. The principal differences in the teaching procedures for different age groups are only those of emphasis.

Many of the approaches to composition presented here are not new; they have been compiled from numerous sources. It is difficult to give credit to any one individual because, in many instances, the same or similar procedures have been independently conceived and practiced by many different people. The author wishes, however, to give special acknowledgment to the late Margaret H'Doubler of the University of Wisconsin, to Martha Hill of Juilliard School of Music, and to the late Hanya Holm, to whom she is indebted for many of the ideas contained in these chapters.

The composition of dance intended for theater presentation invariably encompasses such additional considerations as accompaniment, costuming, staging, lighting, and the use of program notes. In a unified work all of these factors interact in such a way that they cannot be divorced from one another without altering or reducing the total choreographic impression.

Considerable attention has been devoted to the relationship to dance of music and other forms of accompaniment, because this has often been a major concern to both teachers and student composers. The author has purposely employed musical terminology in the chapter that deals with musical accompaniment, in order to make this material also understandable to the musician whose job it is to compose or to improvise for dance. Suggestions for accompaniment have been made particularly with reference to music for beginning choreographers. For advanced dancers and choreographers, the possibilities for differences in treatment of accompaniment are greatly increased, and the choice of particular form and style of accompaniment must rest with the composing artists.

The author is grateful to Maurine Dewsnup, former composer and accompanist for the Modern Dance Department at the University of Utah, for her help and suggestions in writing the original chapter in the first edition, Music and Percussion Accompaniment. The music fragments illustrating different types of piano accompaniment for dance are hers. The writer also wishes to acknowledge with gratitude the considerable contributions of Jon Scoville, current music director for the University of Utah Modern Dance Department and codirector of the Tandy Beal Dance Company, for authoring an update and expansion of the chapter now entitled Music for Choreography.

Emphasis has also been given to discussion of design and construction of dance costumes because this task often falls to the choreographers or the dancers themselves when funding for professional assistance is not available. Special appreciation is due to Ariel Ballif, formerly of the Department of Drama at Yale University and more recently director of Theater 138 in Salt Lake City, for valuable suggestions on costume construction, and to Linda Phillips, former costumer for dance at the University of Utah, for advice in regard to working with a professional costumer.

Because choreographers are seldom expected to hang their own lights, the chapter on lighting focuses largely on how special lighting effects can be achieved and how choreographers can communicate their specific needs to a lighting director. Kenneth White, former stage manager and lighting director for University of Utah Modern Dance, was a coauthor of this chapter. Although post-modern choreographers, in general, have chosen not to follow compositional premises and procedures advanced in this text, it is important to include a discussion of their approaches to choreography. This material has been included in an addendum.

As dance programs in high schools, colleges, and universities have been expanded to include a variety of dance styles and choreographic events, it also seems advisable to address compositional considerations unique to these areas. It is hoped that the second chapter of the Addenda will provide assistance to teachers and students faced with these special choreographic responsibilities. The author wishes to thank Janet Gray, teacher of jazz dance at the University of Utah, for graciously providing helpful information and assistance in presenting the material dealing with choreography for ballet and jazz dance.

Special mention should be made of Margaret Jones, who helped with the editing, and again of the late Margaret H'Doubler, who contributed many hours of her time to the discussion and criticism of the first edition's manuscript. Others who have given valued assistance in the writing of this second edition are Marcia Lloyd, who provided the author with helpful resource materials, and Abby Fiat, Susan McLain-Smith, Mark Borchelt, Gladys Ballif, and Sybil Huskey, who read and critiqued portions of the new material.

The original illustrations in the book were jointly created by Ann Matthews and the author. The drawings for the final plates represent the talented work of Mrs. Matthews.

Without the help of these many generous friends and colleagues, this book would not have been possible.

Elizabeth R. Hayes

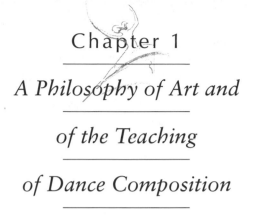

Chapter 1

A Philosophy of Art and

of the Teaching

of Dance Composition

Art expression, like form created by a shifting kaleidoscope, is forever changing, forever new. The myriad of geometric designs that one sees in the kaleidoscope are all made from the same elements, variously shaped pieces of colored glass, but as the relationships of these colored objects to each other are changed, new forms ensue. Although all forms of art are derived from materials inherent in human experience, each work of art varies according to the particular patterning of these materials. As is the case in the kaleidoscope, the possibilities for structural variation are incalculable.

In art, however, an additional variable factor lies in the substance of *individual* human experience. No two persons undergo exactly the same experiences. Not only do the events or circumstances in their lives vary, but even when individuals are subjected to similar experiences, their perceptions of these experiences differ according to the fabric of their particular backgrounds and personalities.

When the substance of these perceptions is again objectified in artistic expression, another transformation of the material takes place. Art expression is never simply an arrangement or a rearrangement of elements selected from human experience; it is also a refinement, abstraction, and intensification of these elements according to the artist's own expressional intentions. Hence, both the selection of artistic substance and the development of expressive form are matters of individual conception; they cannot be governed entirely by detached preestablished rules. There is no objective formula for the creation of a work of art which, if followed meticulously, will guarantee to produce satisfying results. Neither the materials of art nor the creative process can be set down in recipe fashion as one might describe the ingredients and procedure for baking bread. Art is an individual distillation and objective expression of subjective experience.

According to the concept of artistic expression as set forth by John Dewey,[1] aesthetic form resides within the substance of an art; likewise the substance is affected and transmuted by the evolution of its outward form. Although certain principles can assist the composer in evolving art form that satisfies his expressive needs, form in any composition must, basically, arise out of the artist's motivating idea or emotion, perceived in the light of his background of experience and modified by the physical laws governing his art medium.

The Educative Role of the Dance Teacher

In a consideration of dance as an expressive art in education, the problem of defining the teacher's exact role arises. What sort of compositional guidance can he give to the student? How much assistance can he offer without trespassing upon the student's legitimate rights and responsibilities as a choreographer? His realization that the substance of dance expression must stem from individual experience and his conviction that choreographic form should develop from this substance (or content) impose severe limitations upon the teacher's directive function. He cannot tell the dancer *what* or *how* to compose. On the other hand, he can assist the student by acquainting him with his art instrument—his body—and with his art medium; he can show the student how to control the movement of his body so that it will respond efficiently to his expressional needs. In addition, the student can be taught guiding principles of art form which may assist him in composing and in judging his artistic efforts; and he can be exposed to as great a variety of effective creative stimuli as possible, to enlarge his experience and vision as to the expressive potentialities of his art medium.

Content Versus Form

In the guidance of choreographic effort it is of utmost importance to keep clearly in mind the fact that aesthetic content, or substance, and artistic form are interdependent and inseparable. "In a work of art they do not offer themselves as two distinct things; the work is formed matter."[2] Creative art expression is not merely the externalization of a full-blown idea; it is characterized by change and growth. During the creative process, the motivating idea and the gradually evolving expression of it continually interact with and transform each other. Unfortunately misconceptions have occasionally arisen concerning the possibility of emphasizing one of these considerations to the exclusion of the other. At one extreme is the school of thought supporting the theory that externalization of emotion is the only essential consideration in art, discredit-

---

[1] John Dewey, *Art as Experience*, pp. 106–133.
[2] *Ibid.*, p. 114.

ing any necessity for a regard for form. It is from such an erroneous conception that the ill-advised practice of requesting inexperienced students to "dance what the music makes you feel" or simply to "express yourself" has stemmed. Bewildered neophytes without adequate technical resources are thereby placed in the precarious situation of having to jump into deep water before they have learned to swim. The naturally gifted student may have the power to recover himself unscathed; but the student with only average creative ability is apt to suffer the torments of feeling hopelessly inadequate and socially undone, an experience from which he may never fully recover. Even when the dancer has sufficient confidence to be able to allow his emotions to take over, the resulting effect is likely to be somewhat nebulous. Unless the emotional substance of the dance is perceived by the composer with an intensity sufficient to enable him to devise a choreographic form that is suitable to the content, the composition will fall short of its artistic mark.

At the other hypothetical extreme are those teachers for whom the superficial considerations of movement technique and choreographic construction are paramount, and any motivating dance idea is allowed to become completely secondary and is often forgotten entirely. For such individuals, interest in the superficial appearance of movement supplants awareness of movement sensation, the root of choreographic expression. Overstress on *movement technique* tends to develop dancers who can exhibit superior mechanical control without having gained an understanding of how to use that technique for expressional purposes. Instead of becoming dancers in an art sense, they are mere gymnasts, animated automatons who are highly skilled in following directions. Likewise, undue stress upon *compositional structure* in terms of itself, independent of any underlying emotional or intellectual motivation, is likely to produce form that is functionless as art, that is expressively barren.

The attempt to pigeonhole the study of movement technique and that of compositional expression as two isolated and completely unrelated phases of dance also contributes to artistic sterility. When used in this way, technique is bereft of its function as a tool of expression and composition is placed on a metaphorical pedestal, removed from the experience of the average individual and reserved for the talents of the minority. Such complete separation of technique and choreography is particularly undesirable in the field of dance education, which is not concerned primarily with developing specialized performers and choreographers in a professional sense. Realization of the fact that technique and composition are functionally related to one another should help to bridge the abyss that often exists between the teaching of dance technique and the development of creative expression. This understanding should serve to remind those individuals who are absorbed in a frantic struggle to develop skilled technicians that technique in art is not an end in itself. The realization of this relationship should also point the way toward the formulation of practical methods whereby awareness of potential content may be achieved through the experiencing of technique, and whereby interest in technique and compositional form can be motivated by the realization of a need for developing an adequate means of expression.

Upon analysis, one finds that the process involved in the creation of art is identical to that inherent in any type of problem solving. But composition as a creative act may vary widely in the degree of its complexity. According to the definition by Webster, composition is "the act of forming a whole by placing together and uniting different things, parts, or ingredients." Thus a child who selects two blocks and places one on top of the other is experimenting within the bounds of composition. Movement is the building material of which a dance composition is constructed. The term "dance composition," however, if used in the sense of art expression, requires more of the composer than putting together a series of movements to form a unit. Dance, as art, necessitates a selection and transformation of compositional material through reflection and aesthetic evaluation. Dance as fine art demands of the composer both an intensity of emotional feeling and perception and a high degree of sensitivity to and control of his art medium. It is toward these objectives that the student composer needs to direct his endeavor. There is much to be experienced and much to be understood, however, before integrated artistic achievement can be attained. The novitiate will need to begin with simple elements of movement technique and simple problems in composition. Class activities should provide the opportunity for these experiences.

Ideally, the teaching of technique in art should grow out of a felt need for an adequate means of expression; but it is also true that an individual can express himself only in a medium that he understands. It is therefore essential for the young artist first to familiarize himself with his art medium in order to be able to foresee its expressive possibilities. The sculptor, for example, must sensitize his fingers to the texture and adaptability of the clay or stone with which he intends to work in order that he may visualize the artistic potentialities that lie within its scope. Likewise the dancer must know movement for its own sake—that is, he must be aware of movement sensations and of their associative meanings—so that he can use it intelligently as a means of expression. He must acquire through teacher guidance some conception of the infinitude of movement variations and combinations that are possible and that will provide a basis for making his own creative selections.

The practice of teaching dance routines or set movement sequences through imitative procedures robs the student of the creative experience he needs. Such teaching has a limited value in training a student to develop his powers of visual observation and of muscular coordination; if overused, it may endanger the development of his artistic perception and creativity. Although it is frequently regarded as a short cut to technical proficiency, rote learning of movement technique usually denies the student the time and the necessary incentive to analyze movement, either literally or in terms of its psychophysical meanings. Actually imitative teaching is the "long way around" to expressive composition. Choreography evolved from such teaching procedures is likely to be so encumbered with stereotyped movement phrases that it exhibits no more originality than a form letter. The learning of technique should be as creative an experience for the student as the eventual act of composing a dance; it is merely the initial step in the process of expressing an idea. If the student's latent creative powers are to be developed to their fullest, the teaching of technique must be primarily through directed discovery, coupled with a development of kinesthetic perception and culminating in experimental composition that tests the communicative values of these movement forms.

The teacher of dance is concerned not merely with the presentation of subject material. He is also concerned with the students as individuals who have varying personalities and who are at different stages in their artistic development. Age differences affect the interests and psychological responses of students, as any educator knows. But responses are also affected by the students' various levels of artistic maturity.

> The growing artist, like the developing race, passes through progressive levels of artistic achievement. Such a progression may be traced in the evolution of dance. . . .[3] The dancer's growth evolves from dancing for the sheer joy of sensing movement, to the seeking of form and mastery of technique, to dance as the expression and communication of sensory experience, emotion, and creative imagination. . . . In order to lay the background for the next stage, so that one stage may develop normally from the next, we must provide the proper nourishment for every level of growth.[4]

Motivation of Creative Dance Expression

The unrepressed imagination of a young child permits him to plunge self-confidently into unexplored realms of creative endeavor. With maturity, however, he develops an awareness of his technical inadequacies; this awareness, along with the acquisition of exacting standards of artistic

[3] Margaret N. H'Doubler, *Dance: A Creative Art Experience*, p. 103.
[4] *Ibid.*, p. 107.

performance and a fear of appearing ridiculous in the eyes of his class-mates, are tremendously inhibiting factors. A teacher who is working with adults or with adolescents therefore will do well to see that initial excursions into the realm of compositional endeavor are unpretentious ones and that the students have a sufficient movement vocabulary to ful-fill in a modest way their compositional aspirations.

The student must be assured at least a modicum of success in his efforts to solve creative problems, if feelings of inferiority and frustration are not to be the end product of such endeavor. Perhaps, at the begin-ning, student effort might be focused merely on discovering a single new movement that is the organic outgrowth of a movement the student knows already. When the compositional demands of the problem are small, the idea of "creating" does not seem so overwhelming. Given a simple task, the young composer rises to the challenge; he feels less inad-equacy at the thought of expressing himself than potential embarrass-ment at the possibility of admitting defeat. A well-defined problem with an objective approach causes the beginner to concentrate his attention on its solution, and usually he soon forgets to think of how foolish he expected to feel. Group interest becomes that of evaluating movement impersonally, in terms of its expressive qualities, rather than of critically judging individual performers. Thus the initial battle with self-con-sciousness is often won. As the young dancer's understanding of his medium develops, he gradually loses his inhibitions and commences to feel the deep satisfaction that comes with the discovery of a new channel of creative expression.

The primary function of the *compositional study* is experimental; its chief purpose is to teach rather than to communicate or to entertain. A dance study is comparable to an exercise in musical harmony and counterpoint or to a problem in graphic design. Its scope is arbitrarily limited in order that the student, by concentrating his attention on a sin-gle phase of composition, may thoroughly explore its possibilities for creative use. Its place is in the compositional laboratory where it may serve to climax the study of technique or provide learning experiences for students of elementary dance composition.

Compositional problems are valuable for training the student to handle his art medium creatively and for helping h;m to discover new choreographic structure; they may also function as illustrative devices in the presentation of educational dance programs. The results of such studies are often fragmentary in nature and may be rather far removed from any emotional origin because young dancers are usually deeply involved with solving the technical requirements of the choreographic problems. Therefore, compositional studies should not be confused with the *composition of dances,* which are the direct result of a desire to objectify and communicate some significant inner experience. Frequently, however, the creation of a compositional study fires the dancer's imagination beyond the strict requirements of the immediate problem and from that source a dance, as such, is evolved.

Most beginners obtain more enjoyment from composing in groups than from composing individually. With several people contributing their efforts to the composition, there is an exchange of ideas that is especially valuable in these early stages. There is also the social satisfaction of group cooperation, and no individual feels himself isolated and conspicuous. Thus for the timid and inexperienced, group composition provides a highly satisfactory approach. In general, small or medium-sized groups (five to seven people) work together most efficiently. Large groups tend to become unwieldy, since more minds must be brought to a common understanding and more people must be considered in the choreography.

On the other hand, individual composition or group composition directed by a single choreographer is also extremely valuable for the creative initiative that it develops. If the compositional demands are not beyond the level of the student's experience, he will not feel ill at ease at having to depend upon his own resourcefulness. Only when a dancer is in a position to act as choreographer, whether for his own performance or for that of a group, is he able to test completely his compositional powers.

Composition resulting from group planning (especially when the group is composed of individuals who are rich in choreographic ideas) seldom achieves the unity and clarity of a dance or study that has been directed by one person. In any group there are bound to be differences in point of view, and the compromise that results from interchange of thought is likely to be a composite of several compositional schemes. However, on those occasional instances in which several minds can be made to act as one in the production of an art form, the variety of intellectual and emotional experiences contributed to the idea may result in a broadened artistic perception, which is evidenced in increased significance of art expression. The instructor must use his own judgment in deciding upon the type of class organization that will best serve his students in their particular levels of development.

The Teacher as a Dance Critic

The teacher can assist the student materially in his development of a healthy emotional attitude toward creative activity by being sensitive to his occasional moments of discouragement, and by understanding his shortcomings. Constructive rather than negative criticism can do much to help and encourage the beginner who frequently lacks faith in himself. The cynic would argue that the dancer whose artistic drive cannot withstand adverse criticism is not worthy of encouragement. But the educator must constantly remember that his concern is not alone to discover and develop the creative genius whose artistic fire is only quickened by the taunts of critics; his responsibility is also to help the modest layman find an outlet for his creative powers, regardless of their apparent limitations, and to enlarge his scope of appreciation. In so doing, the educator will contribute to the ranks of those who enjoy and understand artistic expression in its greatest forms.

The teacher's function is to guide the student through the uncharted and often bewildering labyrinth of compositional endeavor by offering leading suggestions that will open vistas to new creative horizons for the young composer's own flights of thought. His function is to assist the student in developing a maturity both of expression and of idea. For the artist-teacher whose own compositional powers are highly developed, it is sometimes difficult to resist the temptation to reconstruct a student composition in the likeness of his own art image. Nothing will crush the creative spirit more quickly than dictatorialism in art.

The teacher must constantly readjust his thought processes to the art level of the students. In offering critical advice, he will need to remind himself continually that the inexperienced student cannot learn everything at once. It will be necessary to decide what particular compositional principles are to be taught first and to relegate other considerations to the background.

Although the beginner needs encouragement to give him fortitude to help him conquer his own misgivings, the teacher should never allow his praise to become like an actor's claque, indiscriminate and unintelligent. Vapid flattery serves only to develop in the student a cynical attitude toward the values of criticism, for it in no way assists him; rather, it encourages him to be content with his own unfertile plateau of learning. It is unfortunate that frequently such blanket terms as "interesting," "nice," or "good," are bandied about in place of helpful criticism. It is true, of course, that there is almost always something that is good or interesting in any composition. Those particular features should be discovered, commented on, and praised in the light of their special contributions, but wholesale commendation is valueless for its very lack of any comparative standard for judgment.

What the student really needs is someone to examine his work thoughtfully with him and, in the light of the student's expressive intentions, to help him discover in what instances he has been successful and where his composition has failed. In addition, the student should understand the reasons for these outcomes if the experience is to have any learning value for future reference.

Conclusion

If a teacher of dance composition is to achieve his educational objectives, he must, first of all, be honestly and sympathetically interested in helping the students. Second, he must have a broad vision with regard to the many avenues of approach to the study of composition, in order that he may give the students the greatest possible variety of learning experiences.

Third, he himself must have a comprehension of the art principles that are basic to good composition and must be able to present them intelligently to others. Finally, in the role of dance critic, he must be able to analyze and interpret to the students their successes and their shortcomings and to show them how to evaluate wisely their own creative products.

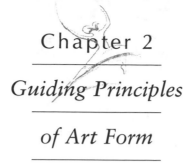

Chapter 2

Guiding Principles

of Art Form

An artist, regardless of the medium he employs, is continually required to make decisions in choosing his ideas, his materials, and his particular methods of execution, and in rejecting that which does not meet his creative needs. All of these decisions are influenced by his purpose or motivating idea and by his own artistic standards of evaluation. While such standards are thought to be intuitively conceived, in reality this artistic intuition has usually been conditioned by an understanding and acceptance of certain art principles that appear to have guided man's efforts since art began. Such principles do not constitute a body of inflexible rules which predetermine art form; they are, rather, factors to be considered in the attainment of aesthetically satisfying composition. Nor are these principles of form applicable exclusively to one art medium of expression. In painting, architecture, literature, music, or dance the same guiding principles point toward the ideal and have done so with varying degrees of consistency down through the ages.

Aesthetic Principles of Form

Unity

The most important and fundamental art principle is that a work of art should have unity. An art object is the end product of a single motivating idea and of a unified form or compositional structure. Furthermore, as stated previously, the form and content of a work of art are not two distinct phases but are one with each other; each influences and transforms the other, producing a single artistic effect. Although a composition may include many sections, in a well-constructed work these parts are knitted together by a unifying thread that is governed by the purpose of the whole. Extraneous material, regardless of its individual value, has no aesthetic justification in a work of art.

The dance composer, therefore, ought first of all to have a very clear conception of his own purpose in creating a dance. With this concept in mind, he should then choose only those movements that will coordinately express that purpose. One should not infer from this statement that each motion needs to have pantomimic significance; rather, every movement, by its quality, range, direction, and temporal and dynamic structure, should contribute in some way to further revealing and enhancing the central dance theme.

As the movement of a dance is evolved and becomes established, the resulting form may in turn alter the composer's original conception of his motivating idea. Nevertheless, despite these modifications and developments, a unified totality of content-form remains the constant objective toward which all choreographic effort must be directed. Between the various parts of a dance there should be a general agreement or coordination of idea, form, and movement style. In a dance drama or suite consisting of several sections, the composer should be aware of an organic reason for the inclusion and the particular organization of these parts under a single heading. The function of each part of a dance or of a dance suite in relation to the whole must be discernible to the observer if that whole is to present an impression of unity and artistic significance.

Variety

Within this unity, however, a second principle, the need for variety, demands consideration. By varying or altering slightly the inherent content and form of a creative work one discovers new material within the original substance. New values and meanings emerge and new insights are disclosed. Without variety, a composition frequently lacks interest and richness of meaning. The painter may achieve variation through differences in form, in light and shade, and in hue. The dramatist may obtain variety through subtle delineation of his characters. The musician may employ change of key or of harmony, may invert his theme or elaborate on a portion of it. Each artist in his way attempts to give significance to his composition by means of variety in the choice and handling of his building materials.

Movement, as a medium of expression, offers endless possibilities for variation. As the choreographer grows in experience and sensitivity, he is increasingly able to perceive the possibilities for diversity. The inexperienced composer usually tries to maintain compositional interest by introducing too much vaguely related material in his composition without sufficient development of any of it.

As an example, one might imagine a dance pattern consisting of an arm movement that introduces a turn and a change of level, which is followed by a jump and a run forward. The novice is inclined either to repeat the pattern numerous times exactly as it was first performed, or never to return to it at all. The experienced composer, however, will reuse significant movements but will vary them according to his compositional needs. In presenting this pattern again he might enlarge and repeat the arm movement and turn, placing them on a moving base; he might omit the change of level, or give it greater emphasis by adding to the movement on that level; he might reverse the order of the movements by performing the jump and run before the turn and change of level; he might elaborate on the run, adding new directions; he might decrease the range so that some of the movement is merely suggested; or he might change the rhythm and quality of some of the movement. With maturity comes the realization that a single movement theme may be examined in all its facets, shortened or lengthened, enlarged or diminished, inverted, transposed, or elaborated on to give greater depth of meaning to the dance statement.

Repetition

Although the artist strives to avoid monotony, it is sometimes desirable that his theme, or a portion of it, be presented a number of times for emphasis. This fact introduces a third art principle, namely, the need for repetition.

Rhythmic activities have long been closely associated with repetition. Although exact repetition is not indispensable to rhythm, repetition does assist in making a specific rhythm increasingly discernible. Hence in arts in which rhythm plays a vital role, repetition becomes an especially important consideration. The poet employs repetition in metrical patterns and in sounds to give pleasing form to his poetry. Repetition of visual line is found to impart strength and clarity to architectural structures. The musician, from primitive to modern times, has used rhythmical repetition of sound as a powerful emotional stimulus. Repetition thus helps to clarify, intensify and enrich an aesthetic experience.

Of all art forms, dance, especially, requires the use of considerable repetition, since the perception of a dance movement is visual and the image received by the spectator vanishes an instant after it has been created. The dance audience has no opportunity to turn back the page or to have a section of the production repeated at will for more careful examination and absorption. Repetition can be helpful in emphasizing significant movement patterns or themes. The choreographer should assist the observer as much as possible by "fixing" the images of important movement motifs through the use of repetition. Repetition of body line plays a part in the clarification of choreographic design, as is illustrated in

Figure 1 (figures are found in the insert between pages 118 and 119). In some instances repetition of sound or of movement may be used to produce a hypnotic effect; in other instances it can create a mood that is permeated with dramatic tension. An example of the latter effect is evidenced in the opera *Emperor Jones,* in the excitement and foreboding produced by the persistent throbbing of jungle drums. Although this illustration is taken from the medium of musical drama, similar results can also be obtained in the dance idiom. Wisely employed, repetition can give rhythmic emphasis, increased meaning, and dramatic power to a dance form without destroying the compositional interest. Furthermore, repetition often provides for both dancer and observer a certain psychological satisfaction in the recognition and reexperiencing of that which is familiar.

Contrast

Usually, as a composition develops, a need for contrast becomes apparent. Although similar to the principle of variety, this principle is not identical with it. Variety aims at diversity in treatment of the material within the theme itself. Contrast implies the introduction of a theme or pattern different in nature from the original, yet related to it, which, by means of its very opposition, highlights the former to result in a new strength of meaning. The visual artist is well acquainted with the psychological fact that complementary colors (extremes in color contrast which, if added together, will produce white light; for example red and green) seen in juxtaposition appear to intensify each other. A dress designer who selects a bright-colored sash for a gown of somber hue capitalizes on the value of contrast as a means of giving emphasis to the costume. The structure of the tripart song form is indicative of the fact that the musician, likewise, is aware of an aesthetic need for contrast in the creation of musical form. One of the earliest and most elemental of the traditional musical forms, its pattern consists of a theme followed by a second contrasting theme, and a return to the original motif. The painter's desire for effective contrast is illustrated in his use of sharply differentiated intensities and colors and in his employment of strong perpendiculars in opposition to a series of horizontal lines. The architect sometimes incorporates this latter plan in his building designs, or often he fulfills the need for architectural contrast by the application of totally different materials of construction (glass, plaster, metal, wood) in close proximity to one another. Contrast, as applied to any art medium, is not merely a difference, but a dynamic opposition, in which the tensions heighten the meaning and increase the strength of each of the opposing but related factors.

The dance composer's means of obtaining contrast are many and varied. Sharp changes of dynamics, or rhythmic scheme, or of spatial design—including range and level—are all contributing potentials.

Contrast ordinarily must be considered in the choice of movement for two or more dancers, or groups of dancers who are appearing together but who are not intended to perform in unison. Stationary movement against activity on a moving base, fast movement against slow, percussive movement against sustained, gentle movement against strong, or accents that do not coincide are some of the possible means of establishing such contrast. In most dances the establishment of contrast between the different movement themes of a composition is also desirable. Furthermore, in dances that have more than one section, the sections usually are designed to contrast with each other. Contrast of this sort can be achieved by changing the tempo, the force, the mood, or, in some cases, the style of the dance movement. In every instance, however, the designer should be guided in his use of contrast and his method of attaining it by the specific needs of his particular dance idea and not by mechanically conceived patterns of construction.

Transition

In order that a work of art may attain the unity so necessary for its success, the contrasting sections must be related to each other by means of subordinate connecting intervals known as transitions. If the parts are to blend together harmoniously into a larger entity, the bridge uniting them must be structurally sound in its relationship to both of the adjacent sections. The musician whose contrasting themes in a symphonic movement are written in different keys finds it necessary to construct a transitional bridge that will carry his listeners auditorially from one to the other with melodic and harmonic ease. The architect or designer occasionally finds it desirable to soften the severity created by sharp linear contrasts and lessen the directional impact by means of clever textural relationships or by means of a third architectural structure to lead from one form to the other. Transition in art represents not only a structural connection but also a condition of "ongoingness"—of artistic growth.

Inherently, movement is the transition from one state of rest, or completion, to another; hence, the very substance from which dance is constructed in reality consists of a series of transitions. The principal concern of the choreographer, however, is that of satisfactorily linking separate movements transitionally with each other. This process is often an extremely delicate one and may sometimes appear to be nothing more than a subtle breath of anticipation of the movement which is to follow.

Such use of transition gives vitality to dance that might otherwise become a series of picture poses, for it animates movement by making one aware of its conception, climax, and conclusion. In some dances a transition may purposely be made sharp for the effect of shock it produces; in other instances, where the intended mood is more serene, an intermediary movement will be required to unite two contrasting activities. Even movements intended to be startling ordinarily will need some preliminary justification (except, perhaps, in the case of comedy). For example, if the composer wishes to introduce a fall into his movement pattern he needs to devise some anticipatory movement to provide motivation for the fall and justify it in terms of the preceding action. Whether the transitional bonds are to be handled boldly in a sharp, crisp manner, or are to be gently flowing will depend chiefly on the demands of the emotional or ideational source of the dance. If the dancer must change from a kneeling base to a standing one, or must change his position from one place on the stage to another, the "how" of getting there is important. He must invent some action that will be appropriate to the movement he has just finished and that will lead into the activity to follow. The use of transition in terms of movement design is illustrated in Figure 2 (figures are found in the insert between pages 118 and 119). The center figure provides visually a transitional link between the reclining one and the standing one.

Transition also applies to the welding together of material within a movement theme. While the untried composer may be inclined to do one movement four times and then another one four times, the experienced choreographer may knit the two movements together, perhaps by doing the first movement twice, the second once, the first once again, the second three times, and ending with a repetition of the first movement. Thus if A represents the first movement and B the second, the pattern instead of being A A A A, B B B B will become A A B A B B B A.

Sequence

Not quite synonymous with transition is the principle of sequence. The former is concerned with the functional connection of one part with another; the latter is involved with a logical placement of these parts chronologically so that they follow each other in significant order. Words in a simple sentence have meaning because of the sequential organization in which they occur. However, if the same words were to be separated and reassembled at random, the meaning would be lost in proportion to the destruction of the continuity of thought.

The dramatist or storyteller is concerned with sequence so his narrative may achieve coherence. Artists in other fields of endeavor are also involved with this consideration. Architecturally, it enters into the practical arrangement of rooms or interrelation of space areas. Tonal and linear sequence and color are the province of the painter. The musician must pattern his melodic lines and harmonic modulations so that note sequences fall on the ear in a satisfying fashion, and his thematic variations must be carefully arranged in sequence to maintain compositional interest and structural continuity.

In dance the sequential plan of the movement series should provide that each movement be a logical outgrowth of that which precedes it, thereby giving continuity and order to the dance pattern as a whole. And in a larger sense, the sections of a longer composition must be tied together by a sense of organic continuation if the total construction is to have meaning.

Climax

Sequential arrangement should contribute not only to the continuity of an art product but also to its artistic development. In considering sequential arrangement the composer must keep in mind the necessity for giving his art expression climax. If the work is to give satisfaction, it must give one a sense of achievement, of having commenced and finally arrived at something significant. Climax is the key statement in an editorial, or is the moment of complete suspense in a play or a mystery novel, or is that portion of a musical composition in which the composer reaches the zenith of emotional power or structural effectiveness.

In the visual arts the term "dominance" has the same relative meaning. The designer, for example, may center interest in a room on a particularly lovely or colorful painting, to which all of the other furnishings, by comparative placement and color harmony, are subordinated. Rembrandt is noted for obtaining a similar effect by concentrating light on the chief object of interest in his compositions. But regardless of the art medium under consideration or the method employed, in each case the focus should be brought to bear in some way on a dominant theme or climactic interest. Other parts of an art product should be related subordinately to the climax, serving as preparation for it, as complement to it, or as its denouement. A composition that lacks climax is likely to leave the observer with a distressing sense of confusion and incompleteness. Dances that fail in this regard appear to fall into two categories: one type is the dance that never seems to develop at all, the entire composition remaining on the same level at which it commenced; the other is the dance consisting of a series of minor climaxes, all of equal importance.

The dance composer in establishing climax is called on to decide what portion of his composition, because of its significance to the whole, should be given the primary emphasis. He must then develop and organize his choreographic material so that temporally, spatially, or dynamically the movement will support this point of culmination. Climax in dance composition may be achieved by increasing the tempo, by enlarging the movement range, by augmenting the number of performers, by increasing the movement dynamics, or perhaps by momentarily suspending the movement altogether so that the tension inherent in the frozen activity supplies the culminating force.

Proportion

Pleasing proportion is another consideration that has immediate bearing on the artistic effectiveness of a composition. By definition, "proportion" means the relation of one part to another with respect to magnitude, quantity, or degree. Although a production may conceivably be constituted of parts of equal size or magnitude, the result is likely to be less interesting than one in which the relative sizes are varied. Although proportion is quantitatively determined, its effect in terms of aesthetic satisfaction is qualitative.

Certain numerical schemes have been proposed by various aestheticians as ideals of relative proportion. Possibly the best known of these systems of proportion is called the golden section, in which a given line or space is divided in such a way that the smaller segment has the same ratio to the larger segment that the larger segment has to the whole. Approximations of this ratio may be made by carrying out the following series:

1—2—3—5—8—13—21—34—and so on

Each term is formed by adding the two preceding terms and each pair of adjacent terms is close to the golden section.[1] It has been claimed that this scheme of proportional relationship is to be found in many forms of nature. The Greeks employed in their two-dimensional rectangular structures a proportionate relationship of two to three; this was called the golden oblong, that is, the oblong measured approximately two units on the short side and three on the long.[2] This proportion, to them, was ideal. On the other hand, a few centuries later and with the advent of Christianity, this Greek ideal was abandoned in medieval Gothic art. Rectangular space was elongated to gain, through greater height, the symbolic effect of aspiration. Certain measurements likewise have been set up as ideals of human proportion, but again, proportions that are considered to be standards of perfection for an adult are obviously unsuitable for an infant or a child. Such facts make it obvious that no rule of proportion can be held inviolable for all times and circumstances. Variation in the relative magnitude of parts admittedly will add

---

[1] Albert R. Chandler, *Beauty and Human Nature*, pp. 33–44.
[2] Harriet and Velta Goldstein, *Art in Everyday Life*, p. 63.

compositional interest whenever it occurs, but the specific pattern of proportion should be regulated by the special demands of the artist's intent.

In dance, the principle of proportion refers to the quantitative selection of parts in terms of their relative numbers, dimensions, temporal values, or dynamic emphasis; it applies not only to the individual dance movements but also to the larger dance sections and to the compositional grouping of the dancers. In considering proportion in reference to his dance composition the choreographer will need to ask himself such questions as these: "How many people shall I use in one group if I have five in another?" "Is this movement given sufficient range and intensity to project the idea that I have in mind?" "Is this section too long in terms of its relative importance to the dance as a whole?" If intelligently handled, the choice of proportions should add aesthetic value and interest to a choreographic work by providing pleasing and meaningful variations and contrasts in stress and magnitude among the parts. In addition, the use of proportion should assist in pointing up the significant portions of a dance by giving them increased emphasis.

Balance

Whereas the principle of proportion has to do with the quantitative selection of the component parts of a composition relative to each other, the principle of balance is concerned with the arrangement of those proportionate parts so that a condition of equilibrium is achieved. Balance includes more than their sequential organization; it deals with the arrangement of these parts as they occur simultaneously. The well-known illustration of the placement of objects of relative size on a see-saw in such a way that equilibrium is established between them demonstrates the use of balance as a principle of physics; that same principle may be applied to art. The arrangement may be either symmetrical or asymmetrical, but whatever the solution, the scientific law of balance acts as a guide to satisfying composition.

The painter and the architect are perpetually concerned with manipulating lines, shapes, textures, and colors into pleasing balance in their compositions. The poet considers metrical balance in formulating the rhythmic plan of his verses. The musician utilizes the principle of balance in creating his harmonic structures and in handling the delicate interplay of the various instrumental sections in orchestration.

For the choreographer, balance assumes an extremely important role, not only in the literal sense of movement control, but also in the matter of floor pattern and in the manipulation of dancers and of groups of dancers in relation to each other. The composer must consider the relative strengths of the space areas of his stage (downstage strong, upstage weak), and the relative intensities of contrasting movement sequences, in his endeavor to achieve choreographic balance. By augmenting the number of dancers who perform them, delicate movements can be brought into balance with those of greater dynamic interest; likewise, weak space areas can be equalized with those that have proportionately greater strength.

Harmony

Finally, if all the elements that have gone into the making of an artistic composition have been chosen and adapted with a view to their acting in pleasing accord with all of the other parts, then the last requisite principle of aesthetic form, the need for harmony, has been met. Harmony implies coordination in the interplay of forces among the various parts of a composition. In any selective society, members are usually chosen because of their ability to work in the established pattern without disrupting it, at the same time furnishing something of special significance to the whole that is complementary to the contributions of the other group members. In art, the choice of materials and their particular compositional handling are made on much the same basis.

The term "harmony," although used perhaps most frequently in reference to musical sound and to color treatment, applies with equal importance to every phase of artistic expression. More specifically, a musician, in writing a symphony, selects musical instruments, assigning them scores that, when heard together, produce a total effect of blended tone and timbre richer than the sound produced by any single instrument or melodic line. A painter of murals or a weaver of tapestries is confronted with the task of choosing colors that agree with and confirm one another, and linear configurations that fit with each other as well as with the spatial scheme as a whole. The writer selects word sounds, the combinations of which produce a total effect of euphony.

Selection of movements that are structurally and dynamically in accord with each other is the particular task of the choreographer. When such harmony or agreement of parts is attained, one should feel in the resulting effect not only that a well-blended unity has been established, but also that each part has been enhanced by every other contributing element.

Conclusion

During the process of composition the dancer must consciously or subconsciously deal with these principles of art form. A conscious awareness of their influence on artistic form leaves a successful art creation less to chance and gives the dancer a better means of judging his composition objectively. For the dancer, these principles are utilized not alone in the selection of movement, rhythmic structure, and spatial design; they apply also to whatever accompaniment, costuming, and stage decor is being incorporated into the total composition.

The primary function of all of the aesthetic principles of form—the need for unity, for variety, for repetition, for contrast, for transition, for appropriate sequence, for climax, for pleasing proportion, for balance, and for harmony—is to reveal and illumine the *creative idea,* aiding in its externalization. Balance and harmony of individual movements may give way to states of off-balance and conflict when the theme is one of emotional turbulence; contrast may be sacrificed and variety confined in a dance depicting monotony. These uses must be determined by the compositional idea. These art principles also interact upon each other; therefore, they cannot be considered independently. The artist's particular manner of achieving variety, for instance, may affect his need for contrast; his choice of proportions may influence the compositional balance and may help to determine the climactic emphasis.

Principles of art form serve both as criteria for selection in the initial creation of art and as a basis for an aesthetic evaluation of the product. However, since form and content are interacting, one cannot judge whether compositional principles have been successfully employed without first arriving at an understanding of the composer's creative purpose. The value of each of these principles of art form resides only in the degree to which they give clarity to the expression of the mind image and beauty to the composition as a whole.

Chapter 3

Dance Studies Based

on Movement Technique

That the dancer's art medium is movement is a fact that would seem needless to reiterate; yet overuse of costumes, scenery, music, or picturesque tableaus as a means of choreographic projection indicates that this fact is occasionally forgotten. Unless the dancer exploits movement to the utmost as his source of art expression, the results are likely to fall short of his artistic goal or to encroach on the domain of some other art field.

Movement and Kinesthesia

Kinesthesia is the fundamental means by which dance ideas are communicated. By definition, this term refers to the sensory experience having its origin in bodily movement and tension. End organs located in the muscles, tendons, and joints are acted on by muscle contraction to produce these sensations; as a result the individual becomes conscious of the fact that he has raised his arm, twisted his body, or clenched his fist. He is even aware of the approximate range, direction, and force of the movement, provided he allows his mind consciously to dwell on these conditions.

Much of the physical activity of an individual is never consciously examined. One seldom stops to make a mental observation of how it feels to walk or to raise one's fork in eating. Yet somewhere in the brain those sensations are recorded for future reference—a phenomenon that enables one to relive those sensations through recall. The more keenly an individual is aware of the movements he performs, however, the more accurately he will be able to recall and reproduce them when the need arises.

Kinesthesia, or movement sensation, in addition to presenting a subjective mental picture of bodily activity, often arouses within the individual a particular feeling or state of mind associated with the movement, or suggests to him a situation that may have motivated the movement in previous circumstances and that has become associated with it.

Not only do individuals become aware of the sensation and the significance of movements their own bodies perform, but they are also capable of empathic response to like movements performed by other people. Thus when the dancer leaps or contracts his body, the observer feels as if he or she were leaping or bending, and associative meanings connected with these movements are recalled to the observer. These memories and associations recalled by the movement of the dancer may not be the same for the observer as they are for the dancer; each draws from his own accumulation of experiences. The measure of the dancer's potential success in projecting to the observer, through dance, thoughts and feelings similar to his own will depend largely on first, the universality of the experience he has chosen to communicate, and second, the degree to which the movements he has selected are universally associated with the idea he wishes to evoke.

The dance composer can learn to select his movements wisely by enlarging and refining his powers of observation of movement in living situations and by increasing the range and depth of his own movement experiences. It seems reasonable to presume that when dance technique is taught creatively, this sensitivity to movement can be developed to a greater degree than when it is taught imitatively. Although rate of learning may be accelerated by the latter method, movements that the student discovers and assimilates by a creative, experimental process are likely to be more meaningful and vital in his experience than those that have been superimposed upon him. The student must be given time, however, not only to make these initial creative discoveries, but also to familiarize himself with the kinesthetic sensations of the movement patterns he has devised so that through association he can discover their possible meanings and expressive values.

As stated in the first chapter, the purpose of the compositional study is to further this understanding of the potential expressive power of movement. The process involved is one of experimentally organizing movement "words" into "sentences." Spoken words gain in richness and specificity of meaning as they are used together with other words, a fact that may also be applied to the language of movement. The restricted scope of the dance study permits the composer to focus his attention on the specific potentialities of the tools of expression he chooses to employ; it offers the student an opportunity to apply his understanding of art principles as they are related to his motivating idea and to observe the manner in which they affect the compositional form and meaning. Such studies need not be complete in the sense that dances are complete. Rather, they are developed only to the degree that is necessary to disclose the knowledge the choreographer sets out to discover. The learning which the student acquires from such creative experiences should contribute to his ultimate objectives in terms of art expression.

Dance improvisation, consisting of extemporized movement, is another approach to the study of choreography. It is an approach, however, most successfully employed on the preadolescent level or (at the opposite extreme) with dancers who are relatively experienced movers. Self-conscious adolescents and adult beginners usually feel a need to organize their composition material intellectually before presenting it in overt form. Unless the problem to be extemporized is an extremely brief one, such students are likely to feel inadequate and insecure. Improvisation does have value in accelerating the creative process. Often new movement that might never have been found by means of intellectual visualization is accidentally discovered through the process of improvising. It is important, however, for students to realize that improvisation is not a substitute for composition, that composition is always the result of planning and selection on the part of the composer.

In the primary grades the child's dramatic imagination is so keenly responsive and his expressive powers are so uninhibited that the pupil needs little assistance in discovering modes of expression adequate to his purposes. Unfortunately, much of this natural creative imagination and dramatic spontaneity is lost in the process of growing up. The development of intellectual judgment and emotional self-consciousness causes the adolescent to become progressively more realistic and objective in his thoughts and interests. His powers of discrimination make him increasingly conscious of his technical inadequacies and of the need to enlarge his expressive vocabulary.

Teachers must be cognizant of these psychological differences in interest and need at the various age levels in order to select appropriate subject material and motivation for learning. High-school and college teachers will need to guard against the practice of dressing movement technique in artificial disguises as a method of presentation. Students at these age levels do not need to be flowers or animals or clock pendulums in order to discover movement or to use it expressively. Young people who are endeavoring to put away childish things are only humiliated by such suggestions.

At the high-school level, teachers should learn to build on the student's newly developed intellectual interests with regard to himself and his personal capacities. This period is one characterized by heightened awareness of technique and of pleasure in the study of movement for its own sake. The teacher needs to capitalize on these interests in planning pupil activities. Creative problems such as those of developing variations on a given combination of steps or body movements, of designing a group composition in which a use of contrasting levels is the chief consideration, of inventing a movement pattern to fit a given rhythmic scheme, or of composing a rondo form in dance movement, can be of absorbing interest to pupils of high-school age.

Until the student has gained the technical security he needs to become once more emotionally articulate, it is best not to clutter his mind with dramatic themes. Such themes are likely to obscure rather than to intensify his perception of kinesthetic feeling and of movement control, which are vitally important at this particular stage of his dance development. College students who are experiencing dance for the first time will have similar needs for objectivity. Even with young children, an objective approach to movement should not be ignored, although it may frequently be introduced as an outgrowth of dramatic movement experiences.

The dance teacher who is employed in secondary and higher education needs to understand the theory of kinesthesia underlying creative expression and must be able to transmit this understanding to students so that they may work intelligently. The realization that movement can communicate by means of its sheer dynamic structure will free the dancer from overdependency on imaginative and dramatic themes and will challenge him to explore new areas in composition. Students should appreciate the importance of developing kinesthetic sensitivity and of using it as a basis for artistic discrimination. The more keenly the dance composer is attuned to the subtle meaning inherent to movement itself, the less he will need to depend upon literal pantomime, costume, decor, or accompaniment for the projection of his ideas.

Experimental choreography which is constructed directly upon movement may proceed along any one of a number of avenues of departure. The dancer may choose to concentrate upon the effects created by different uses of space, rhythm, or choreographic structure. Since, however, the beginning dancer in high school and in college is concerned first with acquiring a movement vocabulary, it is logical for beginning composition to develop as an outgrowth of the kinesthetic study of movement for its own sake.

Obviously, dancers can bring to a creative problem only that which they themselves have experienced. If experience is limited, the compositional problem must resolve itself into those few elements that are familiar. The study must be restricted to the level of the students' understanding, yet should stimulate them to further growth. Even though the technique involved may be relatively elementary, the creative exercise may be presented in a way that is challenging to their interests.

The following creative problems derived from the study of movement for its own sake are presented as suggestions for choreographic experimentation. The material has been classified under two general headings: locomotor movement and body movement. It should be pointed out, however, that no locomotion can take place without body movement, and little bodily activity in dance exists without some locomotion. The differentiation is merely a matter of emphasis.

Locomotor Movement

Variations on a Given Step or Step Sequence

One of the most elementary examples of a compositional problem is that of creating a variation on one of the fundamental steps, for example, a skip, a walk, or a run. Even when the problem is thus simplified, the beginning student needs to have the elements that make for variation in movement discussed and clarified before he can work intelligently. He needs to understand that the controlling factors which determine the resulting structure of any movement are *time*—including relative duration and tempo, *space*—including distance and focus and direction, and *energy*—including intensity and accent, and that manipulation of any one of these elements results in a new movement form.

At first, it is probably wise not to bombard the inexperienced person with too many of these variables at one time, or he will be overwhelmed by the complexity of his task. Even for the experienced composer, compositional results are obtained with greater ease and often with greater clarity when some of these controlling movement factors are stressed and the rest are subordinated. The instructor may be of valuable assistance in helping the student explore thoroughly, one at a time, the variations latent in each of these forces governing movement.

A step pattern consisting of a combination of several fundamental steps presents variation possibilities of increased complexity, for example: step, hop, hop, step, hop, hop, run, run, run, jump. Given a locomotor pattern such as this, the student will find that each step requires special consideration as to manner of execution. For instance, it will be necessary to determine whether the free leg on the hop will be raised forward or backward or to the side; whether the knee will be bent or straight; whether the ankle will be extended or flexed. The jump may be taken with the feet together or apart, in wide or in long stride; it may involve a great deal of elevation or only a small amount. The directional plan of each part of the step pattern must be established, and the related action of the arms and body must be considered. Even without the addition of such special considerations as range, intensity, quality, and specific style to complicate the problem, the beginning student will find that the conceivable combinations of movement variables are innumerable.

In handling such exploratory exercises the instructor cannot expect the student to happen on all of these variables by chance. It is the teacher's responsibility to draw out the student through leading questions, helping him to realize by his own thought processes the variables that movement offers to the dancer. Such remarks as "What directions could you use other than forward?" "Could you do the pattern turning around?" "Try bringing the free leg in front on the second hop this time," "How else could you jump?" can suggest to the student possibilities that he may have overlooked. These movement variations then need to be experienced and their kinesthetic sensations observed. Only by this means does the young composer gain sufficient control and understanding of his medium to be able to make intelligent selections in constructing complex movement studies and, later, dance forms.

It will be discovered, in some cases, that certain variations are more practicable than others. For instance, heaviness in contrast to lightness may appear out of place in steps of elevation. There would be very little artistic value in a heavy hop or leap. The instructor's own knowledge about and experience with movement furnishes a basis for helping the student to eliminate quickly the ineffectual variables so that he may concentrate on those that are more satisfying to perform.

The creation and selection of movements and the arrangement of these materials into an organic whole are processes that are sometimes difficult for the beginner to envision. The instructor may need to illustrate such procedures with a few pertinent examples. Sometimes a simple demonstration is sufficient to make the problem clear. Occasionally the teacher may find it necessary to direct the class in the actual experiencing of one or two movement sequences based on the particular material being explored.

By way of illustration one might take this example. The step pattern is presumed to be

(w–walk; j–jump; h–hop; r–run; stp–stomp).

In order to help the students to realize some of the ways in which they can vary this pattern, the teacher might suggest to them the following directional ideas:

For the first two measures:

1. Move forward, forward, back, back, forward; and repeat all, facing sideward.

2. Circle right on the first measure; left on the second measure.

3. Move forward, forward, side, cross, side; repeat, moving side-ward the opposite way.

4. Combine any two of the above patterns.

For the third measure:

1. Jump hop into opposite diagonals.

2. Circle right, freeing the left leg and turning away from it on the first hop, freeing the right leg (knee bent), and turning toward it on the second hop.

For the fourth measure:

1. Move backward on the runs, and do the stamps moving forward.

2. Do two runs forward, pivot to face the opposite direction and do two runs and a stamp, pivot again, and stamp in the original forward direction.

In the case of each of the measures given above, numerous other variations, which the students should be permitted to discover for themselves, are possible. Out of the sum total of their discoveries the class members can then select the variations they like best and put them together in a final pattern. It should be kept clearly in mind, however, that directed activity by the teacher has a place in the educational approach to dance composition only when it serves as a stimulus for creative work on the part of the student.

Arrangement of Given Steps

After the beginner has experienced the fundamental steps, both individually for their own specific motor coordinations, and in certain definite combinations, the problem of sequential arrangement may be considered. Given a prescribed number of locomotor steps, the student may be asked to arrange these into a sequence and rhythmic pattern of his own choosing. To illustrate: the student might be allotted two walks, four runs, and two leaps as basic movement material for composition, the assignment being to construct with these steps a locomotor sequence that is pleasurable to perform. The meter may be defined by the problem, or it may be left to the composer's discretion. There are, of course, numerous possible solutions for such an assignment. Four examples are given below.

Two different sequential arrangements of the designated steps related to 3/4 meter:

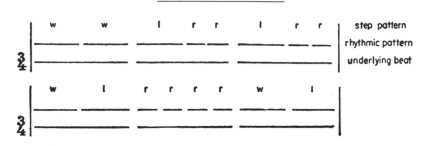

The second sequential pattern given on the previous page now related to 4/4 and 5/4 meters:

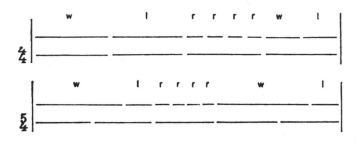

Some students may arrive at the same solution in step sequence, but the rhythm or manner of execution of the pattern may be different. Others may select the same rhythmic pattern, but the step sequence may vary. In some cases the resulting patterns may be identical, but in each instance the experience has been a creative one for the student if he has arrived at his result through his own selective procedure.

Some locomotor steps are not practicable to perform in close proximity to certain other steps. For example, a leap, when it is preceded by a hop, is placed in a position of mechanical disadvantage. Consequently, the instructor must be sure that he has selected locomotor material adaptable to more than one or two possible arrangements.

Use of Traditional Step Combinations

As the student of dance experiments within the bounds of locomotor movement, he will undoubtedly come upon step sequences that others before him have discovered and performed, some of which have been handed down to posterity under the heading of "traditional dance steps." But to the young dancer they will be new discoveries, and in their moment of re-creation those conventional combinations will be given new vitality and meaning. It is his privilege, if he chooses, to use these traditional forms, constructing upon them as his fancy directs. It may not be possible to reproduce the old forms in complete authenticity, since only people who belong to the cultures from which these forms arise can give them their original meanings. But one can dance them in the light of his own reactions to, or feelings about, these movement patterns, or in accordance with his concept of how they might have been performed. For the beginner there is a sense of security in composing upon such a definite structure. The problem then becomes one of achieving sufficient variation for interest within the limits of the chosen dance pattern or its ideational conception. Such step combinations as the polka, the schottische, the waltz, the mazurka, the polonaise, and the more modern tango, rhumba, samba, and jazz forms are all good material for creative experimentation.

One might use the tango by way of illustration. The traditional step has a basic meter of 2/4, employing two more or less typical rhythmic patterns (given below), although there are many other rhythmic variations.

The tango is ordinarily performed with smooth, gliding steps, and with the knees bent, lowering the center of gravity. When the tango is removed from the less spectacular confines of the social dance idiom, it often achieves a strikingly sinuous quality with considerable movement in the hip joint. The arm action tends to be flowing, in keeping with the general movement quality. Interest is heightened by the contrast of slow and of rapid movement stimulated by the rhythmic structure.

Such a general deduction of what constitutes characteristic tango movement must be made by the student from his direct experience with some of its specific forms. On this foundation the structure of new creative patterns may arise.

Body Movement

Body movement refers to activity that is performed primarily on a stationary base or with less emphasis upon the locomotor phase of the movement pattern. The study of dance technique should acquaint the student with actions such as flexion, extension, and rotation that are possible within each of the body joints. It should include not only the discovery of what movements the body can do, but also an analysis of the specific tensions, rhythms, tempos, and spatial factors that are employed, as well as a recognition of the kinesthetic values inherent to these techniques. This knowledge and experience provide the substance with which the young composer may construct studies that will contribute to his increased understanding of movement as an art medium.

Compositionally, body movement may be examined with many of the same general considerations as those proposed for locomotor movement. Variation of a given pattern may be obtained by altering the temporal, spatial, or dynamic relationships. Likewise, permutations of a given order of movements are achievable.

Use of Specific Types of Body Movements

Because movement is, by definition, a change of position, for the beginner the simplest possible creative problem in body movement is to find a means of getting from one assigned position to another. He need not go from one to the other directly, but may choose to construct a devious and elaborate transitional bridge between the two positions. In exploring movement possibilities, the student will probably discover a number of alternative solutions from which he may choose the pattern which best satisfies him. In that sense, the assignment becomes a compositional problem.

Specific exercises in technique may also provide usable subject material for beginning composition. By studying the movement quality that characterizes a given technique and by then reorganizing, distorting, and adding to the original movements, the beginner may sometimes create short dance studies that have emotive connotations. Likewise, movements that are associated with certain everyday activities may provide the dance composer with choreographic material adaptable to abstraction. Studies of this type are discussed in further detail in Chapter 7.

As the student's technical experience grows, he will be able to cope with problems of increased complication. A compositional exercise that is relatively simple yet challenging to the beginner is that of creating a movement sequence or theme from a group of specified bodily activities, such as rotation of the spine, trunk flexion, and a choice of lateral movement. Even thus limited, the composer has considerable latitude in his choice of timing, level, quality, consecutive arrangement, and exact control of the designated movements. It is often amazing, even to the initiated, to observe the variety of excellent movement material embodied in such a simple problem. This type of study may be expanded to include locomotor movement as well, or it may be constructed upon such choreographic material as runs, change of level, and focus. Before such assignments can be meaningful to the student, however, he must have had first-hand acquaintance with the movements thus specified.

It is occasionally desirable to delimit a compositional problem by assigning to it certain anatomical restrictions. For example, the dancer may be asked to compose a study in which only the arms and the upper body are used. Or the student may be assigned a compositional problem in which the use of arms is to be minimized and the emphasis placed on action of the rest of the body. By stressing areas in which students are technically or expressionally weak the teacher may, with such studies, contribute to the dancers' choreographic development.

Development of Movement Sequences

In another type of creative problem the opening movements for a short movement phrase or theme may be set by the instructor and presented to the class as a whole. Such introductory movements can be as simple as a jump and a clap and four runs forward. Or again, the pattern may consist of a quick lift of the left leg (straight) into the left diagonal, a shift of weight onto that leg in a diagonal lunge, and a slow raising of the right arm sideward to overhead with the body leaning way from the arm, the focus following the hand. Proceeding from this common experience, each individual student may then complete the phrase according to his own tastes and aesthetic understanding. He must select movements that, in his judgment, grow organically from the preceding ones, and that add interest through variation or contrast. The assignment may be confined to body movement exclusively, or it may also include locomotion. In addition to its compositional values, such a problem contributes to the dancer's appreciatory powers as well. It demonstrates undeniably the fact that although no two individuals will react identically to the same stimulus, the creative results may be equally convincing if they have been conceived with artistic discrimination and are performed with sincerity.

Organized along a somewhat parallel plan is a very simple group study that has proved interesting and instructive to students. It is one of constructing a movement "sentence" or "paragraph" by allowing each person to contribute successively to the whole. A similar verbal game is often played by children who invent stories, each child in his turn adding a word to help complete the narrative. The first person's job, of course, is the easiest, because his part does not have to relate to any preceding movement. Each succeeding participant must start his pattern from the last position of the movement sequence preceding his own. The movement selected must be a transitional outgrowth of the previous movement and must add interest—rhythmically, dynamically, or spatially—to the whole as he "inherits" it. The last person has the most difficult task, since he must draw the total pattern together into a satisfying conclusion. In a movement study of this sort it is usually desirable to keep the group small in size, since a structure too long is likely to lack unity because of the beginner's untutored search for variety. Also, if the group as a whole is expected to present the completed pattern in unison, it should not become too long to be remembered easily. As an illustration, a group consisting of four people may be assigned to create one measure apiece of 5/4 meter. The purpose of the first dancer's movement may be to establish the meter and to focus attention on a floor pattern. The second dancer may choose to emphasize variation in rhythmic pattern; the third may introduce a turn and change in level; and the fourth dancer, utilizing this new level, and perhaps repeating some of the previous movements, may attempt to fulfill a possible need for dynamic contrast.

The value of this kind of group organization lies in the fact that each member of the group is held completely responsible for creating one small part (usually not more than four to six counts) of the total pattern. Thus individual initiative and social responsibility are fostered, and overactive leadership by any one member of the group is discouraged. From the standpoint of choreographic accomplishment the chief weakness of such a plan lies in the fact that artistically unified results are difficult to attain when the compositional directorship is passed from one individual to another.

Use of Specific Movement Qualities

Another phase of movement that can stimulate creative imagination is the manner in which the energy of motion is released, that is, the movement quality. Such qualities may be classified under the general headings of swinging (which also includes swaying and pulsating), sustained, percussive (including explosive, staccato, and vibrating), and collapsing movement.

The swing is probably the most familiar of all the movement qualities, because the body is constructed to operate naturally in that way. Also, since gravity contributes a portion of the functional energy, effective results are obtained with relatively little fatigue. The ease and the pleasure with which swinging movement may be accomplished make it an ideal introductory activity for compositional study. Certain of the other movement qualities may at first seem foreign to the beginner because of their less frequent natural usage. This is particularly true of percussive and collapsing movements. Active acquaintance with the control of such motions and observation of motor sensations connect-

ed with them is necessary before they can purposefully serve the choreographer. However, once the dancer has consciously familiarized himself with these movement qualities, he frequently finds them to be intimately tied in with emotional overtones that may be readily sensed and
later capitalized on in the making of dance compositions. The following suggested creative studies, stressing the control of quality of movement, can provide useful learning situations for the prospective dance
composer.

Obviously it is possible to construct a movement pattern that
utilizes one of the movement qualities alone as, for example, a study
based on sustained movement, or one in which percussive movement
is dominant. The value of such a problem lies in its simplicity, which
enables the student to concentrate on the expressive assets peculiar to
that quality.

A more complex organization involving two people is based upon
the use of the antiphonal or question-and-answer form described later
on page 81. One dancer commences the study by improvising a very
short movement phrase or "statement" based on a specified movement
quality. The second dancer answers with a complementary phrase in the
same quality. The first dancer again takes the initiative, and the partner
replies. In a problem of this type confined to the use of swinging movement, for instance, the dancer might invent the following movement
phrases:

> The first dancer, kneeling on one knee sideward to his partner,
> begins by swinging his arm across his body away from his partner,
> with an elbow lead (3 counts); next, he swings both arms toward his
> partner (3 counts); then rising, he swings his free arm and leg direct-
> ly backward (3 counts); and finally, he turns around in place toward
> his partner with an elbow lead (3 counts).

> The second dancer, who is standing, picks up the last turning move-
> ment from his partner (3 counts); finishes the movement by swing-
> ing both arms sideward (3 counts); then he moves backward away
> from his partner with three steps while swinging both arms to the
> rear (3 counts); and ends his pattern with a lift of one leg and both
> arms forward toward his partner (3 counts).

From there the first dancer will continue with a new phrase of
swinging movement and his partner will devise a suitable response. Such
an experiment is entirely one of improvisation within the limitations of
the assigned quality, but because the movement statements are short, the
beginner does not feel the insecurity often associated with improvisation. It calls for the development of sensitivity, on the part of both
dancers, to their interrelationships with each other—sensitivity that may

be evidenced in choice of movement, in use of focus, and in even more subtle responses. It also provides a valuable learning experience in the use of dominance and subordination in movement. The dancer, awaiting his turn, must still maintain an active part in the pattern, but his movement must be subdued in relation to that of his partner. Although the general scheme of the dance study remains constant, its outward aspect will change completely each time the attention is focused upon a different movement quality.

Because these various qualities are so completely different in their effects upon motion, a study in which they are all used in juxtaposition is valuable for the contrast it illustrates. Here, especially, the dynamics of the pure movement often call up rich emotional associations in the mind of the dancer, which may suggest dramatic content. A simple example of a combination of movement qualities is diagramed below.

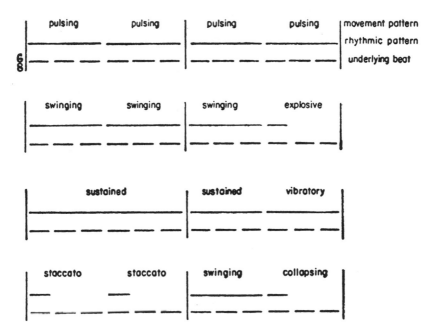

Such compositional studies are only a few of the many possible ones that have proved practicable and instructive for the student of dance. There are undoubtedly others just as valuable. The teacher should bear in mind that however movement is used as a creative stimulus, the solution of the study should contribute to the dancer's enriched understanding of the expressional values of movement. It should direct the composer to greater efficiency in using his artistic material in a simple, understandable, and aesthetically satisfying style.

Suggested Problems for Compositional Studies

Studies Based on Locomotor Movement (for groups of approximately three to six individuals)

1. Compose a dance study based entirely on walking. Vary the walk by changing the direction of movement, the rhythm of stepping (such as two fast steps and one slow), the size of the steps, and the use of the arms and body while walking. Place the emphasis on pure movement, avoiding character impersonations. Relate all of the movement to some definite metrical scheme (for example, 4/4, 5/4, or 6/8).

2. Using skips and slides only, compose a dance study similar to the one described above.

3. Choose any three fundamental steps and create a dance study, using only those three steps. Interest in the movement pattern can be increased by performing one combination of these steps against another. Relate all step combinations rhythmically to a definite meter and spatially and dynamically to each other.

4. Create a movement sequence using the step pattern diagrammed on page 28, or any other similar pattern. Perform the movement first, in unison with everyone moving in the same direction; second, in unison but with some of the dancers facing in a different direction from the rest of the group; third, with part of the group commencing with measure 3 and dancing the measures in the following order—3, 4, 1, 2 —while the rest of the group dances the regular sequence of measures. (It may be desirable to repeat this third section.) Develop the pattern so that the group can perform all three sections continuously without stopping to adjust positions on the floor.

5. Combine variations of the 6/8 polka with skips, with slides, or with both skips and slides, as the basic material of a dance study:

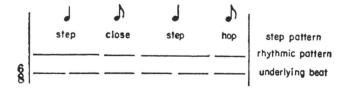

6. Create a satirical dance study which contrasts the frankly bouncy quality of the 2/4 polka with the low, gliding, sinuous, and sophisticated character of the tango, which is also in 2/4, the basic rhythm of which is merely a transposition of the polka rhythm:

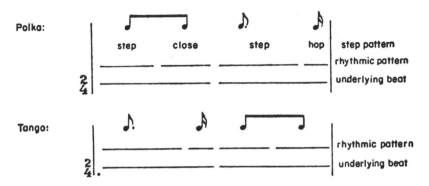

7. Combine movements that can be related to a waltz rhythm with the traditional waltz step or with the running waltz and develop them into a dance study.

8. Invent a series of movement combinations in 3/4 meter, vigorous in character, which establish an accent on the second beat of the measure, and combine them in a dance study with the traditional mazurka steps.

9. In a dance study based on 3/4 meter, contrast the waltz rhythm, in which the accent falls on the first beat of the measure, with the mazurka rhythm, in which the accent falls on count 2. Establish the contrast by changing frequently from one rhythm to the other and by performing one rhythm against the other. Use both the traditional waltz and mazurka steps and other movement patterns appropriate to the rhythmic structures and movement qualities of these traditional steps.

10. Using the rhythmic structure of the rhumba (or the tango, the samba, the bolero, the jitterbug, boogie-woogie, and so forth) as a base, devise a dance study in which the movements are built, either in a strict sense or in a free sense on this rhythm.

Studies Based on Body Movement (to be done singly or in groups)

1. Build a dance study that involves primarily the use of the hands, arms, and upper torso.

2. Create a movement study in which the use of hands and arms is minimized.

3. Develop a dance pattern in which the major portion of the movement consists of rotation (twisting) or is motivated by rotation. Include rotation of different parts of the body such as shoulder, hip, spine, and so forth.

4. Select three localized areas of the body, such as the right shoulder, the left hip, and the left hand, from which all of the dance movements are to be initiated. Use both a stationary and a moving base.

5. Compose a movement sequence by permitting each member of the group to create one measure of the pattern according to the plan described on pages 33 and 34. When the movement sequence is completed it can, if desired, be presented in the manner suggested for Problem 4 under "Studies Based on Locomotor Movement."

Studies Based on Movement Qualities

1. Select a single movement quality, such as swinging or sustained movement, on which the entire compositional study is to be built.

2. Improvise or compose a question-and-answer form such as that described on page 35, using a single movement quality throughout the study. If the pattern is to be improvised, it will be expedient to use only two people in the composition; if the pattern is to be composed, a large number of people can be employed to perform the movements.

3. Using the same question-and-answer form referred to above, improvise a movement pattern in which the leader or "first speaker" may choose any movement quality that he desires to use and the answering person must respond in that same quality; or if preferred, the answering person must quickly choose for response a movement quality different from that of the questioner. The speakers may interrupt each other and may vary the length of their movement phrases. The chief problem is to be aware of each other and of the movement qualities being used.

4. Create a movement pattern to fit the following scheme or a similar plan, such as that given on page 36.

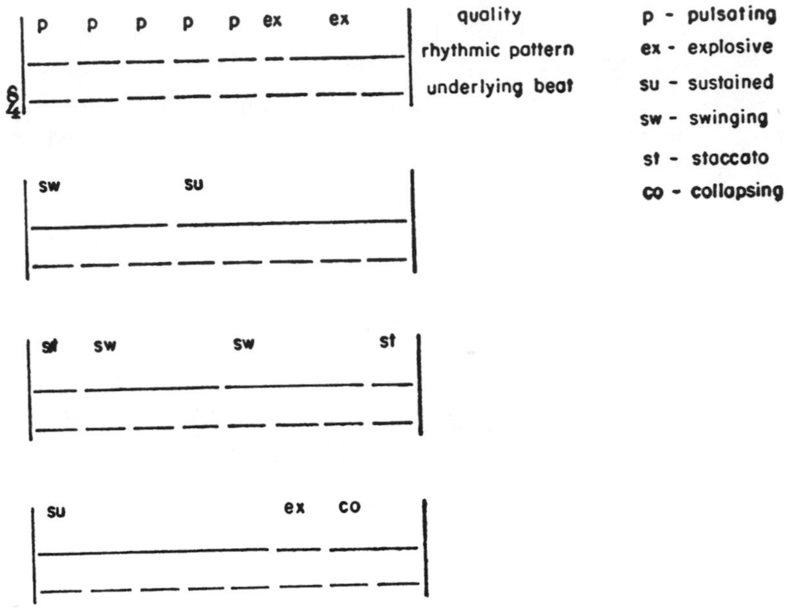

p p p p p ex ex	quality
——— ——— ——— ——— ——— ——— ———————	rhythmic pattern
——— ——— ——— ——— ——— ——— ——— ———	underlying beat

$\frac{6}{4}$

sw   su
——————— ———————
——— ——— ——— ———

st   sw   sw   st
—— ——————— ——————— ——
—— —— —— —— —— —— ——

su   ex   co
——————————— —— ———
—— —— —— —— —— —— ——

p - pulsating
ex - explosive
su - sustained
sw - swinging
st - staccato
co - collapsing

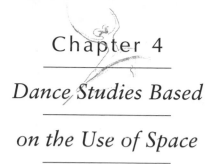

Chapter 4

Dance Studies Based

on the Use of Space

Space becomes a significant factor in the life of man from the moment he is born. As the individual grows, his feelings with regard to space may change or may develop in certain ways as a result of his experiences. Some people have intense emotional aversion to small spaces whereas others find great satisfaction in the sense of protection that sheltered areas afford them. In our present-day existence the human mind is continually bombarded by dramatic extremes in dimensions—from microscopic measurements to distances in interstellar space. Living becomes a process of perpetual adjustment to the towering height of the skyscraper, to the tremendous acreage of the modern factory, to the confining limits of the one-room flat.

Elements of Space

In comparison with his sensitivity to smell or touch, or with his kinesthetic awareness, man's powers of visual observation and discrimination are acutely sensitized. This increased visual discernment may be the result of practice, since much of man's learning is motivated by visual stimuli. Whatever the reason, the fact that the spatial approach to dance appeals to the visual as well as to the kinesthetic sense makes it one of the easiest and most tangible types of choreography for the novice to comprehend. The use of space, as an essential characteristic of all movement, includes such special considerations as direction, focus, planes, density, range, and specific design.

Direction

Direction has had significance for man ever since he first set out to go from one specific place to another; it has both literal and abstract connotations. Its literal meanings are graphically expressed in maps and charts; its abstract meanings are revealed in the linear designs of the artist.

The application of direction to movement includes two basic considerations. First, there is the path that the moving body cuts through the surrounding space. When viewed with reference to locomotion, it is the floor pattern. But any movement that the body can perform has a directional bearing on the space area through which it moves. In addition to the path itself, direction applies to the relation of the body of the dancer to the path. For example, it is possible for the dancer to face the side of his space area and move forward into it (Diagram 1A), or he may face the front of his space area and walk sideward, relative to his own body (Diagram 1B). Although the dancer travels in the same direction in both instances, each of these two uses of direction is a different movement experience.

A.   B.

DIAGRAM 1. *Dancers Moving on a Sideward Path*

The anatomical structure of man is such that certain directional patterns are more easily achieved than others. It is more natural, for instance, to raise the arm horizontally forward or sideward than to raise it to shoulder height backward. Again, partially because of the fact that the dancer can see where he is going and partially because of the structural mechanism of the body, most locomotor activities are performed more comfortably in a forward direction than backward or sideward. Consequently, the body must be trained in the performance of the less familiar movement experiences if direction is to be fully explored and utilized in all of its phases.

Generally speaking, movement directions may be identified as either straight or curvilinear. Combinations of straight lines result in squares, rectangles, triangles, zigzags, and numerous other linear designs. Interesting floor patterns and body movement sequences may be built on such an elemental plan as the use of the forward, backward, and sideward directions alone. The problem may be made slightly more complex by the addition of diagonals or movement up or down. At first it may be desirable for the teacher to limit the locomotor activity to movement that is done forward into the line of path. When the student becomes more secure in his directional bearings, the problem may be further complicated by adding changes in the relation of the dancer's body to the compositional path. Thus he may move sideward on a forward path or backward on a floor pattern to the side.

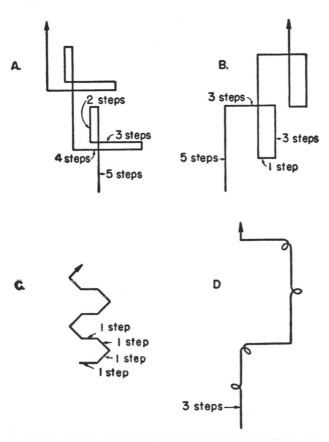

DIAGRAM 2. *Straight-Line Floor Progressions*

Diagram 2A illustrates a straight-line floor progression in which the body turns to face the path throughout the pattern. The dancer takes five steps facing forward, starting with the right foot, two steps facing backward, three steps facing sideward right, and four steps facing sideward left, and then repeats the pattern. In the patterns illustrated in Diagrams 2B, C, and D, the floor progressions employ different relationships of the body to the path. In B, the dancer takes five steps forward beginning with the right foot, three grapevine steps sideward, three steps backward, and one step sideward, and continues to repeat the pattern. The dancer does not change the direction in which his body is facing. The same is true of pattern C. Here the dancer takes one step to the side right, one step crossing over diagonally forward right, one step crossing over diagonally forward left, and continues, repeating the pattern on alternate sides. In pattern D, the dancer turns to face different directions. Beginning with the right foot he takes three steps forward, pivoting $1/2$ turn to the left on the third step; now facing backward, he takes three steps backward (continuing in the line of direction), pivoting $1/2$ turn to the left on the third step to face forward again; finally he takes three grapevine steps sideward, and is ready to repeat the pattern on the opposite side, starting with the left foot.

Curves include many of the same considerations as those enumerated for straight lines. They also introduce the added factor of the pull of centripetal force. If one attempts to move in a circle at a high rate of speed, the centripetal attraction tends to cause the body to bank or lean inward and to lower the center of gravity. To maintain a strictly vertical relationship over one's feet is not only uncomfortable but also literally impossible. The greater the speed, the greater the body lean. On the other hand, it is also possible to oppose that centripetal force with the upper body by leaning laterally away from the center of the curve and allowing only the hips to shift inward. One may move in large or small circles, in figure 8's, in spirals, in scallops, in serpentines, or in any of the combinations that are possible to these patterns. The body may move forward or backward into the line of path, turning with it; or it may face continuously in one direction of the space area, which constantly changes the relation of body to path. Diminished size in circular path eventually introduces the pivot turn, the technical handling of which has innumerable possibilities.

Three curved-line floor progressions are illustrated in Diagram 3. In the pattern in Diagram 3A, the dancer makes a five-step half circle moving forward, commencing with the inside foot; then he makes a five-step half circle moving backward, leaning toward the center of the circles. The pattern is repeated. In pattern B, the dancer makes a five-step half circle forward again, starting with the inside foot; makes a $1/2$ pivot turn (one step) and a five-step half circle, moving backward; then he repeats the pattern on the opposite side. The body leans in toward the center of the circles throughout the pattern. In pattern C, the dancer makes a five-step half circle, leaning away from the center, beginning with the inside foot, and a three-step half circle leaning toward the center; the pattern is repeated.

An experimental study was once made to discover what emotive qualities, if any, were generally associated with certain types of linear patterns. The results of the study indicated, among other things, that straight-line patterns, especially those in which there were many sharp changes of direction, were felt to be more stimulating and powerful than most curved-line patterns. Straight lines were predominantly associated with active, intense emotions, whereas most curved lines were considered to be somewhat yielding, soothing, or playful by nature.[1] The results of this experiment may be explained, in part, by the physical laws governing the direction of motion. A straight line affords the most speedy and efficient route to an objective. Since both starting and stopping of movement require a greater expenditure of energy than that needed to maintain it, directional patterns that include many angles obviously call for more force than those that continue in one direction or change direction gradually (Figs. 3 and 4; figures are found in the insert between pages 118 and 119).

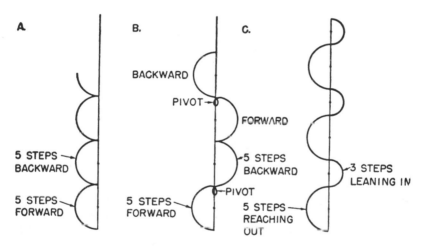

A.

B.

C.

BACKWARD

PIVOT→

FORWARD

5 STEPS→
BACKWARD

←5 STEPS
BACKWARD

←3 STEPS
LEANING IN

5 STEPS→
FORWARD

5 STEPS→
FORWARD

←PIVOT

5 STEPS→
REACHING
OUT

DIAGRAM 3. *Curved-Line Floor Progressions*

Such experimental evidence is not conclusive and should not be used as a basis for the establishment of compositional rules; nevertheless, it does indicate the necessity for the composer to understand the associative tendencies that exist with reference to linear patterns in order that he may select the types of linear design that will reinforce his creative ideas. Diagram 4 shows two examples of floor patterns that involve the use of straight lines or of curved lines exclusively.

[1] Elizabeth R. Hayes, "The Emotional Effect of Color, Lighting and Line in Relation to Dance Composition." Unpublished master's thesis, pp. 85-88.

There is yet another phase in the consideration of direction which is important for the composer to recognize. In designing composition to be viewed by an observer, the composer must consider his directional plan in terms of its relation to his prospective audience. He should recognize the fact that psychologically, forward-moving directions are potentially strong and assertive, whereas retreating directions are potentially weak (p. 125). Again an understanding of these facts should not stereotype the manner in which direction is used in compositional form, but it should awaken the choreographer to the need for counteracting these inherent characteristics when he wishes to create other types of impressions.

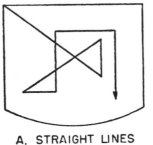   

A. STRAIGHT LINES   B. CURVED LINES

DIAGRAM 4. *Floor Patterns of Contrasting Design*

After the student has explored the possibilities for movement contained in arbitrarily limited directional studies (such as those suggested for straight line) he can eventually draw upon these experiences in creating longer compositions. These studies, although retaining their emphasis on straight or curvilinear directions, will be limited only by the student's own artistic integrity. Emotional overtones organic to the movement itself are sure to be evidenced if the movement is performed throughout with an awareness of motor sensation.

Focus

Although focus is intimately associated with direction, its contribution to the total conception of space and movement in space is something distinct and special. The power of focus to communicate is demonstrated by everyday instances in which someone who is staring at an unusual sight or looking for a lost object automatically attracts the gaze of passersby to that point on which he is focusing. In dance, focus frequently gives added impact to the direction of a movement, or, occasionally, establishes new direction in opposition to body and locomotor movement. Focus not only indicates direction, but also suggests dimensional boundaries by the adjustment of the eyes to focus at a distance or at close range. In addition to establishing a focal point literally by use of the eyes, the dancer can direct the body in various ways to suggest focus kinesthetically. Thus focus may be subtly implied by particularized uses of the arms or legs, by general body lean, or by body tension.

In any type of choreography, if directions are to be made clear, focus must necessarily enter in; but there are also interesting compositional problems that deal with focus specifically. Perhaps the simplest of these is a study involving focus on a single point. Such usage is already within the experience of every individual who has ever related himself to an outside objective in curiosity, affection, fear, or veneration. The chosen focal spot may be located wherever the composer wishes it to be. It may be on the ceiling, on the floor, or in any of the compass directions, but wherever it is, the feeling of affinity to the point of focus should influence every movement of the dance form if the idea of focus is to predominate.

The addition of a second focal point introduces new complications. The pull of two opposing forces tends to call up feelings of conflict or indecision. Such emotional associations are not necessarily inherent to the problem, however. For example, in a group study an entirely different result may be obtained if the problem of focus is solved by having a single dancer relate her movement to a focal point directly overhead while the rest of the group focuses on the solo dancer (Fig. 5; figures are found in the insert between pages 118 and 119.

A third suggestion for the use of focus is the type of compositional exercise in which the point of focus is shifted constantly, although it is clearly established in each new direction. Movement inspired by such use of focus might conceivably carry with it emotional overtones suggestive of restlessness, searching, or inconstancy, because of the very nature of the problem assigned.

Regardless of the exact assignment, focus as a phase of dance experience generally extracts a very sincere and unself-conscious response from beginning dancers because of the concentration it requires.

Planes

Space may also be considered in a planar sense. A plane may be established in any direction one selects. However, certain planes, such as the vertical, horizontal, lateral, or diagonal, have a directional explicitness that makes them easy to identify in terms of abstract spatial design and, in some cases, in terms of their symbolic meaning. A compositional study based on the definition through movement of all these planes can be used effectively to amplify the dancer's awareness of the relation of his movement to space.

The selection of a single directional plane as the basis for composition causes the choreographer to explore thoroughly the range of possibilities that lie within its scope. In the vertical plane the emphasis may be placed on any one of a number of different details. Effort may be directed toward establishing an impression of height, or of depth. Or again, the choreographer may stress contrasts in level, developing variations in the manner of change from one position to another and exploring the movement possibilities relevant to each level. Ordinarily, students should guard against the tendency to change level continually (like an elevator running from floor to floor) without accomplishing anything on any of the planes. Change of level should be motivated by choreographic need, and choice of level should be made on the basis of its significance, literally or abstractly, to the whole. If the study is composed for a group of dancers rather than for a single performer, the opportunity for obtaining interesting contrast of level is increased. If the group pattern involves four dancers, for example, it is possible to have three of the dancers perform movement on a kneeling base while the remaining one is doing locomotor activity. Then while two of the three dancers who have been kneeling rise, the one who has been standing may join the other dancer who has been on the floor, on another intermediary level. Under ordinary circumstances, compositional organization of this nature is more interesting than that in which the dancers are all kneeling or standing or lying down at the same time. Falls, of course, are very efficient and effective level changers, but because they are so kinetically startling, the student must be guided in his use of them so that their dynamic punctuation is organic to the composition and not superimposed as a sort of technical display.

The horizontal plane, the natural evidences of which are familiarly seen in strata of rock and earth or in the broad expanses of midwestern topography, calls for a new spatial handling of movement. One may concentrate effort on utilizing a large compass of movement possibilities within one horizontal plane, or on establishing interest through the interplay of various levels of horizontal movement.

Another problem of conceivable interest is that of employing two planes of contrasting directional force (for example, vertical against horizontal) as a basis for experimental construction. The planar use of space as a stimulus for creative discovery should provide the student composer with an enriched understanding of space as a three-dimensional medium.

Density

Space may also be considered by the dancer from the standpoint of its relative density. Movements, for example, that an individual performs in space occupied by air produce different sensations, kinesthetically, when they are performed under water. Different tensions are established between the individual and the space through which he moves. The dancer's imagination may permit him to transform the air into substances of different textures and densities (such as water, molasses, sand, mud, sponge, or fruit cake), which will in turn affect his movement quality and its expressive values.

Range

Range, of necessity, is inseparable from other spatial factors in its actual existence as a part of movement; but, like the others, it may be emphasized experimentally in order that the dancer may discern, through kinesthesia, the exact effect its specific use has upon movement.

Large range is closely associated with a feeling of expansion which, in dance, may be translated into movements of extension; small range is likewise frequently associated with contractive movements, although it is not limited to this association. Range, or dimension, in its literal application to dance movement denotes the relative amount of distance covered by the body in action. It includes both the dimensions of the floor pattern and the size of the body movements. The nature of large and expansive movement is such that it tends to call up kinesthetically to the dancer ideas and emotions that are free, extroverted, and open (Fig. 6; figures are to be found in the insert between pages 118 and 119). Small range and contractive movement act to the contrary and are inclined to arouse associative feelings of confinement and introversion, or to create effects of meticulous precision or of ornamental detail.

Compositional studies based exclusively on the use of large, expansive movement, or on small range or contractive movement, or on a gradual progression from contracted to expansive movement, or from small range to large range and vice versa, or on sharp contrasts in dimension, are equally practicable as space problems. Such studies may be approached either from the literal sense, in which the use of space is realistically defined by imaginary walls or barriers or by ideational content, or they may be handled abstractly, for the purpose of studying the effect of range on movement for its own sake. Particular stage sets often create unusual space areas that influence the range of the dancer's movement and affect the relationship of the dancer to the space in which he moves.

Design

Any composition study, regardless of the exact movement approach, will have an overall spatial structure or design that is the result of conscious planning and selection. Compositional design may be classified as symmetrical or asymmetrical. A symmetrical pattern is one in which movement (viewed from the front) taking place on one side of the dance area is structurally mirrored on the opposite side of the area. An almost classic example of symmetrical arrangement is frequently to be observed on family mantelpieces where a clock or a bowl of flowers appears neatly in the center, with vases or candlesticks placed equidistant on each side. Asymmetrical patterning in choreography involves a lack of symmetry, wherein equilateral repetitions of the movement are not employed. Symmetrical design has traditionally been associated with classic formality; asymmetry is generally less formal, although it is not necessarily so. The use of asymmetrical arrangement, so characteristic of modern dance, has probably developed from the same forces that have influenced modern architectural design. The spatial form of both is functionally determined according to the needs of the creative idea, rather than being regulated by conventional patterns.

Folk dance forms are among the most familiar examples of symmetrical design. Double lines, circles, and squares are some of the patterns they frequently employ. Perhaps because of previous acquaintance with these folk forms, or perhaps because group composition often commences with a sort of group-circle discussion, beginning students are inclined to adopt symmetrical circular formations in their early compositions. Young composers need to learn to be discriminatory in the use of such formations. For social group dances, which are not concerned with audience interest, or for certain types of ritualistic dances, closed square and circular group arrangements are often highly desirable. When dances are intended to be seen by an audience, however, such formations, if used extensively, are usually too enclosed to project well unless they can be observed from above.

Any symmetrical pattern seems to be easier for the novice to comprehend and cope with than an asymmetrical arrangement. In the former type of design, spatial balance is automatically taken care of to a large extent and complexity of patterning is reduced, because both sides of the design are the same. Nevertheless, once the student of composition has been introduced to asymmetrical arrangement, the unexpected and exciting spatial relationships that can be evolved often cause him to discard the symmetrical somewhat contemptuously. It probably will be expedient that he have experience in composing studies concerned exclusively, first with one, then with the other of these two types of spatial arrangement so that he may become aware of the potential usefulness of each. With maturity and adroit teacher guidance, the student will learn to use each kind of spatial design where its expressive values are most appropriate: the symmetrical for the more formal, ceremonial, and obviously ordered moments; and the asymmetrical to lend interest, delight, and surprise to any dance form.

Diagram 5 illustrates the use of symmetrical design in the construction of a floor pattern; Diagrams 6 and 7 illustrate the use of asymmetrical design. In Diagram 5A, two dancers enter from opposite sides of the stage, move toward the center and then downstage; in 5B, two more dancers enter and repeat the floor pattern established by the first two, while the first two progress away from the center and then upstage; in 5C, the first two dancers move diagonally toward center stage and then diagonally away from center stage, progressing continuously downstage while the other two do just the opposite; in 5D, the first two dancers, who are now downstage move slightly upstage and then directly toward the center while the second two dancers reverse the pattern by moving away from the center and then downstage.

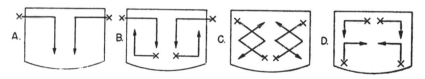

DIAGRAM 5. *A Symmetrical Floor Plan Designed for Four Dancers*

In Diagram 6A in the downstage right area, a man spins in place while three women dance on a stationary kneeling base; in the upstage left area, a woman encircles a man who dances in place. In 6B, the three

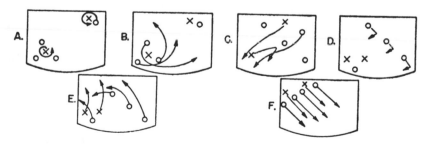

DIAGRAM 6. *An Asymmetrical Floor Plan Designed for Two Men and Four Women (x=man; o=woman)*

women move to form a diagonal line in the center of the stage while the others move in place. In 6C, the two dancers in the upstage left area pass through the diagonal line of women and are joined by the other man. In 6D, the diagonal line changes position slightly while the others dance on a stationary base. In 6E, all dancers move upstage right to form a group, the women in a diagonal line, the men behind them. In 6F all of the dancers move downstage left en masse, ending approximately center stage.

In Diagram 7A, the two dancers in the upstage right area move while the three in the second group remain quiet; in 7B, the second group moves; in 7C, the two groups move around each other to exchange positions on the floor; in 7D, each group makes a half circle to the right, and the two groups then pass through each other.

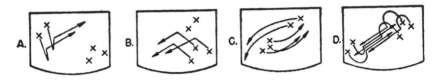

DIAGRAM 7. *An Asymmetrical Floor Plan Designed for Five Dancers*

Conclusion

Throughout the consideration of movement studies based on space factors, two points should be kept clearly in mind. First, the student must have a sufficient foundation of the technical experience in movement that is basic to these problems so that he is adequately prepared to achieve their solution. Second, it must be remembered that regardless of the complexity or high degree of artistic handling of such spatial problems, they are still only studies, the purpose and value of which are to enlarge the dancer's concept of the many compositional uses of space at his command. This enriched experience of movement is the fertile substance from which dance compositions can emerge into expressive art forms.

Suggested Problems for Compositional Studies

1. In a group of four to seven people, compose a movement study in which the principal attention is directed to a floor pattern limited to straight lines. The dancers may progress forward,

sideward, backward, or diagonally, face any direction they please, and each may move in and out among the others in a fashion somewhat similar to the pieces of a chess game. All of the dancers need not be moving across the floor all of the time. Keep the movements simple, but clear-cut, using focus to help establish the directions.

2. In a group or line of three to five dancers, with one person as the leader, move in unison in a curved-line path. Eventually, as the pattern develops, individuals may break away from the group to make new curved patterns of their own; then, gradually, they may relate to each other in twos or threes until finally the whole group is moving together again with a new leader.

3. With any number of people up to seven, compose a movement study in which the dancers relate themselves to a single focal point which both attracts and repels them.

4. In a group of five or six people, continually shift the focus from one point to another, with each person moving individually as if searching for something. Make the focal points definite. Increase the tempo and bodily tension until the whole pattern becomes quite frantic. Finally, establish a single goal or objective to which each of the individuals, one at a time, is eventually drawn.

5. By means of focus, change of body level, and body movement, establish a feeling of unattainable height in one area of the space and a feeling of penetrating depth (such as one might feel on looking into a well) in another area. The problem may be solved individually or by a group.

6. In a group of five or six people, compose a study in which each member of the group makes use of two or three levels. Take advantage of opportunities to contrast one level with another, but see that the movements of the dancers are also related to each other. Make good use of each level chosen. Include also some floor pattern that will permit the spatial relationships among the members of the group to be changed.

7. In threes, choose two parallel vertical planes. One individual is to relate all of his movement as completely as possible to one of the planes while the other two people relate themselves to the second plane. Keep all movements as flat as possible in order to emphasize the two-dimensional character of the planes.

8. Create a group study using movement on at least three different levels to establish an impression of horizontal planes. Give some of the movement a locomotor base where it is possible to do so.

9. Divide the dance space into three sharply defined areas. The density of one area is to be thin, permitting the dancer to extend his movement to its fullest range with a minimum of bodily tension; the space in the second area is weighty, pressing in upon the dancer's body causing it gradually to contract, or permitting it to expand only as a result of intense muscular effort; the third area is not weighty, but there are strong air currents that periodically carry the dancer in unexpected directions. As the dancer moves from one area into another the change in the characteristics of the space should be reflected in the dancer's movement.

10. Create a movement study with groups of four or five people in which the movement range changes in one of the following ways, from

(1) large to small;

(2) small to large;

(3) large to small to large;

(4) small to large to small.

11. Working in couples or in threes, move on the inside of some imaginary three-dimensional form such as a cube, a cone, a sphere, or narrow tunnel that widens suddenly at one end. Define the shape of the enclosure by means of the dance movement.

12. In a group of four or six people organized in partners, compose a short study in symmetrical design. Partners, working on opposite sides of the dance area, are to mirror each other's movement and must try to keep an equal distance from the center line; they must also be sensitive to their relationships with the other couples. Emphasize floor pattern, but include also some change of level.

13. Draw a linear design, varying the intensity of the lines. Use the design as a floor pattern, choosing locomotor and body movements that are strong for the accented portions of the design and movements that are correspondingly less forceful for the unaccented areas.

14. Place several objects of contrasting forms (such as a tall standard for a volleyball net, a large, low platform or box or table, and a set of movable steps) in different parts of the dance floor. Working individually, but as one of a large group, improvise dance movement that will include most of the dance area. Respond kinesthetically in some active fashion to the shapes of the objects on the floor whenever they are close by. (Climb the steps or emphasize their broken diagonal line by means of body movement, and so forth.) Also, be sensitive to spatial relationships with other dancers. Two people who find themselves together momentarily should recognize each other, respond to the movement quality, rhythm, or directional pattern of the other individual, and continue together until the need for moving together has been satisfied.

15. Using from ten to twelve people, begin a dance study with all of the participants centered in a closely knit group. Gradually break up the mass by having the dancers, singly or in groups of three, two, or four move away from the original mass, one group at a time. The floor patterns of the newly formed groups may encompass any part of the dance area. As the small groups pass near or through one another some of the dancers may transfer from one group to the other, thus constantly reorganizing themselves into new group relationships. Make the movement pattern of each group as interesting as possible, including such considerations as change of level, dynamic variation, and so forth. At the same time, be conscious of the relationship of the movement of each individual group to that of adjacent groups and to the group as a whole.

16. Organize into five groups as indicated in Diagram 8A. The level on which each group is to begin moving is specified.

Groups 2, 3, and 4 are to move in place for four counts; they are then to use sixteen counts to move to their next positions on the floor (Diagram 8B).

Groups 1 and 5 are to move in place for eight counts and then use sixteen counts to move to their next positions on the floor (Diagram 8B).

After reaching the position indicated in Diagram 8B, all groups are to use eight counts to move in place and sixteen counts to progress to the final position indicated in Diagram 8C.

Groups 2, 3, and 4 move in place for eight counts. Groups 1 and 5 move in place for four counts. Throughout the dance study each group moves in unison. When progressing from one place to another on the floor, the groups may choose whatever path they prefer but should

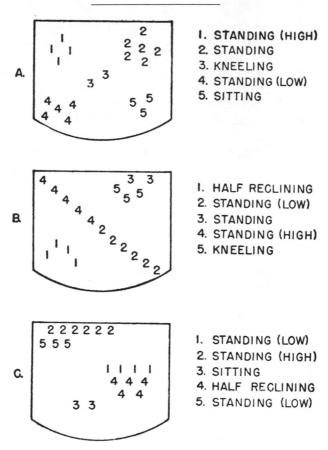

DIAGRAM 8. *Problem in Floor Pattern and Change of Level*

assume responsibility for helping to balance the space as a whole. Groups that pass by or through other groups should recognize and react to the other group by means of its dance movement. Keep the movement patterns very simple, but make them definite.

The problem may easily be adapted to include a greater or lesser number of people.

Chapter 5

Dance Studies Based

on Elements of Rhythm

Rhythm is a property intrinsic to all of man's activity and to all of his environment; it might be defined as the measuring of time, space, and energy. One perceives rhythm in the relationship of one object or element to another in terms of time and distance and intensity. Since the individual ordinarily perceives distance by means of eye movements, distance is also measurable in terms of the time required to move the eye from the beginning to the end of a space unit. Therefore, the study of rhythm, for all intents and purposes, resolves itself into a study of measured time and energy.

Kinesthetic Perception of Rhythm

All movement is rhythmic, whether or not it is recognized to be so. The more regular and obvious the relationship with reference to time and energy between the parts of a pattern, the more easily is one able to recognize and define the rhythm. Subtle or complex relationships sometimes create an impression that rhythm is lacking. For example, the relationship between the dance movement of the Native American and his drum accompaniment is often so complex and difficult to define that the uninitiated might at first feel that one or the other was out of time. Yet the relationship is there; it needs only to be understood. As stated in Chapter 2, exact repetition is not an inherent characteristic of rhythm; repetition does, however, increase one's ability to identify a rhythm by intensifying one's awareness of the rhythmic organization. The student of dance must learn through experience just how subtle his rhythms can be and how much repetition is necessary to permit the observer to comprehend his rhythmic dance structures and to appreciate their expressive values.

The rhythm of movement in the human organism is kinesthetically perceived and governed. The muscular contractions that produce move-

57

ment in the body consume time and energy. The rhythmic structure of movement is determined by the relationship of the specific amounts of time and energy expended in the various parts of the movement sequences. Kinesthesia enables one to know *how much time* and energy has been expended. Thus the development of kinesthetic sensitivity which will enable the student to recognize and to regulate the expenditure of time and energy in his dance movement is supremely important to successful choreography.

In working with movement, untrained dancers are often inclined to drift into loose habits of analytical thought, employing a kind of "dancer's count" as it is ignominiously called. In such cases, the dancers are usually found to be numbering the separate movements of the pattern regardless of their relative timing. The count sounds something like 1, 2–3 (pause) 4, instead of an even 1, 2, 3, 4, representing the steady beat which temporally measures one movement with another. Until the dance composer is conscious of the rhythmic structure of his dance movement he lacks the ability to control it.

The following suggestions for rhythmic studies are given in the hope that they may provide movement experiences for the young composer which will heighten his kinesthetic awareness of rhythm, will develop his ability to control rhythm and to use it ingeniously, and will increase his appreciation of the potentialities of rhythmic expression.

Meter and Accent

Simple Meters

The beat is the dancer's smallest unit of temporal measurement. The grouping of beats by means of accent, called "meter," is probably the simplest conceivable form of rhythmic organization, yet it offers more in the way of compositional stimulus for dance than one may at first realize.

To begin with, each specific meter, for example 2/4, 3/4, 4/4, or 6/8, has its own definite character, which is determined by its particular tempo and rhythmic structure. Normally, a moderate 6/8 or a fast 3/4, for example, is likely to suggest a swinging movement response because of its tempo and ternary organization; on the other hand, a brisk 4/4 may prompt a sharper, more direct quality of movement—again because of its particular metrical structure. In composing a study based on a definite meter, the student may take advantage of these innate qualities and enlarge upon them. Conversely, for purposes of experimentation and divertissement, he may deliberately defy the inherent nature of accepted movement style of the meter. Studies entitled "Waltz in 4/4" or "March in 3/4" are illustrative of this latter approach.

It is also important for the student to become acquainted with less well-known meters, such as 5/4, 7/4, 9/8, or 12/8, the potentialities of which are yet to be fully appreciated by the average person. Frequently, in long measures, secondary metrical accents play important roles. An alteration in the placement of such secondary accents can change the rhythmic character of a metrical pattern by rearranging the grouping of beats in the measure. For example, in a 5/4 rhythm, a secondary accent might be placed on either the third or the fourth beat in the measure. If it were placed on count 3, the sub-organization would be two beats followed by three beats, as illustrated in the metrical pattern below.

$$\frac{5}{4}\Big| \overset{\diagup}{\rule{2em}{0.4pt}} \rule{2em}{0.4pt}\; \overset{\diagup}{\rule{2em}{0.4pt}} \rule{2em}{0.4pt}\; \rule{2em}{0.4pt} \Big|$$

If it occurred on count 4, the subgrouping would be three and two.

$$\frac{5}{4}\Big| \overset{\diagup}{\rule{2em}{0.4pt}} \rule{2em}{0.4pt}\; \rule{2em}{0.4pt}\; \overset{\diagup}{\rule{2em}{0.4pt}} \rule{2em}{0.4pt} \Big|$$

The total rhythmic effect of the 5/4 measure is thus materially changed by such a shift in accent. Interesting rhythmic structures on which to compose movement may be created by alternating measures of the same meter in which the beats have been grouped in different ways as a result of the placement of secondary accents.

Mixed Meters

Modern dance, like modern music, frequently incorporates a number of different meters in the same composition. They may appear as contrasting sections of a single dance, or the change may occur in closer proximity, such as a measure of 3/4, followed by two measures of 5/4, and then by one of 4/4, and so forth.

There are at least two methods of approach in developing a study of this sort. The dance composer may plan the metrical organization before composing the movement; or he may let the meter be determined freely by his choice of movement, keeping in mind that change in meter is to be the desired source of rhythmic interest. The value of the former approach lies in its rhythmic discipline. The latter approach is more natural and less confining than the former, since choice of movement is not inhibited by a prearranged rhythmic frame, and the results may seem less mechanical. For the beginning student whose acquaintance with dance and musical form has been with the conventional single-meter type, such compositional experiences can be both enlightening and enriching.

Cumulative Meters

Occasionally a specifically ordered arrangement of measures of different meters is desirable, because of the particular dynamics established by such organization. A pattern of measures in which the number of beats in each successive measure is increased or diminished in a definite arithmetic progression, such as

```
       2      3         4          5            6
 1.  |— —|— — —|— — — —|— — — — —|— — — — — —|

       1    3      5         7          5       3    1
2. or |—|— — —|— — — — —|— — — — — — —|— — — — —|— — —|—|

         5       2      4      2    3    2    2    2  1
3. or |— — — — —|— — |— — — —|— —|— — —|— —|— —|— —|—|
```

is sometimes identified as "cumulative meter." Although the metrical accent actually occurs on the first beat of each measure, there is often a tendency in working with cumulative meters to *feel* accent, instead, on the last beat of each measure. This phenomenon may be explained by the fact that emphasis tends to be directed to that point in the measure which represents the cutting off or completion of that particular grouping of beats. In movement, also, additional energy is sometimes expended at this point, to check the direction of an established movement preparatory to the introduction of a new direction in the following measure. Actually, the accent may be placed on *either* the first or the last beats in the pattern, provided the chosen plan is followed consistently. The resulting choreographic effect, however, may be quite different in the two cases. One rhythmic plan emphasizes the introduction of each unit of movement, whereas the other stresses its arrest or completion. The metrical pattern tends to become proportionately more dynamic as the metrical accents occur in increasingly rapid succession. Hence, as the number of beats in each measure is diminished, rhythmic excitement increases; and, conversely, as the measures are lengthened, rhythmic tension is gradually dispelled. Spatially, on the other hand, measures are inclined to become stronger in proportion to their greater number of beats, since the lengthening of time between accents permits the range of movement to be enlarged. The effectiveness of a cumulative metrical plan is the more apparent when it is contrasted with a steady meter in the adjacent sections of the composition. It is important that the student of dance discover the characteristics of cumulative structures through studying such forms, so that he may take advantage of their contributions to dance expression.

Meters in Counterpoint

Both modern dancers and modern musicians occasionally find compositionally desirable the simultaneous employment of two unlike meters. For instance, in some modern music the score indicates one meter in the treble clef, and another for the bass. Such a combination effects an interplay of accents between the two meters that creates a rhythmic impression of complementary action or of orderly conflict. A similar result is obtained in the dance idiom when two dancers or groups of dancers present simultaneously movements based on different meters. In a study in metrical accent that employs two groups of dancers at the same time, for instance, one group might be accenting the first of every three beats, basing its movement on 3/4 meter, while the other group accents the first of every four beats, working in 4/4 meter. Even though the metrical accents are at variance, the underlying pulse that is shared by both rhythms establishes a temporal relationship between the two meters. In building composition on such a rhythmic organization, the choreographer will need to remember that special care must be taken to interrelate the different groups through a wise choice of movement and use of space. Otherwise the pattern is likely to fall apart, becoming two dances concurrently exhibited.

Resultant Rhythms

When two different meters are performed simultaneously, a third rhythmic structure which has an identity of its own is created by the sum of their accents. This particular rhythmic structure is known as a resultant rhythm. For example, if a 3/4 meter is superimposed on a 5/4 meter, the sum of their accents results in a 15/4 pattern of irregularly accented beats. This latter structure is the resultant rhythm.

The syncopation established by such an irregularly accented rhythmic structure may motivate the choreographer to discover correspondingly interesting movement forms. The presentation of a resultant rhythm suggests a number of compositional possibilities. The rhythm might be performed by an entire group in unison; it might be presented simultaneously against movements constructed on one of the meters from which it is derived (for example, resultant rhythm against 3/4); all three rhythms might be danced concurrently (resultant rhythm, 3/4, and 5/4); or the three rhythms might be danced successively or transferred from one group to another. The choreographic plan of the resultant rhythm might be designed to show its relationship to the simple meters by incorporating the accented movements of these two meters into its compositional scheme; or it might be comprised of movements that oppose or contrast with the movements of the simple meters. If the dancers are well-disciplined to maintain their pattern against rhythmic distractions, the effect of syncopation may be further enhanced by employing accompaniment that does not follow exactly the accents of the dancers' resultant rhythm. Accompaniment that is built on one or the other of the basic meters involved, but with an independent and slightly syncopated rhythm of its own, or one that is built on a third, unrelated meter, can provide an effective counterpoint to the movement which will add to the total rhythmic excitement. Thus the resultant rhythm derived from 3/4 and 5/4 meters, for example, might be performed successfully to a syncopated 4/4 accompaniment.

Arbitrarily Imposed Accents

Accents other than metrical accents may also be employed to increase the rhythmic interest of a pattern. The composer is then free to select the beats or portions of beats on which he wishes to establish these accents. Syncopation, the placement of accents on normally unaccented beats or portions of beats, has a stimulating effect on the senses, activating motor response. Such superimposed accents can be placed according to some definite scheme of organization. The following accent patterns in 4/4 meter illustrate that an accent might be placed regularly on the second count (pattern 1), or it might be shifted from the first beat to the second, to the third, and to the fourth in each successive measure (pattern 2). Or the accents might be arranged irregularly to suit the composer's personal fancy. Very simple rhythmic problems of this type are capable of providing many worthwhile creative opportunities for the student choreographer. (See the following three examples.)

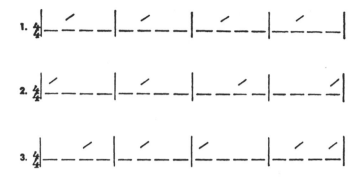

A sixteen-beat measure, or two measures of eight beats, is a very workable frame on which to superimpose accents. At first, the dance study might be limited to movement that can be done on a simple walking base—one step to every beat—eliminating any further rhythmic complications. The problem then would be merely one of finding effectual ways of establishing accent while walking. The student will discover that accents can be created by movements of the arms or body, by change of direction or of level, by increased force or size of step, or by variation in the manner of performance in walking. When these possibilities have been explored, the limitations might be expanded to include modification of step pattern (for example, substitution of leaps, hops, or jumps for the walking steps on the accented beats). Later, the composer might be permitted to vary the length of the intervals in the rhythmic pattern— prolonging the accented intervals and dividing unaccented beats, or omitting some unaccented intervals altogether and thus giving himself still greater compositional freedom. The following illustrates a rhythmic variation of accent pattern 3 given above.

Interesting duets may be composed by employing contrapuntally two dissimilar patterns of accent. For example, a dancer may compose movement to fit pattern 1, while her partner's movement is constructed to conform with pattern 2.

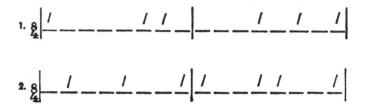

Again, the dynamic quality of all such studies is increased when they are presented against a syncopated background accompaniment in which the rhythms are not completely identical with those of the dance form.

Rhythmic Pattern

Thus far, the discussion of rhythmic stimuli for compositional effort has been limited primarily to meter and accent. Variation in the relative duration of the time intervals (or in note values) has been purposely omitted or considered only incidentally. Rhythmic pattern, which involves the organized patterning of beats, combined beats, or their sub-divisions, presents so many alterable factors that it is impossible even to visualize all of the conceivable rhythmic combinations. The fact that two quarter notes and two eighth notes may be arranged in six different ways

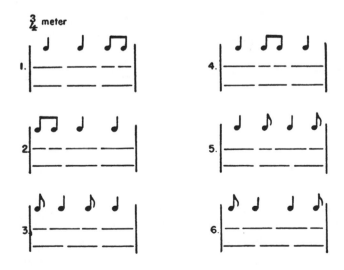

relative to one measure of 3/4 meter exemplifies the infinitude of rhythmic variations existent for those who are interested in finding them.

As an element in dance composition, rhythmic pattern is tremendously important. The application to movement of dynamically interesting rhythms can often transform dance that might otherwise seem trite and ordinary into highly pleasing choreography.

The use of the rhythmic pattern as a basis for compositional endeavor offers the young student excellent discipline in rhythmic precision, a virtue frequently lacking in the untrained individual. It is of paramount importance, then, for the instructor to require strict accuracy in rhythmic response if the problem is to fulfill its educational purpose. It is usually expedient in the beginning to make rhythmic problems brief, so that emphasis is not placed on the learning of a pattern but rather on the accurate choreographic planning and performance of it. Later, rhythmic problems can be lengthened to include several measures. Two examples of simple rhythmic patterns follow:

It is important in composing a rhythmic pattern to make sure that the pattern can be felt as a rhythmic entity when it is completed. Unless the rhythm can be readily sensed as a whole, it is difficult to comprehend and to use. Often, more satisfactory results may be obtained by tapping out a rhythm that sounds or feels good and then writing it down, than by working out the rhythm first on paper.

The arbitrary rhythmic restrictions imposed by a complex rhythmic pattern may inhibit spontaneity of movement until the composer becomes mentally and bodily saturated with its particular rhythmic organization. Nevertheless, the composition of studies based on such a stimulus can be extremely challenging, and there is real intellectual—as well as physical and emotional—satisfaction in their successful achievement. In addition to its disciplinary values, a rhythmic pattern, in a positive sense as a stimulus for dance, is frequently evocative of new choreographic material. The attempt to compose within restrictions set by a particular rhythmic pattern often leads the dancer to the discovery and selection of movement that is fresh and original in form and intrinsic meaning.

A very simple rhythmic pattern can be interesting as a round when the measures are designed to contrast with each other. The following rhythm is an example of a pattern suitable for a round, provided appropriate movement is also selected. (The composition of rounds is discussed in further detail on pp. 88–90.)

Likewise, two simple rhythms may be presented in counterpoint with pleasing effect. Two illustrations, one in 3/4 and the other in 4/4, follow. In each instance the first rhythm might be presented simultaneously with the second, one group of dancers performing pattern 1 while another group performs pattern 2. Then, if desired, the groups may exchange rhythms, perhaps giving the patterns new movement interpretations.

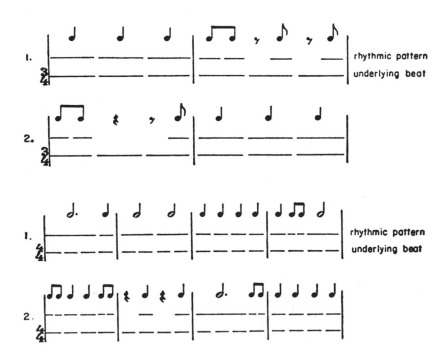

The fact that two patterns are being performed at the same time introduces sufficient rhythmic complication so that the rhythmic patterns themselves need not be elaborate. Effort should be directed instead toward establishing effective rhythmic contrast between the two patterns. Again, in composing the movements for the two rhythmic patterns each group must consider how its movements are going to relate to and contrast with those of the other group.

Interesting rhythmic patterns exist within such familiar movements as shaking hands or scrubbing clothes; these may be discovered, analyzed, and then used as a basis for developing movement variations on that rhythmic structure. The systematized movements of the assembly-line worker may provide usable rhythmic material for the dancer; he may create rhythmic variations of the original utilitarian movement by changing the rhythmic structure, the underlying meter, or the tempo of a familiar movement sequence. Rhythmic patterns may also be derived from environmental sounds and visual designs: from poetry and nursery rhymes; from the rhythmic sound of shoes being polished; from the rhythm found in an ornamentalal border design. The illustrations below are of rhythmic patterns that may be developed from these three sources.

1. Rhythmic pattern derived from poetry. (See page 68.)

2. Rhythmic pattern created by the motions and the "slap slap" sounds of a shoe-shine polishing cloth being brushed back and forth over a shoe.

3. Rhythmic pattern derived from a border design as a result of tracing the linear outlines.

Diagram 9. *Border Design*

SING SONG by Christina Rosetti

```
| Mo - ther   shake   the   cher - ry            tree |   Verse
                                                         rhythmic pattern
4/4                                                      underlying beat
```

```
| Su - san   catch   a   cher - ry |
```

```
| Oh   how   fun - ny   that   would   be |
```

```
| Let's   be   mer - ry! |
```

BREAK, BREAK, BREAK by Alfred Lord Tennyson

```
| Break,        break,   | break,            On   thy |
6/8
| cold   gray   stones,   O |   Sea!          And   I |
| would   that   my   tongue   could | ut - ter        The |
| tho'ts   that   a - rise   in |   me. |
```

Tempo and Intensity

Rhythmic patterns serve also as excellent structural foundations from which to conduct compositional experiments involving tempo and intensity. Both of these rhythmic elements are properties of movement that cannot be divorced from it. However, for purposes of creative experimentation the dance composer may manipulate the tempo or the intensity independently in order to discover, exactly, its special contribution to movement expression. Obviously, the quality of slow, strong movement will change if either the tempo is increased or the intensity diminished. It is important for the young choreographer to observe these qualitative changes so that he may learn to regulate his use of tempo and intensity in later dance forms in accordance with his expressive needs.

"Twice as Fast and Twice as Slow"

A type of study designed to illustrate the effect on movement of contrasting tempos is one that has been called "twice as fast and twice as slow." As the name suggests, each measure or phrase of the rhythmic structure is repeated in a tempo exactly twice as fast and, again, twice as slow as the original motif. The rhythm is first presented in a moderate tempo, in order to establish a basis for contrast; it may or may not be repeated between the two temporal extremes. In the following illustration the first measure exemplifies a rhythm in moderate tempo; the second, a rhythm twice as fast as the first; the third, a rhythm twice as slow as the first.

Other measures may be treated in a like manner to make a rhythmic study of desired length.

If the movement pattern that has been selected for the measure of moderate speed is repeated identically in fast and slow tempos, the student can learn a great deal by observing kinesthetically the effect each rate of speed has on the movement. He will discover the necessity for selecting movement that is practicable and that retains its interest when repeated in the three different tempos. Highly intricate movements or those involving large range may prove unfeasible when the tempo is doubled; likewise, leaps and jumps or movement requiring difficult balance may be ill-suited to a slowed tempo.

Another challenge which the novitiate will encounter is that of making his rhythms *exactly* twice as fast or twice as slow as the original pattern. This problem is made easier when the total pattern at all three tempos can be related to a constant underlying beat, as in the previous illustration.

The study offers comic possibilities as well, especially if the three tempos are represented by three dancers whose natural body structures predispose them to move at different rates of speed (a tall, rangy person taking the slow rhythm and a very petite individual the quick tempo).

Various Tempos and Intensities in Combination

A movement sequence built on a definite rhythmic pattern may present a variety of choreographic impressions as a result of alteration in both the tempo and the intensity which govern the movement. For example, a movement pattern that, in the original, was performed at a moderate speed with moderate intensity might also be performed in fast tempo, weak force; moderate tempo, strong force; slow tempo, weak force; fast tempo, strong force, and so forth. It may be enlightening to students to describe in words the impressions that are suggested to each of them through kinesthetic association as a result of performing the movement sequence in different tempos and intensities. For example, movements that are danced slowly with little force might be termed "stealthy" by some and, perhaps, "soothing and caressive" by others. The same movements, vigorously performed in a rapid tempo, may seem "frenzied"; or, when performed slowly with strong intensity they may present an impression of "defiance" or "aggression." Another experimental possibility is that of contrasting different tempos and intensities within a given movement sequence.

Various combinations of speed and force may also be applied to rhythmic patterns for which no specific movements have been designed. The composer may then select whatever movement he feels is appropriate to the particular tempo and intensity that has been assigned for the rhythmic pattern. With each modification of speed and force differences in the creative results, both in terms of style and in choice of movements, will undoubtedly be observable.

Rhapsodic Rhythms, or Breath Rhythms

Rhapsodic, or breath, rhythms represent a type of rhythmical structure that cannot be metronomically defined or regulated. Just as the rhythm of breathing is quickened or retarded by the individual's state of physical or emotional excitement, so also may the rhythmic structure of his movement be affected. For that reason, rhythms of this type are sometimes referred to as breath rhythms. The rhythmic structure is flexible in both tempo and intensity, permitting gradual or sudden acceleration or retardation of the rhythmic count, and a modification of intensity according to the dictates of the inner dynamics of the movements as performed by the dancers. Rhythms of this sort are to be found in musical compositions of the rhapsodic type in which the flexibility of the rhythmic organization allows the artist a certain latitude for individual interpretation. No rhythm that is humanly performed can be completely devoid of slight variations in tempo and intensity. In a rhapsodic rhythm, however, such variations are deliberately sought for their expressional values. Because the rhythmic structures of rhapsodic, or breath, rhythms are for the most part subjectively established, group work on such compositions necessitates repeated rehearsal until all of the performers can sense, kinesthetically, a mutual pulse and dynamic organization. Although it can be a highly effective form of rhythmic expression, rhapsodic rhythm must be used with integrity and not as an excuse for careless rhythmic construction resulting from indolence or sentimentality.

Conclusion

One should not infer from this discussion of composition based on elements of rhythm that awareness of rhythmic form should be confined to these studies alone. The composer should be held accountable for an exact analysis and understanding of the rhythmic structure of every dance form he creates. Only with the security that is derived from complete understanding can a group of dancers work together with rhythmic unity, or communicate the rhythmic structure of their dance pattern to their accompanist and to their audience. Keen rhythmic awareness, exacting discipline, and a broad background of rhythmic experience are essential to all significant dance composition.

Suggested Problems for Compositional Studies

1. In small groups, compose a movement study in 3/4 meter and give it a marchlike quality. As an alternative, compose a study in waltz quality to 4/4 or 5/4 meter. (Of the two meters, the 5/4 is more nearly like a waltz rhythm since they both contain an uneven number of beats.)

2. Create a movement study in 7/4 meter, organizing the rhythm of the movements in such a way that the subgrouping of the seven beats is not always the same. Part of the time the groupings of beats in the 7/4 measure may be presented as 4 and 3; part of the time as 3 and 4; sometimes as an unbroken 7; and occasionally as 2, 2 and 3; 2, 3, and 2; or 3, 2, and 2.

3. Compose a movement phrase or series of phrases using the digits in the telephone number of a member of the group as the basis for the metrical pattern. If the telephone number were 334-8256, for example, the metrical pattern would be two measures of three beats, one measure of four beats, followed by a measure of eight beats, a measure of two beats, a measure of five beats, and a measure of six beats. This pattern may be repeated if necessary.

4. Compose a movement study in cumulative rhythm according to the following metrical scheme: 1, 3, 5, 7, 5, 3, 1, 4, 4, 4, 4, 1, 3, 5, 7 (the numbers represent the number of beats in each measure). Accent the last beat in each measure, except in the measures of four beats, in which the first beat is to be accented.

5. Fashion a study in resultant rhythm, using 3/4 and 5/4 as the two basic meters (see patterns on p. 62). With a group of five or six people, begin the study by having some of the dancers perform five measures of 3/4 meter while the others perform simultaneously three measures of 5/4 meter, accenting strongly the first beat of each measure. All other beats remain unaccented. Continue the study, with everyone performing the resultant rhythm in unison twice. The same movement or different movement may be used for the repetition. Conclude the study by presenting once more the 3/4 meter against the 5/4 meter, but with different groups of people performing the two meters. Present the whole study against a syncopated 4/4 accompaniment.

6. In twos, create a movement study using a steady rhythm of four measures of 8/4 as a base. Establish rhythmic interest by accenting certain beats at irregular intervals in the pattern by means of strong, well-defined movements. The two individuals dancing together should not accent the same beats except occasionally, when it seems compositionally desirable. Partners should endeavor to interrelate their movements.

7. In groups, create a movement study based on the rhythmic pattern of a nursery rhyme. Do not pantomime the nursery

rhyme, but use purely abstract movement. The rhythmic pattern may be passed from one individual or a portion of the group to another, or it may be performed by everyone in unison. Be sure that there is a movement for every syllable of the nursery rhyme or interval of the rhythmic pattern. Try to guess the nursery rhyme that was chosen by each group by observing the rhythm of the dance movement.

8. In couples, compose a dance study built on 3/4 (or 4/4 or 5/4) meter. The two participants are to create unlike rhythmic patterns which they perform in counterpoint. Although the rhythmic patterns of their movements are not the same, the dancers should relate their movements to each other spatially and dynamically for the sake of compositional unity. Brief examples of rhythmic counterpoint are found on page 66.

9. With a group of sixteen dancers, arranged so that there are four dancers in each corner of the dance area, give the entire group a simple four-measure pattern based on walks and claps. Make each measure of the pattern sufficiently different in movement and sound so that the measures provide interesting contrast to each other. Now have the group of dancers in one corner perform the pattern as given. Begin another foursome with measure 2, doing measures 2, 3, 4, and 1. Begin the third group with measure 3, and the fourth group with measure 4. All groups are to begin at the same time and move toward the center of the dance area. When the dancers reach the center (at the end of their pattern) they must each run to a new corner and begin again, moving toward the center but this time performing the pattern assigned to that particular corner. There can be only four dancers in any one corner. Continue changing corners with each repetition of the pattern. A sample of the type of pattern which could be used is given below.

| step clap step clap step clap | step | step | clap | step | clap | clap |

3/4

clap step step step step step		movement pattern
		rhythmic pattern
		underlying beat

The problem may be further complicated by making a completely different pattern for each corner. Then the dancers must learn all four patterns in order to be able to change from one corner to another.

10. In groups of three or four individuals, devise a very simple rhythm pattern of four measures of 4/4 meter such as the following:

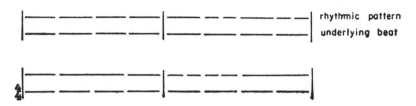

Create a movement pattern to fit the rhythmic structure of the first measure; repeat the same movement pattern, exactly twice as fast; then do it once again, in moderate tempo; and, finally, repeat the pattern, exactly twice as slow. Proceed from there to work out each of the succeeding measures in like fashion. Be sure to select movements for the pattern in moderate tempo that can be adapted comfortably to a tempo that is twice as fast and also twice as slow. Select various members of the group to perform the moderate, twice as fast, and twice as slow rhythms; they may be the same or different people each time. Portions of the pattern may also be performed by more than one member of the group. Include some floor pattern, but use body movement also in working out the movement pattern. The problem may suggest comic possibilities.

11. Construct a simple four- or eight-measure rhythmic pattern in 4/4 or 5/4 meter. Divide the class into groups of from two to six people, to compose on this rhythmic structure a movement pattern that is designed to be performed according to one of the following schemes:

(1) slow tempo, strong intensity;

(2) fast tempo, weak intensity;

(3) slow tempo, weak intensity;

(4) fast tempo, strong intensity.

Each group may choose its own tempo-intensity combination. Notice the effect these different combinations of tempo and intensity have on the choice of movement and on the movement quality and style.

12. In couples, improvise movement on a designated meter. Each individual is to decide whether the intensity of his movement is to be strong or weak. If one dancer's movements are relatively weak and his partner's are strong, he should assume a subordinate role and passively relate his movements to those of his partner. If the movements of both individuals are concurrently weak, no sense of relationship may be present between the dancers; rather, they may give a feeling of drifting apart. If both dancers' movements are simultaneously strong, a feeling of conflict may result. The individuals may change roles at any time. Try to be sensitive to the differences of movement intensity displayed by the other dancer.

13. In small groups, develop a movement study based on breath rhythms, in which the rhythmic structure is not related to a metronomic count, but is entirely determined by the inner dynamics of the dance movement.

Chapter 6

A Structural Approach to

Dance Composition

The previous chapters have reiterated the premise that the structure of an artistic creation and its motivating idea are interactive and interdependent. However, the creative process in art is, as a rule, initiated by the conception of an idea. For an artist to begin with a form and then to decide what he wishes to convey with it is to reverse the natural creative procedure. Only when the form, itself, is the idea, is such a plan justifiable in art.

Certain types of structural organization are, however, more or less universally employed because they seem to be organically suited to the expressive needs of composition. As a result of this universal usage some of these forms have been given identifying labels, such as "A B A" or "theme and variations." In the study of dance composition it is advisable to see that the student has a firsthand acquaintance with all of these conventional structures. With the inclusion of some study of these forms, the student can investigate for himself the potential choreographic values that each possesses. Thus it becomes necessary here to focus attention specifically on the structural organization of dance.

Compositional structure in terms of dance falls into two general classifications: the first category concerns the *dancers,* with reference to their numbers, arrangement and movement relationships to each other; the second concerns the movement *themes* of a composition in terms of their structural organization and interplay of patterns.

Group Relationships

Any dance involving more than one participant necessitates a consideration of the mutual relations of the dancers—spatially, temporally, and dynamically.

The Duet

Although relatively simple, a duet introduces certain choreographic aspects that are not present in solo composition. To compose a duet that is actually a composition for two dancers is not as simple as it might at first appear. The choreography must be of such a nature that it cannot be presented as effectively as a solo, a trio, or a quartet. Two people—no more, no less—should be necessary for its consummation. It is possible, of course, for the two dancers to perform the same movement pattern. However, a constant use of parallel repetition of movement or of symmetrical opposition (one dancer mirroring the other) in a duet can make the movement of the second dancer seem redundant and unnecessary to the projective meaning of the dance. Choreographic interest is usually heightened when the two dancers perform different but complementary and related movements (Fig. 7; figures will be found in the insert between pages 118 and 119). Each dancer thereby becomes a vital and indispensable part of the compositional design. Both parallel and symmetrical repetition have a place in duet choreography; however they should be used discriminatingly as a means of emphasizing a particular movement sequence, of engendering variety within the total composition, or of satisfying the special demands of the dance idea.

If the student is to become creatively proficient in his use of the duet form, he will need to be given opportunities for experimentation. Improvisation with a partner is one valuable source of experience. By this active exploratory means, dancers extemporize new couple relationships that can be used in later compositions.

A good introductory problem in couple improvisation is the one described on page 35 in the discussion of composition based upon qualities of movement. Each of the two participants alternately initiates an extemporaneous movement phrase while his partner assumes a subordinate or less active role. The problem of improvisation may be given limitations, such as ascribing the special quality of movement or the length of phrase to be employed; or the setting of limitations may be left to the accompanist, or, more appropriately, to the dancers themselves to determine as the improvisation progresses. In the latter instance, the problem becomes a sort of game of Follow the Leader, with the two dancers alternately taking the creative initiative.

Another variant of the same idea is extemporization in which one partner remains the continually dominant member and the other is consistently passive or subordinate. This type of organization sometimes suggests dramatic connotations—perhaps hypnosis, tyranny, or imitative adulation. Dramatic ideas, of course, may be capitalized on, although the dancers should be encouraged to consider the problem also in its more abstract phases of spatial, temporal, and dynamic relationship. The follower should experiment with all types of response to the leader's movement stimuli. He may repeat the motion in parallel or sequential imitation; he may, as his partner's reflection, mirror it; or he may follow the movement command or idea that is intimated in the leader's actions.

A third plan for improvisation involves a more subtle partner relationship than that described in either of the two previous suggestions for studies; it is one in which the roles of leader and follower are not specifically assigned. Instead, each dancer must become sensitive enough to his partner's movement to know instinctively whether to assume the initiative, whether to relinquish it to his fellow dancer, or whether to counterbalance his partner's movement with equally aggressive movements of opposition and contrast. A problem of this nature develops not only the dancer's creative abilities, but also his sense of rapport, or sympathetic accord, with another person's movement, a characteristic that is essential to all successful group composition.

Such preliminary experiences in improvisation contribute greatly to the student's complete understanding of the duet as a dance form, understanding that will later be of assistance to him in fashioning duets that are reflectively planned with a view to their meaningful content.

The Trio and the Quartet

The trio and the quartet become increasingly complex in compositional structure as the number of performers is augmented, but the possibilities for choreographic variation are likewise expanded. Here, again, the problem is to make each dancer essential to the choreography. Improvisation for such a scheme is more difficult than for the duet form, since extemporaneous adjustment to two or three people is harder than such adjustment to only one. Improvisation may lead to the discovery of much excellent choreographic material, but satisfactory results with the trio and with the quartet are likely to be most successfully achieved on a premeditated basis.

Large-Group Compositions

The large-group dance has perhaps the most versatile possibilities of all the choreographic forms for group arrangement. Smaller groups may be made by dividing the large one, thereby continually changing group relationships and numerical proportions. Group arrangement in a quartet is limited to 4; 3–1; 2–2; or 2–1–1. On the other hand, a dance involving nine participants may be arranged as 9, or (to mention only some) divided into groups of 1–8; 2–7; 3–6; 4–5; 3–3–3;1–3–5; or 2–3–4, not to mention them all. There is danger, of course, in breaking a large unit into too many small ones. Such compositional organization can be distracting to watch if no center of interest is established. In general, when there are several groups, one of these should be made temporarily dominant. Even when there are only two groups, it is usually advisable to focus the attention alternately on one or the other, or else to select clever contrast movement by means of which each group will point up the other.

Movement in Unison. The simplest use of a large group is one in which all of the participants move in unison. Unison tends to give strength to dance choreography through repetition of action and of spatial design. Imagine, for example, a dance in which the interest is centered on a given point in the space area. As the number of dancers who move in unison toward or away from that point, and who focus on it, is increased, the dramatic intensity is proportionately heightened. However, with added experience, the composer will realize that not all movements are well adapted to unisonal organization. Some activities that are extremely significant when performed by one individual may lose their effect when presented en masse. The upward thrust of an arm, for example, if executed by a single dancer, can project a feeling of height and verticality. If performed by a group of dancers, however, this movement loses some of its vertical significance because of the horizontal effect of the mass formation. In occasional instances the subtleties in the design of a movement sequence may be swallowed up in the group presentation. Only by experimentation can the composer really know whether or not a movement may be effectively performed in unison. The important point is that he realize that such judgments must be made in order to insure successful choreography. Unison of movement can be truly powerful if it is skillfully incorporated; it can also be meaningless and dull when it is indiscriminately applied.

Sequential Movement. If dancers do not act in unison, they may move either sequentially, alternately, or in simultaneous contrast. Motion that is passed in succession from one dancer or one group to another is called sequential movement. The successive action of the members of a chorus line is an example, although the use of sequential movement need not always be so obviously employed. Sequential repetition of a movement automatically establishes an effect of unity among the performing groups. Often such close interrelation of parts is choreographically desirable; however, sequential movement may grow monotonous if it is continued too long, unless it is interspersed with group unison or other forms of group organization. The wavelike progression of sequential movement is full of potential dramatic connotations since it calls attention to the effect of one dancer's movement on that of another.

Antiphonal and Responsorial Movement. Alternate action of lesser groups within a large one is built on the natural structure of man's conversational instinct—exchanging question and answer, or statement and statement. The terms "antiphonal" and "responsorial," which describe this type of organization, have been borrowed by dance from church ritual. The former refers to the alternate singing of two choirs in different parts of the church; the latter, to the alternation of soloist and group, as, for example, a minister and his congregation. In a similar sense these terms apply to dance, and the resulting structural forms are among the most frequently used types of group organization.

As in ordinary conversation, the length of the action phrases may vary according to how much the participants have to say. Use of irregular phrasing helps to combat structural monotony. Contrary to practices in polite conversation, however, it is often desirable in dance to permit the "listening" group to interrupt the "speaker." Such overlapping of dance movements on the parts of the two groups prevents the total composition from becoming disconnected and choppy. The listening group, likewise, need not always remain entirely quiescent. Regular alternation of activity and complete inaction tends to result in a mechanical type of choreography. Furthermore, it is difficult for the dancers to keep their dance parts "alive" during sustained periods of immobility. Instead, subordinate movement that will not distract from the dominant theme may be incorporated. Such subdued action is often preferable to complete inactivity, unless the special dramatic character of a dance idea demands the latter type of organization.

Contrasting Movements Simultaneously Presented. Two or more groups, on occasion, may be made to appear equally and simultaneously important. Choice of movement for each group must then be such that it enhances or intensifies that of the other groups. The pattern of each group will need to be sufficiently different from that of the other groups that each can be easily distinguished. However, all of the patterns must in some way be related or they will distract from each other and frustrate the observer. By making the rhythmic scheme of one group support and point up that of another, by interrelating the floor patterns of the various groups, and by adroit use of focus and direction of movement, the composer may achieve a sense of unity among the groups. This type of group choreography is perhaps the most complex to direct, but it is also one of the most effective when successfully handled.

Each kind of group arrangement has its own intrinsic values which the student composer must explore. Only by such means does he acquire the variety of resources necessary for adequate choreographic expression.

Thematic Structures

The thematic organization of a dance composition, if the composition is to be considered an artistic achievement, is invariably regulated by aesthetic purpose. Those thematic arrangements which have become traditional are apparently basic to certain timeless and universal expressive needs. Many of the thematic structures employed by dancers are not necessarily peculiar to dance alone, but are reflected in other forms of art expression and in ordinary patterns of living.

The Theme

A dance theme is a movement pattern that is comparable to a simple sentence in writing or to a design or motif in the graphic arts. Although a movement theme is only part of a dance composition, it exists also as an entity, complete in itself, possessing a beginning, a middle and an end. The particular movement sequence that constitutes the theme needs to have sufficient individuality and expressive significance that it can be grasped immediately and forcibly by the observer. A good dance theme, like a well-constructed sentence, is long enough to be complete and short enough to be perceived easily in its entirety. The movement material is economically selected, with special attention to its harmonic relationship to the whole, and is so organized that it will present a unified total impression. Learning to recognize and appreciate good thematic organization in the compositional works of others can be of assistance to the young composer in creating successful dance themes of his own.

When first introducing to inexperienced students the problem of thematic invention, the instructor may, as a helpful approach, present one or two opening movements of a theme and request the students to complete the pattern (p. 33). This approach has two advantages for beginners: first, it limits the compositional requirements; second, it enables members of the class to judge what constitutes a satisfactory theme by comparing the different solutions to an identical problem.

A B Form

A need for contrast is apparently intrinsic to man's nature. Action is alternated with rest, and work with play. Monotony, unrelieved and long endured, can drive man to insanity. With rare exception, contrast is an inherent necessity for all good composition. The most natural method of satisfying this need is by the establishment, in composition, of a second theme or section which introduces new values differing from those already set forth. This use of a second part, designated by the letter B, to contrast with that of a first, designated by A, creates what is known as an A B form, a common type of thematic structure. The familiar tune, "Yankee Doodle," is an illustration of this form in music. The A section consists of the first four phrases; the B section of the four remaining phrases. In such a scheme, the composer's chief concerns are to create patterns that supplement and enhance each other, and to bridge them transitionally, so that the total composition is unified. The thematic material in each part must be simple and lucid enough so that no later repetition of it is necessary for complete understanding. Such requisite simplicity limits the use of the A B form to very short compositions in which the composer does not find elaboration on his original material necessary. When introducing this type of structure, the teacher may wish to assign the entire problem at once; or, for reasons given in the preceding paragraph, he may find it advantageous to have each of the class members compose a B theme to contrast and harmonize with an A theme that has been previously established.

A B A Form

In performing certain daily activities an individual frequently feels the need for a brief change of occupation before finishing the work he has begun. A short walk in the middle of a period of concentrated thought may sharpen a thinker's perceptive abilities. Possibly the walk may enable the individual to see the problem in a different perspective when he returns to it. The structure of the A B A form is designed to meet a similar psychological need in art expression. Musically, the A B A form is perhaps most frequently to be observed in such lyric songs as "Drink to Me Only with Thine Eyes," and in simple instrumental works; it is also used occasionally in musical compositions of greater complexity. In dance, this type of structure, like that of the A B form, is especially suitable for compositions in which the ideational material demands a direct, uncomplicated form of presentation.

The structural framework of the A B A form, as the name indicates, employs a repetition of the first motif after both movement themes have been presented. Such repetition tends to confer increased emphasis on theme A, theme B becoming subordinate. This type of compositional structure enables the composer to focus attention specifically on his principal idea, and the repetition of theme gives the work a satisfying sense of conclusion. It is important for the composer to realize, however, that the first theme does not necessarily have to be repeated **exactly** as it was originally stated. Slight variation is not only permissible, but also is usually highly desirable. The motif may be somewhat altered, or it may be abbreviated or lengthened. The composer must use his own discretion in deciding how it is to be handled. The B theme, although usually subordinate, is not merely the handmaiden for A. It should have an individuality of its own; it should be composed carefully to supply the needed contrast for A, and yet blend with it to form a unified composition. The special movement qualities contributed by this secondary theme often disclose new values in the primary motif. In some compositions the B section may actually become the climactic portion of the dance as a result of its dynamic movement qualities.

Rondo

Although contrast is essential to satisfactory living, some activities are sufficiently important that one finds it necessary to return to them again and again. The pattern of man's daily life serves as a good illustration. Each day may provide a different kind of living adventure, yet each night man returns to his bed to sleep. The need for frequent reiteration of an idea or theme is observable in radio advertising and in the traditional structure of the popular ballad which consists of many verses and a single recurring chorus.

Dance choreography that is built on one principal theme, repeated at intervals and with contrasting episodes between the repetitions, is known as a rondo. The framework of the pattern may be symbolized as follows:

$$\underline{A}\ B\ \underline{A}\ C\ \underline{A}\ D\ \underline{A}\ E\ \underline{A}$$
or
$$A\ \underline{B}\ C\ \underline{B}\ D\ \underline{B}\ E\ \underline{B}$$

In the layman's language the rondo is like a club sandwich: bread, ham, bread, cheese, bread, tomato, bread. Each new theme should further enhance the primary motif by means of its special attributes of contrast. These themes should also possess sufficient individuality that they are clearly distinguishable from each other as well as from the principal theme. When employing this type of thematic organization, the composer must bear in mind the fact that the principal theme is to appear a number of times and must consequently be made interesting enough to justify such repetition. This characteristic reiteration of one theme makes the rondo particularly adaptable to compositions that necessitate persistent emphasis on a principal dance idea, or to compositions that require a unifying interlude to establish the relationship between a series of dramatic episodes. As an example of this latter use of the rondo, we may think of a series of fragmentary scenes portraying various phases of city life, each of which is eventually swallowed up by an interlude pattern representing the crosscurrents of people at a busy street intersection. The repetition of the street-corner theme provides the transitional bond that ties together the separate episodes.

Rhapsodic Form

Living does not always conform to the conventional patterns that have been established by previous experience. Particularly when strong emotion governs the actions of an individual, the plan of living may take on a kind of order that is highly irregular according to tradition. Similarly when art is the expression of ecstatic feeling, this intense emotion often bursts through the regulative bounds of conventional forms and establishes form that is definable only in terms of itself. In music and dance such compositions are known as rhapsodies and the various forms that are the results of these outbursts of ecstasy are called rhapsodic forms. George Enesco's *Roumanian Rhapsodies I and II* and George Gershwin's *Rhapsody in Blue* are excellent examples of this type of musical structure. Narrative compositions, too, whether pertaining to music or dance, ordinarily belong in this category, because compositional form, in such cases, is the direct outgrowth of the narrative subject matter.

While such compositions may at first glance present an impression that connotes absence of planning, actually there is a considerable difference between irregular structure and no structure at all. The emotion itself acts as the principal unifying force that welds together the various parts of the composition. Choreography of this sort demands much of the dance composer in terms of intensity of feeling and aesthetic sensitivity. The flexibility of the rhapsodic dance structure gives the choreographer the creative freedom he is justified in claiming. On the other hand, he cannot afford to permit liberty to become license, thereby allowing rhapsodic form to dissolve into vagueness and disorganization. The task of creating rhapsodic form (except for narrative dances, in which form is partly determined by content) is not always suited to the abilities of beginning composers who need the help of established limitations to enable them to present their movement material clearly and concisely. However, when the dance student is sufficiently disciplined to regulate his compositional activities intellectually as well as emotionally, and when he has gained an adequate understanding of the interrelationship of movement and emotion, he should be mature enough to use the rhapsodic structure with artistic integrity and discrimination.

Theme and Variations

For most individuals, most of the time, living appears to be a series of variations on a theme. People sleep, eat, work, and play according to a general regulative plan. But they do not always perform these activities in exactly the same way. The variety they are able to achieve within this plan makes living continuously fascinating and pleasurable. In dance, also, a single theme may be self-sufficient as a basis for claiming interest, but its significance increases when it is examined and projected in its corresponding variations. It is essential in the creation of such a dance structure that the theme be composed with a view to its future adaptability in the construction of these variations. The theme should be simple enough so that the variations can expand upon this basic structure. The separate movements in the theme should be distinctive in pattern and direction so that they may be engraved upon the mind and may be recognized easily in the variations fashioned upon them. As a rule, the composer should make the character of the theme somewhat general, reserving specific qualities or styles such as that of a folk dance, a dirge, or a preclassic court form, for the variations. Occasionally, however, the theme may be developed on a definite narrative structure, the variations being used to represent specific phases of the dramatic scheme. Repetition of movement, whether performed on the same side of the body or to the opposite side, ordinarily should be reserved for the variations, since it is not the function of the theme to elaborate on itself. Finally, the theme, although utilizing space, should not progress too far in any one direction without returning; otherwise, later repetitions of the theme will tend to carry the dancers out of the performing area. When the theme is first introduced, it needs to be presented with utter simplicity, permitting no contrapuntal embellishments to distract the observer from absorbing its full significance.

In creating variations on a theme, the composer may change any part of the pattern by whatever method he may select; but he must also retain enough of the original theme that the source of the variation can still be recognized. If one element of the theme, such as the directional plan, is permitted to remain constant throughout all of the variations, the relationship between the theme and its variations is made increasingly apparent. Variation on a theme may be achieved by changing the quality of the movement or its general style or mood; or it may be achieved by altering the tempo, the rhythm, the dimensions, or the directions in which the pattern is performed. The theme may be inverted, thus changing the order in which the separate movements are presented; or certain portions of the theme may be repeated or lengthened and others omitted entirely. If the composition is a group dance, variations may be further differentiated by changing the number and the organization of the dancers who perform them.

A theme and variations, because of the intricate nature of the structural form, is frequently performed as "absolute" dance designed especially for intellectual enjoyment. The construction of a theme and variations has value not only in disclosing the potentialities it possesses as a basic dance form; it is also an excellent disciplinary device for training the choreographer to handle his compositional materials with resourceful economy. It encourages him to become ingenious in the discovery of new movement material within a single limited source. Invention of variations on a theme should not, however, be misconstrued as a simple creative problem. Short creative exercises, such as that of designing a single variation on a given theme, can provide the beginning composer with the type of experience he requires to develop his compositional powers; however, the creation of a fully developed theme and variations of artistic merit demands an extensive background of movement technique and creative experience to provide the choreographer with adequate resources for devising numerous variations.

Ground Bass

The ground bass might properly have been included in the discussion of group relationship (p. 77) because a group of dancers is required for its performance. However, because the ground bass is also concerned with thematic organization, it seems advisable to discuss it here. The theme of a ground bass might be likened to the heartbeat as a vital living function that continues uninterrupted, against other changing and varied human activities. Although the term "ground bass," like "rondo" and "canon," has been borrowed by dancers from music, the structure was not adapted from music, but originated independently in fulfillment of elemental choreographic needs. Musically, a ground bass is defined as a phrase or a theme in the bass staff that is continually repeated to accompany a constantly changing melody and harmony; in dance, it has been adapted to signify a type of structure in which a single movement theme is constantly reiterated throughout the composition against contra-movement performed by other members of the group. An example of a simple form of ground bass is to be found in certain Native American dances in which the women provide a constant background theme by shuffling their feet or by vibrating their bodies. Against this basic movement pattern the men execute difficult and varied dance steps as the principal center of interest. The ground bass theme need not always be presented by the same dancer or group of dancers. It may be passed from one individual or group to another—as a ball is tossed from one player to his neighbor in a game of catch, or it may be performed by the entire group in unison. Structurally, the ground bass theme should be composed with enough ingenuity so that it does not become tedious with repetition; or, if the function of the ground bass is merely to provide background movement, the other movement patterns needs to be designed to sustain the compositional interest. The ending of the ground bass theme should be of such a nature that the dancer can return smoothly and easily to the beginning of the pattern. Because variations do not have to be built on it, the principal motif in a ground bass may have a more specific style than the fundamental motif of a theme and variations.

Because of the fact that the theme itself is constant, the composer is called on to keep the total movement design fresh and interesting by varying the other factors in the composition. The different accompanying motifs may be utilized to enhance the basic theme and to alter the total effect of the group pattern. Rhythmic counterpoint, as well as contrasting spatial design (differences in level or range, for example), may be established through this interplay of thematic materials. Change in the numbers and in the spatial relation of the dance groups is another source of choreographic interest. Even the ground bass theme itself may be presented with different effect by changing the direction and the group arrangement of the dancers performing it. It is important that the composer select movement to accompany the ground bass which will harmonize with it in design and in general quality or style when the two are seen together. The development of artistic judgment in the selection of harmonic contrapuntal movement is a primary product of this dance experience. Here again, the compositional problem is a complex one and not generally suited to the level of completely inexperienced students; but it is both stimulating and valuable for those who are capable of handling it.

Round or Canon

A living counterpart of the round or canon, the last of the conventional forms to be discussed here, is displayed in the continuity of life itself, with its overlapping generations. A single life moves forward from infancy, to childhood, to youth, to maturity, and finally to old age. Yet the total pattern of human existence in the world at any one moment is a curious configuration of all of these stages of man's development with their contrasting directions, tempos, and emotional drives.

A round or canon consists of a melody (in music) or a movement theme (in dance) presented by two or more performing groups, which introduce the theme successively, a few beats (or sometimes a measure or more) apart. In dance, the round or canon form produces a rich tapestry of movement composed of all the various parts of a theme viewed simultaneously in a kind of rhythmic montage.

In a strict round the rhythmic structure, the movement design, and the floor pattern are identical in every voice. If the different voices enter one phrase apart, eventually all the phrases in the theme will appear concurrently, provided there are as many voices as phrases.

1st voice 1—2—3—4
2nd voice   1—2—3—4
3rd voice   1—2—3—4
4th voice   1—2—3—4

This fact necessitates a consideration of the harmony of the phrases or sections of the thematic pattern, not only as they occur sequentially, but also as they are presented simultaneously. Each part of the pattern needs to be distinctive enough so that it does not appear to be a duplication of any other part. The composer should consider the rhythm, the movement, and the space pattern of each portion as it is to be viewed against the others. Fast rhythms may be contrasted effectively with slow ones; low levels with high ones; and movement on a stationary base with locomotor activity.

From the standpoint of the rhythmic construction, the composer will need to guard against the occurrence of dead spots, that is, areas in the combined pattern in which no rhythmic interest has been provided by any of the voices. The last beat of any measure is particularly vulnerable to this weakness, since there is a natural tendency to end measures with unbroken intervals (undivided beats). Each part of the total contrapuntal pattern should have acquired some rhythmic vitality from at least one of the voice parts. When the performers are relatively inexperienced rhythmically and when the basic tempo is fast, it is usually advisable to build the rhythmic structure entirely on either a binary or a ternary division of beats. Since the rhythmic difference between these two kinds of beat divisions is minute, one or the other of the two rhythms is apt to appear slightly offbeat when they are seen or heard simultaneously unless they are presented with the utmost precision. In general, both the rhythm and the movement for a round or canon should be kept relatively simple and clear since the interplay of voices, in itself, creates sufficient complications. A very simple but usable rhythmic pattern for a round appeared at the top of page 69. Another example is given below:

After the movement theme for a round has been completed, the composer must determine how he wishes to arrange the different voices, or parts, spatially in relation to each other. When the arrangement is such that the various voices, or dance groups, perform in separate space areas without intermingling, the compositional difficulties are few. The chief problem becomes one of interrelating the groups in some fashion so that a total impression of unity is achieved. When the floor pattern and the placement of groups is such that the groups do intermingle, compositional interest is, as a rule, greatly heightened but compositional difficulties are proportionately multiplied. The choreographer is faced with the problems of keeping his stage balanced and of preventing one group from covering or crowding another. In directing this latter type of canon arrangement the composer may have difficulty in visualizing mentally the exact relationships of the performing groups to each other before they actually occur, because no two groups are dancing the same part of the pattern at the same time. If the choreography becomes too entangled spatially, complications can sometimes be relieved by reducing the number of voices to three or even two. Sometimes considerable experimentation is necessary before a completely satisfactory arrangement can be found. Slight changes in the movement range or in the directional plan of the original pattern may be indicated. In placing the dance groups in the performing area, the composer will also need to decide whether or not he wishes the voices to face in the same direction or in different directions; he must also assign the particular order in which they are to enter. Again, he may need to try several possibilities in order to determine which plan is the most satisfactory. Theoretically, in a strict canon, the number and group arrangement of the dancers and the direction of performance should probably be identical in each voice. However, such exactitude is seldom followed because it makes the choreographic pattern too mechanical. Usually the numbers and the relative placement of the dancers in each group will be determined by the effect desired for the total organization.

Occasionally, further liberties may be taken with the structure of the canon form. In some instances the rhythmic pattern is the only constant for all voices, each group performing a different movement sequence built on this rhythmic scheme. Such a composition is a canon or round from the standpoint of its rhythmic organization only, since the movement pattern and the spatial design are handled in free counterpoint. In long canon forms it may also be desirable to include a section that is performed in unison to contrast with the main polyphonic design.

Conclusion

Understanding and appreciation of dance structure is indisputably necessary to the success of creative composition. Both the structural organization of groups and of movement themes needs to be clearly discerned and projected if the choreographic results are to be more than accidental. Such studies as these are not only valuable as teaching aids with reference to the organization of compositional material, but they also furnish potential outlets for the dance composer's creative ideas. Neither student nor teacher should lose sight of the fact, however, that structural form is usually only the means to the end; its function ordinarily is to clarify but not to dominate the motivating idea.

Suggested Problems for Compositional Studies

1. Compose a dance study using three people in such a way that the pattern cannot be performed with fewer than three, nor can the number of dancers be augmented to choreographic advantage.

2. Working in groups of four, with a leader designated, improvise a pattern of movement that is passed sequentially from one member of the group to another. The leader should invent one measure of movement which, when completed, is imitated by the second member of the group, by the third, and finally by the fourth member. The leader now establishes a new measure of movement which is passed on sequentially; he does so two more times. Each member of the group should be given an opportunity to act as leader. When the group members have become proficient in reproducing movements created by their fellow dancers, the leader may present his second measure immediately without waiting for the first movement to be performed by the others. In this way the dancers who follow him will be required to observe the second movement while they are performing the first one. Try to make each measure of movement an integrated outgrowth of the preceding one.

3. Construct a dance study in antiphonal form, using two groups of dancers, three or four persons in each group. Vary the length of the movement phrases and permit the movements of one group to overlap slightly with those of the other. Use the movement pattern of one group to motivate the ensuing movement response of the other group. Break the basic rhythm

sufficiently to establish rhythmic variation. Consider the need for interesting floor pattern as well as body movement.

4. In a group of five to seven people, select a leader who directs the movements of the other group members, indicating what they are to do by means of his own dance movement. Try improvising the pattern first and then give it an established form. The movement pattern may be purely abstract or it may take on dramatic significance.

5. Using a group of moderate size, fashion a movement study on an A B A form. Develop the A section on a moving base, in a sustained movement quality, with a minimum use of arms; construct the B section primarily on a stationary base, including both sustained and percussive movement qualities and emphasizing movement of the arms.

6. Use from four to seven people to compose a rondo consisting of A B A C A. Give the A theme a lively folk quality, the B section a strong martial quality, and the C section a quiet semireligious quality or mood. Try to guard against making the transitions from one section to another appear choppy and unmotivated. Seek interesting ways of making one section lead into the next.

7. Compose, individually, a four-measure pattern for a theme and variations. Present each of the patterns for class examination and criticism. Select two or three of the patterns (depending upon the size of the class) that appear to possess the most interesting variation possibilities. Work in groups of five to seven people on one of the chosen themes. Develop two variations of the theme, basing the quality and mood of these variations on two colors (for example, yellow and slate blue) that may be chosen by the group or assigned by the teacher.

8. Using a group of moderate size, compose a ground bass dance form in which the ground bass consists of a simple, constantly repeated background movement on which other continually changing movements of major interest are superimposed.

9. Create a dance study in which the ground bass theme is of primary interest and the other movement material is designed to complement this principal theme. Try to present the ground bass theme in as many different ways (in terms of direction, numbers of performers, and relationship to other movements as possible.

10. On pages 66 and 89 are two rhythmic patterns for a round; select one and compose a simple movement pattern, endeavoring to establish as much contrast as possible between each of the measures. See that the movement pattern progresses across the floor part of the time and employs several different directions. Present the pattern as a three- or four-part round, first, with all of the voices entering from the same place in the dance area. Second, try having the groups begin in different places on the floor, facing in different directions. Some slight adjustments in the spatial pattern may have to be made to balance the "stage" and to eliminate collisions.

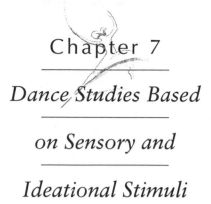

Chapter 7

Dance Studies Based

on Sensory and

Ideational Stimuli

Thoughts, ideas, and emotions basic to art expression are born of man's knowledge of himself and of his environment as reported to him through his physical senses. The more keenly his senses are attuned to his surroundings the more intense and abundant his overtly expressed responses are likely to be. Consequently, the development of an acute sensitivity is requisite to artistic growth. All of the senses contribute to this awareness of environment, although certain of them are more naturally associated than others with certain art media. For example, the musician is likely to be more keenly responsive to auditory stimuli than he is to visual or kinesthetic sensation, because tone is his medium of expression. This fact, however, does not preclude his use of other sense impressions. Rachmaninoff, emotionally moved by Arnold Boecklin's painting, "The Isle of the Dead," used it as an inspiration for his symphonic poem of the same name. The impelling source of Mendelssohn's *Incidental Music to a Midsummer Night's Dream* and of Tschaikowsky's *Romeo and Juliet Overture* was literature.

The dance composer, likewise, may draw on sensory impressions conveyed to him by any of his sense organs: he sees; he hears; he smells; he tastes; he feels; and he is aware of his own movement. The choreographer is fortunate in that dance is both a spatial and a temporal art. Thus, not only experiences which take place in time, but also objects or stimuli spatially perceived can furnish material that is directly translatable into dance. Music, poetry, or simple rhythmic sound, all of which share with dance the common element of time, can provide much valuable rhythmic substance which may be used as the actual basis for dance construction or as rhythmic inspiration for the choreography. Visual design, which shares with dance the use of space, may reveal linear patterns and space relationships that can be translated into floor patterns, group arrangements, or body movement. The visual and the auditory senses are, consequently, important supplementary aids to the dance composer. Of all of his senses, however, the dancer's kinesthetic sense should be the one most keenly receptive to sensation and most active in providing choreographic motivation. This "sixth sense" is responsible for informing the individual of body motion—the dancer's medium of art expression. The dance composer must first be fully cognizant of his own art medium and of the sensory impressions created by movement before he can make intelligent use of other kinds of sensory stimuli.

Kinesthetic Stimuli

The performance of movement, regardless of its purpose, induces kinesthetic sensations that may be pleasurable or disagreeable. Movement that is efficiently performed automatically produces pleasurable sensation. However, in addition to kinesthetic sensation, motor activity frequently stimulates various emotional overtones which are associated with the movement as a result of previous experience. Either the kinesthetic sensations themselves, or the feeling-states thus aroused by the movement sensations, or both may motivate the dancer to create choreography expressive of these sensations or emotions. By way of illustration one might take this example: the dancer experiences, kinesthetically, movement that employs strong tension achieved by the resistant action of opposing sets of muscles. The action may possibly consist of a sharp twist of the upper torso and then a strongly "reluctant" lowering of the body to one knee while focusing upward; this movement when performed with control can be pleasurable to the dancer, but it may also arouse disagreeable feelings and emotions which he associates with exaggerated tension. The movement in and of itself has no literal meaning; however, the muscular tensions inherent in the movement recall to the dancer similar states of physical tension that were experienced, perhaps, in connection with an emotional state of agitation, terror, or unfulfilled longing. Thus pure movement takes on new connotative meaning and becomes evocative of emotions, moods, or ideas that may inspire dance production.

Literal Movement as the Basis for Dance Pantomime

Daily activities offer the composer a wealth of familiar movement patterns which may be used either as ideational stimuli for dance or as basic material with which to construct abstract movement themes.

Literal, everyday movement is performed with either of two general aims in view: first, for the accomplishment of a specific utilitarian objective such as sweeping the floor or walking to the office; second, entirely for the pleasurable sensations inherent in the movement itself, for example, jumping on bed springs or swinging in a swing. As kinesthetic stimuli for dance, movement of both kinds may be drawn upon. When these movement patterns are performed for communicative symbolism instead of for their literal intentions, they become known as pantomime. Thus a person may go through the motions of sweeping a floor without actually holding a broom. Pantomime, however, if it is to be artistically employed in dance or drama, cannot be simply transplanted in its realistic form into art. The literal movement must be altered, by exaggeration or understatement, elimination of unnecessary detail, and reorganization of rhythmic structure, to become more artistically significant than the original.

Overstatement, or exaggeration of literal movement, often creates a humorous effect as in a caricature or a cartoon. For example, in dance or other forms of theater an exaggerated lope or an extreme hip movement may provoke laughter from an audience because it undermines the dignity of the performer. Likewise, extreme *understatement* may arouse amusement, depending on how it is handled. Such use of understatement may be illustrated by a dance sequence representing two political parties, the radical and the conservative. The radical group characterizes its behavior by a vigorous flag-waving movement of the arm, while the conservative party reduces the same movement to a diminutive wave of the forefinger. The minimized range not only illustrates the idea of conservatism, but also produces an intended comic result by its sheer contrast with the movement of normal range.

Frequently actors and dancers employ understatement to project serious dramatic meaning. The actor who wishes to convey annoyance, instead of stamping on the floor and shouting at his adversary, communicates the intensity of his irritation by drumming his fingers on the table. The dancer need not fling himself to the ground or wring his hands to portray grief; instead, he may move his body with restraint from side to side, or he may move his arm up and down within a very small range, but with extreme intensity. The significance of the movement is implied rather than fully expressed. The dancer stores up a reserve of intense inner feeling which gives his external expression an augmented source of dynamic motivation. Such artistic restraint impels the observer to provide empathically some of the emotion implied but purposely withheld by the artist. The communicative bond between the dancer and his audience is thus strengthened, and through this mutual sharing of dramatic experience poignancy of artistic feeling is more fully realized.

A dance composer should study a movement as it exists in living situations—observing it, performing it—in order to discover its essential form in terms of expressive meaning. Often a subtle momentary "freezing" and intensification of a movement at its point of climax can heighten artistic import by means of temporal and dynamic emphasis. Thus an upward reach, preceding a fall, might be held in suspension to increase the dramatic implication. Realistic detail that contributes nothing to the meaning of a movement has no justification for existence choreographically; its presence merely clutters and obscures the essential significance of a dance form. The composer needs to be like a maker of fine perfumes, a distiller of essences.

A dance composer should endeavor to avoid the use of movements that draw particular attention to the dancer as a person. The literal performance of such action as smoothing the hair or slapping the body, or extreme use of facial expression tends to overpersonalize movement as artistic expression and rob it of its universal meanings. Although dances in the folk idiom may be treated somewhat broadly in most composition, dance movement involving physical contact necessitates subtlety of handling. Usually choreographic results are most aesthetically pleasing when such physical relationships are merely suggested by the dancers. Facial expression, the chief reflector of human emotions, need not be completely masked out; it should support the dance idea without sentimentalizing it and without distracting from the primary expressive medium, which is movement.

The invention of pantomimic dance requires careful observation, abundant experimentation, and a discerning selection of movement. Generally speaking, the sooner students of dance realize that dance pantomime is more than realistic gesture with a few skips or polkas thrown in for embellishment, the better their chances of achieving artistic success. Pantomimic choreography must be *dance* movement that has been kinesthetically and ideationally inspired by gesture, and which, by means of artistic distortion, reflects the mind impression of the dance composer.

Literal Movement as a Basis for Abstract Dance

Everyday activities may also contribute basic movement material that can be used in abstract choreography. The composer, in such instances, is no longer interested in retaining the original significance of the source material; he is concerned only with the patterns of movement found within that activity in terms of their rhythmic structure, spatial design, and kinesthetic feel. By distorting and rearranging this familiar movement material, the dancer enlarges his expressive vocabulary; out of the old forms, he creates new movement patterns that are kinesthetically and visually satisfying to him. These movements, modified and refined by the dancer's selective processes, when set forth in compositional form may be enjoyed and appreciated purely for their kinesthetic, rhythmic, and spatial effectiveness.

Activities that contain a wide variety of movements are especially adaptable to the process of abstraction. The more parts of the body involved in the original source material, the greater are the number of potential derivatives. Sports activities, such as the game of basketball, have endless possibilities for abstraction. Tennis, although usable, is slightly less ideal than basketball for purposes of abstraction, because one arm consistently receives much greater emphasis than the other. Such limitations, however, can be compensated in the reshaping of the movement material by supplementing the natural pattern, or by occasionally overstating the movement performed by the weaker side. Ordinary daily activities such as taking a shower, working in a garden, pitching hay, or housecleaning contain an abundance of resource materials for dance composition that merely await discovery. Familiar dance movements such as a spiral turn or a mazurka may themselves serve as bases on which to mold new variations. Even *action words* representative of generalized types of movement, as for example, push, brush, poke, give, and take may sometimes inspire pleasingly original action patterns.

Beginning choreographers frequently need assistance in freeing themselves from the limitations set by the established structure of a literal idea. They may need to examine separately the spatial design, the rhythm, and the movement quality of the source material. If the total movement pattern is performed in sustained slow motion, thereby neutralizing the effect of change in quality and rhythm, the spatial organization becomes sharply discernible. The choreographic design may seem completely satisfactory as it is, or the composer may wish to alter some of its outlines. Small movements may be transformed into large ones, and vice versa. A pleasing movement within the total pattern may seem worthy of repetition. Movements performed on a stationary base may be given a moving base. When the spatial pattern is set, variations in quality, in tempo, and in dynamic interest may be reintroduced—but not necessarily in a manner corresponding to the original pattern. In some activities, the quality of the movement pattern or its rhythmic structure may appear to be the dominant feature, rather than the spatial design. The composer may wish to retain one of these elements as his constant factor and to vary the others. Such objective examination of movement helps to lead the student away from literal meanings and to focus his attention on movement itself as a source of kinesthetic and visual satisfaction.

Auditory Stimuli

Historical evidence discloses that music or rhythmic sound has always been intimately associated with dance. Sound or music has served as both a stimulus for dance and an accompaniment to it. The two arts have at times been so interrelated that it is sometimes difficult to conceive of one without the other. The fact that both sound and movement are predominantly temporal in organization is probably one reason for their mutual association. In addition, because music has an extremely direct appeal to the emotions, there has been a tendency among dancers to rely on it as a sort of catalytic agent with which to quicken their emotional responses. It is a mistake, however, to allow any art form to become completely dependent on another. Music or sound may be used legitimately as a stimulus for dance, as may any other kind of sensory stimulus, but the dance composer should not permit music to dominate his creative impulses to the extent that he is inspirationally barren without it. Nor should the subsequent dance form be merely musical structure mechanically transposed into another medium. If sound is to be used as a stimulus for dance, the resulting choreographic form should be the reflection and embodiment of the composer's particular intellectual and emotional response to that stimulus.

Auditory stimuli may be chiefly rhythmic or principally melodic in interest, or both. Sounds produced by percussion instruments—drums, temple blocks, wood blocks, castanets, rattles, gongs, cymbals, triangles, and so forth—are usually made with special view to their rhythmic effects and to contrasts in instrumental qualities. Other musical instruments, because of their wide range of tonal variations, stress melodic and harmonic structure as well as rhythm.

Percussive Instruments

There are a number of different ways in which percussion may be used as a stimulus for dance movement. A previously composed percussion orchestration may motivate the dancer's creative impulses; or, again, the tonal quality of a single type of percussion instrument may stimulate him to find movement appropriate to that sound. For instance the sound of gongs is likely to suggest movement very different in design and quality from that which is motivated by drums or by wood-block percussion. The prolonged tone of the gong calls for an expansive and smoothly sustained type of movement response, whereas the abrupt staccato sounds of the wood blocks invite the use of sharply checked, percussive dance movement.

The motor activity involved in the playing of various percussion instruments may also serve as a stimulus for dance. Although such movement may be so completely abstracted that the percussion instruments are no longer necessary to the dance, often the choreographer may choose to include the actual playing of the instruments as a part of his composition. Castanets, tambourines, and rattles have always been used in this manner, but some of the larger instruments have intriguing possibilities also. Drums and gongs that are light enough to be carried by the dancers are adaptable to such purposes. Or, if the instruments are too large to be carried, they can be placed on the floor in an interesting spatial organization so that the dancer may play upon them as an integral part of the choreographic plan.

The composer need not limit himself to the use of percussion sounds made by playing upon traditional instruments. Special tonal effects, such as that of fingernail rhythms on a hollow box or a metal wastebasket, can be devised by means of experimentation. A little inventiveness will enable the dancer to create interesting and unusual effects through the use of instruments made of unorthodox materials; these, also, can be utilized both as dance stimuli and as choreographic accompaniment.

Melodic Instruments

Some instruments are capable of producing a large variety of tones and therefore can produce melodies. In such instances the dancer is not only influenced by the special quality of the sound produced but also by the melody. The tonal quality, the rhythm, and the melody combined provide inspiration for the movement response, although the dance composer must guard against the tendency to "ride" the melody (moving upward or downward in a parasite fashion with the change of pitch in the music) if the dance is to be more than a musical exercise.

Among melodic instruments that have been used frequently, both as a stimulus and as an accompaniment for dance, are the piano, the flute, the violin, and the cello. There are probably several reasons for their popularity. In the first place, these instruments are usually more readily available to the dancer than are some of the other orchestral pieces; in the second place, it is probable that more music adaptable to dance has been written for them. Perhaps another explanation of the popular use of these instruments is that each possesses a certain timbre that is especially appealing to those interested in movement as a medium of art expression. Research in the field, however, may disclose to the dance composer a number of other musical instruments that can provide desirable accompaniment and motivation for dance composition. Greek dancers frequently used the lyre in connection with dance. The harp, its modern prototype, can, when it is available, be an effective stimulus for dance. Rare or ancient instruments such as the cithara, the celesta, and the harpsichord also have engaging possibilities.

The Human Voice

In considering instruments of sound one must not overlook the human voice. Both movement and vocalization are produced by the same expressive instrument, the human body; it is natural therefore, that they should work together in close accord. In scientific terms, alternation of muscle tension and relaxation through the torso forces air to pass through the vocal cords. Vocal sound would thus be produced by dance movement were it not subconsciously inhibited. Such sound, if it is made audible by the removal of these inhibitions, can provide a vocal accompaniment for dance that is intrinsically related to the movement quality. For example, strong, contractive body movement normally causes a sudden expulsion of air from the lungs, which, if vocalized, might be heard as a grunt or in some cases a cry or a wail. Varied muscle tension alters tonal pitch as well. Sometimes this type of vocalization resembles a sort of inarticulated chant, depending on the character of movement stimulus. Vocal sound resulting directly from movement is likely to present an effect of primitivism, since it is governed by physical rather than by intellectual forces. Because of its highly emotional quality, such sound may need to be somewhat abstracted for complete artistry of effect. The dramatic results, however, can be intensely expressive because of the fact that both the movement and the accompanying sound are inherent to man's organic nature.

Varying degrees of muscular tension in the throat are required to produce different vowel and consonant sounds. The throat muscles are tightened, for example, in the production of such sounds as long *e* or *k;* they are comparatively relaxed, on the other hand, during the production of a long *o* or a *sh* sound. The sounds *t* and *p* have an explosive quality. A sigh is associated with a feeling of relaxation, a sneeze with accumulative tension and an ultimate explosion. In working with wordless sounds in connection with dance, the composer may approach the problem from at least two different standpoints. He may commence with the movement and endeavor to discover the sounds that are a natural outgrowth of the movement; or he may select certain sounds from which to evolve the dance movement. Both procedures can produce interesting and sometimes rather surprising results. The former, however, requires a considerable degree of introspection and a lack of inhibition on the part of the performer, a fact which may make it difficult for beginners to handle successfully.

Vocal sound that is artistically planned for melodic and harmonic enjoyment, such as the *song* form, may also serve as a type of stimulus and as accompaniment for dance. As a stimulus, it functions like that of any other auditory sensation; as accompaniment, however, it must be limited in use by the fact that the dancer can rarely accompany himself successfully by means of song. Usually the conflicting demands of the singer and the dancer for breath control make the combination of expression impractical. On the other hand, very pleasing results can be attained when the song accompaniment is presented by a singer or by a group of singers who are not involved with the movement.

Verbal Stimulus

The use of words as a stimulus for dance immediately introduces a problem of verbal meanings. Sound is no longer heard for its own sake, but rather with a view to its specific communicative function. Even words arranged primarily for their effect of euphony, such as those in the verse of Gertrude Stein, cannot be completely dissociated from their functional meanings. The choreographer needs to bear this fact in mind whenever he chooses to share his word stimulus with his audience. Unless the resulting movement harmonizes with the verbal meanings, the observer is likely to become confused by the two conflicting sets of stimuli. If the choreographer does not wish to be expressionally restricted by his verbal source material, he would do well to use it only as a personal inspiration and eliminate it from his final projective form. In such cases the words serve as the source of the dance idea, but the ensuing dance form must project the meaning with sufficient adequacy that the verbal expression is no longer necessary.

For the most part, dance should not be dependent on words to explain its meanings. However, each of these two expressive media can, on occasion, enhance the other without sacrificing artistic independence. Words may sometimes be spoken or written as a preface to the choreographic work, to set the mood or to state its purpose. In such instances, the words precede the dance and do not interrupt or accompany the movement pattern once it has been started. Frequently, the verbal stimulus is incorporated as an organic part of the dance expression. The words might be spoken by the dancer or by a group of dancers, or they might be read offstage by a speaker or by a choral-reading group. Whatever the specific organization, the dance composer needs to guard against the natural tendency to use movement as mere pantomimic gesture to illustrate the verbal meanings. If dance is to be the dominant form of expression, the words should be used only to state essential facts or ideas that cannot be communicated by means of movement, or to provide basic ideational material for the choreographer to use as his point of departure. Often, the verbal passages may be somewhat fragmentary in form, since their function is a supplementary one. The words and the dance movement can be presented alternately or simultaneously. When the words actually accompany the movement, however, the composer must bear in mind that words or verbal statements differ in the extent of their activating force. Some words are mild; others are like projectiles, dramatically impelling the dancer through time and space with their emotive power until the inspiration derived from the word stimulus has been expended. Because of this fact, the words accompanying a dance cannot always be read or spoken without pause or interruption. Frequently the verbal accompaniment must be suspended to allow the dancer to develop further in movement an idea or emotion that has been inspired by the words. This is an artistic necessity which the inexperienced composer often fails to consider.

If the verbal stimulus is extremely powerful, an attempt to create a dance form of similar intensity may be inappropriate, as it may serve only to compete with the verbal effectiveness. In such cases, movement may be used to better advantage as an accompanying background for the prose or poetry. In this role, the choreography would reflect and support the words by means of understatement. An instance of this kind might be choreography for such a poem as Edna St. Vincent Millay's "The Murder of Lidice." The words of the poem are so vivid and dramatic in themselves that much of the time any effort to compete with them choreographically would be disastrous. Yet simple movement, well chosen, which is appropriate to the mood of the poem, might furnish an additional sensory value that the words alone could not provide. Whenever the verbal stimulus is presented simultaneously with the dance response, the composer is compelled to decide which of the two is to be made the dominant interest. An attempt to compromise is likely to result in redundancy and confusion.

Visual Stimuli

The visual sense can bring to the human mind the perception of contour and linear design and an awareness of color in all its varying hues and intensities.

Pictures and Linear Designs

Because dance is a spatial art as well as a temporal one, visual design is necessarily of supreme importance to the choreographer. As an artist, the composer must become sensitive to line and to visual structure as potential means of expression. The development of such sensitivity also increases his awareness of visual design in his environment, which may serve as a stimulus for dance composition. Visual stimuli may be either pictorial or abstract in form. In general, pictures are inclined to suggest dances of episode or of mood, whereas abstract designs, as might be expected, are more likely to affect the dancer's specific use of floor pattern and spatial design. Very simple linear patterns can motivate the dance composer's creative imagination to a surprising degree. A spiral or a zigzag line, or each of any number of other possibilities is often all that is necessary to provide a creative stimulus for dance. Sometimes the choreographer utilizes the dynamic quality of the linear design as a basis for his composition; at other times, he may associate a specific idea with that particular linear pattern and this idea will motivate the dance form. Diagram 10 offers examples of designs that might inspire movement responses. An individual viewing C, for example, might see the frenetic excitement inherent in its many sharp changes of direction and might select movements to reflect this spirited agitation; another individual, viewing the same design, might be reminded of lightning and, as a consequence, select movements suggestive of the turbulence of an electrical storm. Design A might impress the observer with a sense of weight and positive direction; B might suggest to him grace, as well as self-containment and introspection. Design D, although equally graceful, is fluidly active and progressive. The symmetrical, ascending pattern of the Gothic arch in design E would probably suggest serenity and aspiration even if religious associations were not present. These are only a few examples of linear patterns that have evocative symbolism. Patterns observable in one's daily environment, such as the course laid out on a croquet green, may also provide material for choreographic expression.

A series of such simple linear patterns can be used as a basis for a game that beginning composers usually find to be both stimulating and entertaining. Each individual or small group selects one of the designs without disclosing the choice to others. When the dance study is presented, the observers try to guess which linear design was used as the stimulus. This procedure not only taxes the student's creative ingenuity, but also enables him to test the projective power of his movement ideas.

A.   B.   C.   D.   E.

DIAGRAM 10. *Linear Patterns*

Color

Colors, as well as linear designs, are associated with definite ideas and emotions. Rarely can an individual look upon a color with complete objectivity. Fortunately for the creative artist certain general reactions to color are more or less universal within a culture. A test was given to a group of high school and college students in which they were shown a series of colors.[1] As each color was presented, the student was asked to write the first word that entered his mind in response to what he saw. Although the answers varied, certain general associations recurred among the total responses. A list of five words representing some of the most typical reactions to each color follows:

White	Red	Orange	Yellow
purity	fire	oranges	sun
snow	heat	gaiety	gaiety
holiness	fury	warmth	bright
peace	strife	brilliance	lemon
blank	barn	vigor	cowardice

Green	Blue	Violet	Black
grass	sky	royalty	death
spring	water	death	grief
trees	calm	night	silence
Ireland	contentment	sorrow	mystery
cool	cool	meditation	night

Other studies have been done along this line with similar results.[2] Some of these associations are traceable to man's natural environment in which the sun appears to be yellow, the grass green, and the sky and ocean blue; others have been established through customs which associate red with barns and fire engines, black with funerals, and purple with royalty. But associations fixed by custom are absolute only within the particular culture that creates them. Chinese culture decrees the use of red for weddings and white for mourning. Hence, white or red, symbolically employed, would have different connotations for a Chinese and an American.

The only unalterable characteristics of color, not directly traceable to custom and environment, are certain physical and physiological features that have been more or less scientifically ascertained. Colors at the red end of the spectrum—red, orange, and yellow—are known to attract more heat from the sun's rays than the blues and violets at the opposite

[1] Elizabeth R. Hayes, "The Emotional Effect of Color, Lighting and Line in Relation to Dance Composition."
[2] Michel Jacobs, The At of Colour, pp. 29-31.

end. Green is somewhat neutral, depending on its exact hue. Black is warmer than all of the colors, and white, its opposite, is colder. Psychologically, the warm colors are considered by most authorities to be stimulating, whereas the cool colors are soothing and suggestive of repose. These particular characteristics of color have enabled psychologists to use color as a form of emotional therapy with considerable success.

The dance composer's reaction to color is undoubtedly a fusion of all of these influences. His emotional response will naturally reflect his individual background of experience. But he must not base his artistic interpretation of color on highly personal experiences if it is to be understood and appreciated by others.

The use of color as a stimulus for dance is excellent motivation for inexperienced composers because of its universal emotional appeal. As with linear design, the old guessing game of "Which color am I?" can be both fun and an excellent teaching device for individual composition and group work.

Combinations of design and color can add interesting complications to the use of visual apperception as a stimulus for dance. Other visual objects, such as a fanciful costume or a grotesque or expressive mask may also serve to motivate the student choreographer. Teachers need only draw upon their own imaginations to discover other visual stimuli in everyday environment from which students may gather creative inspiration.

Tactile Stimuli

The sense of touch, as a potential source of experience that can be applied to artistic creation, has been generally ignored by most artists. Yet, if the student will consider some of the various substances and textures with which his tactile sense has acquainted him, he may find that a number of them can stimulate interesting movement forms. For most people the sense of touch works in partnership with the visual sense. Each of the two kinds of sensory impressions serves to verify the other. The visual sense in human beings, however, seems to be the more highly developed of the two. Because of this, individuals are inclined to rely more on visual sensation and to become less sensitive to tactile stimuli. Impressions received through the tactile sense can sometimes be sharpened by temporary removal, through the use of blindfolds, of visual assistance. Then a pine cone, a glass ball, or a pompon of yarn becomes, respectively, more prickly, more firm and smooth, or more soft and fluffy to one's sense of touch than it was before. Substance, texture, and surface contour are brought into focus so that when the objects are seen again, the total experience is intensified.

An interesting compositional problem for students of dance is to examine an object while they are blindfolded and then to attempt to present that sensory impression by means of movement. If the blindfolds are kept on while the students experiment with movement, the results are likely to be truer to the tactile impression than they would be otherwise. Visual assistance is thereby completely eliminated from both stimulus and response. However, in a lengthy compositional form, the mechanics of movement may be so hampered by blindfolds that their use becomes impractical.

Different cloth textures, such as velvet, taffeta, satin, chiffon, calico, and corduroy are good contrasts of tactile sensation that can be used as stimuli for dance movement. Water, in its varying physical states of vapor, liquid, snow, and ice offers other excellent possibilities. In some instances, the composer's response will probably be influenced, to a degree, by his visual memory of these objects in motion (the falling of snow or the breaking of waves); nevertheless, if the student's attention can be directed to observing how these objects or substances feel to the touch, his sensitivity will be developed in one more direction.

The experience of handling physical objects may also inspire the creation of dance forms in which those objects are used as properties. The manipulative use of a banner, pole, hoop, ladder, basket, or rope induces a different type of movement response, which may be of dramatic significance or of aesthetic interest. Experimentation along these lines can provide useful material for the development of both individual and group choreography.

Olfactory and Gustatory Stimuli

Sensations of smell and of taste have also been generally ignored as art stimuli, except, perhaps, by the poets. The theater, at one time, conducted some experiments in which an attempt was made to use odor as a means of establishing mood or of increasing the realism of certain stage sets. Odors appropriate to the various dramatic scenes were introduced through theater ventilating systems. Although the idea may have been artistically sound (a highly controversial issue), execution of such a scheme was difficult to regulate since the odors persisted long after the scenes for which they were needed had terminated.

It is quite possible for the dance composer to use olfactory or even gustatory experiences as stimuli for dance. The smell of new-mown hay, or of chili sauce in the making, or of some especially enchanting perfume, may be sufficient to motivate choreographic response. Smells, however, are almost invariably associated with the environmental situations in which those odors were either first, or most intensely, experienced. Seldom is one's response to olfactory stimulus completely objective. The odor of burning leaves reminds one of autumn, possibly one particular autumn. The smell of clean clothes may recall a line full of washing flapping in the sunshine, or perhaps the way it feels to slip between cool, freshly laundered sheets after an exhausting day. Even the smell of perfume is colored somewhat by the intimative title applied to it. These associations, provided they are sufficiently universal in character, usually help to clarify and enrich, rather than to confuse, the dancer's creative movement response. Both smell and taste are highly intangible in themselves. The ability to analyze one's apperception of these sensations and to objectify one's response effectively requires an acute sensitivity and a fertile imagination.

Ideational and Emotional Stimuli

The workings of the human mind are of such complexity that it would be unwise to attempt more than broad generalizations in discussing ideational stimuli for dance. Artistic ideation ranges from nebulous moods to definite dramatic situations; it may include historical dance as well as contemporary themes. The choreographer's only limitations in choice of subject matter are imposed by the boundaries of his own experience and understanding, by his technical limitations, and by the particular restrictions of his art medium.

Moods or State of Being

Perhaps the most natural medium for the expression of mood has always been movement. Uninhibited, man jumps or claps his hands when he is happy and belligerently flails the air with his limbs when he is angry. Moods are such an inherent part of human behavior that they are shared by artist and appreciator alike. Only the abnormal individual has not been happy or frightened or angry at some time in his life, and even a child suffers grief at the loss of a favorite toy. One can therefore employ mood as a stimulus for composition with complete assurance of its intrinsic universality of appeal, provided it is impersonally presented; however, if he expresses the mood in a trite, uninteresting manner, he has contributed nothing new or valuable to the field of creative endeavor. The composer must endeavor to find a fresh approach which sheds new light on the familiar topic. At the same time, the movement must remain true to the motivating idea or the dance will fail in its communicative purpose. Novelty, for its own sake, without meaning, is artistically worthless.

The substance of a dance of mood is sometimes given increased objective significance and interest if the mood is presented with reference to its motivating cause, rather than as a general state of being. A dance entitled "Fear of High Places," or "Lullaby for a Young Soldier," has more specific meaning than one entitled simply "Fear" or "Lullaby." When the choreographer can concentrate on a single phase of a mood rather than on generalities, he is more likely to comprehend its emotional subtleties and to discover new ways of expressing them. These remarks are not intended to imply that generalized moods are inappropriate as ideational dance material. Excellent dances have been created on such general themes as "Lament," "Warning," or "Celebration." The success of these dances, however, is ascribable to both the choreographers' and the dancers' breadth of human understanding and artistic ingenuity of expression.

If beginning students have difficulty thinking of danceable ideas, the instructor can sometimes stimulate creative thought by the introduction of a series of forceful or picturesque adjectives. Words such as "visionary," "hesitant," "festive," "petulant," "generous," "frenzied," or their corresponding nouns may suggest choreographic material which the dancer had not thought of before. Once the composer has selected his idea he will need to search the attic of his memory for all experiences that can enrich the meaning of his chosen topic. Suppose, for example, that he has selected "friendship" as his compositional theme. His own experience as a friend and as one having friends may disclose evidence to indicate that friendship involves similarity of tastes, identity of beliefs; or it may involve complementary rather than similar personalities. Friendship may also mean sympathy and understanding and the desire to share. These characteristics thus become the *specific* dance ideas that are to motivate the composition, and it is the dance composer's task to find their counterparts in movement.

When students are inexperienced in working creatively with movement, simple means of assisting them to explore movement as expression without overtaxing their creative powers may be needed. As such a means, the plan of providing the students with a definite movement pattern and asking them to perform it with a particular mood in mind may be employed. The specified pattern, for instance, may consist of a gradual rise to the feet from a half-kneeling position, a slow walk forward, a sharp change of direction that may be introduced by a full turn, a walk accelerating into a run in the new direction, to be followed by a jump, a step, and a fall or quick change of level to the floor. Variations and embellishment of the walk and of the other movements, the exact rhythmic pattern, and the dynamic organization are left unspecified. This leeway permits the student to vary the basic structure to fit the mood he wishes to express.

For experienced composers, an enjoyable and worthwhile class experience may be introduced by placing single words on separate slips of paper and arranging them so that each dancer can select a slip without having seen the word written on it. The dancer then attempts to communicate that word or idea by means of dance movement so that the other members of the group can identify the intended title. Such a plan is not only entertaining for the participants, but challenges the creative imagination and skill of each performer more than if he were to select a word for himself; it also provides the dancer with an objective means of verifying the communicative effectiveness of his movement expression.

Human Relationships

The social relationship of an individual to his fellow beings, or of one group to another, is a matter of utmost importance in every culture. This interrelationship of human beings provides the living source material for all dramatic expression. The playwright and the dance composer are, of all artists, perhaps the most directly concerned with these patterns of human interplay. The dramatist is interested in the portrayal of particular characters in particular situations, although his drama may also have universal implications. The dancer, however, can work directly with the abstract concepts of these human relationships. In some instances, the choreographer may wish to portray the dramatic situation in a fairly literal, though universalized, fashion. In other instances the composer may choose to distill from this literal situation the crosscurrents of dynamic action created by the characters and to present these in a completely abstract manner, devoid of specific narrative meaning.

There is an abundance of choreographic material in the social patterns that surround every individual. The relationship of the possessive mother to her child; of the dependent child to his parents; of one competing group to another; of a prosecuting attorney to the prisoner, or of an attorney for the defense to the jury—each of these phases of the human drama calls for a particularized kind of behavior that can be represented through dance movement. Relationships differ also according to the personality types involved in each situation. For example, the response of a people to their leader is not always the same; it is determined in part by the personality of the leader, who may be a tyrant, a religious leader, a benevolent dictator, a puppet ruler, or a democratic educator. The social pattern in each case differs according to the effect on the group of the leader's personality. The environmental situation is another factor that affects human behavior. Deprivation, for instance, causes people to respond in a manner that is contrary to their conduct in times of plenty. The behavior of the housewife at a bargain counter may bear little resemblance to her actions on an ordinary shopping day. Again, the movements of a person entering a cathedral are different from those of one who is entering a bank or a post office. If the dancer can sensitize himself to the intricate patterns of social relationship and the subtle variations in human response that are a part of the life around him, he should never be at a loss for choreographic inspiration.

Dance Dramas

The term "dance drama" encompasses a variety of choreographic forms. Its boundaries may range from pantomimic dance-ballads to profound dance-epics. The choreography may be inspired by historical or legendary incidents, or by contemporary happenings. The significant characteristic all of these dance forms have in common is the fact that each attempts to describe an event or series of events through the medium of dance movement. As previously stated, a heterogeneous collection of dances which, at the last moment, are grouped together under some pseudotitle does not constitute a dance drama. The work must have a continuity of idea governing all of its lesser parts and determining their ultimate form.

A dance drama almost invariably entails group choreography, and it usually involves a series of episodes. For this reason, a supervisory coordinator of the entire dance production, who can view the work from the standpoint of its total effectiveness, is necessary. It is his responsibility to see that the dance has unity of idea, a logical sequential plan, harmony of structure, and variety and contrast among the various sections. He must also help the individual performers to understand the relation of their separate parts to the dance idea as a whole.

Because dance drama attempts to tell a story, there is sometimes a tendency on the part of the composer to resort to pantomime as the principal means of projecting his idea. Although pantomime is probably the natural source from which to derive meaningful dance movement, the composer will need to guard against using literal pantomime as a substitute for dance. There is also a temptation, when large groups are involved, to lean toward the use of pageantry in place of dance. Choreography is necessarily limited when adequate space in which to move is lacking. Unless floor space is unconfined, the director may have to decide whether his production is to become a series of tableaus involving masses, or whether it is to be a dance drama in the true meaning of the term.

History and literature are among the composer's richest sources of thematic material for dramatic dance forms. For example, incidents arising out of the American Civil War, or events and emotional drives and responses pertaining to the settlement of the western United States (the spirit of adventure, the physical labor, the loneliness, the recreational activities, and in some instances, the religious fervor of the pioneering people) offer splendid opportunities for dance expression. Characterizations of historical or legendary individuals, such as Carrie Nation or Rip Van Winkle, suggest further movement possibilities. Such famous and infamous personalities as, respectively, Abraham Lincoln and Lizzie Borden have served as inspiration for a number of well-known choreographic works. Sometimes local history contains anecdotes and folk tales on which the dancer can draw for compositional material. Myths, such as the story of Orpheus; fairy tales such as *The Little Sea Maid, Cinderella,* or *Ali Baba and the Forty Thieves;* and cuttings from epic poems, such as *America Was Promises,* by Archibald MacLeish, or from volumes of poetry such as *The People, Yes,* by Carl Sandburg, contain countless narrative and dramatic possibilities for dance. Certain modern plays have been written which, like the ancient Greek dramas, incorporate dance movement as a significant part of their dramatic structures. *Three Plays for Dancers,* by William Butler Yeats, and *The Great American Goof,* by William Saroyan, are dramas written expressly to be performed by dancers. In addition, a limited amount of narrative or descriptive music can sometimes provide the needed impetus for the dance composer. Mussorgsky's *Pictures at an Exhibition,* Prokofiev's *Peter and the Wolf,* Saint-Saën's *Carnival of the Animals,* Gershwin's *An American in Paris,* and John Alden Carpenter's *Skyscrapers* and *Birthday of the Infanta* are well known works in this category. Such musical writings as Aaron Copland's *Billy the Kid, Ballet Suite,* and *Rodeo;* Morton Gould's *Interplay;* and Leonard Bernstein's *Facsimile, Fancy Free,* and *Age of Anxiety,* although long and sometimes rhythmically and structurally complicated, are particularly suitable to movement because they were composed specifically as dance accompaniment. However, the dancer's most effective source of dramatic motivation is often to be found in the contemporary events and relationships that surround and affect his life as an individual and as a member of society. Regardless of the source of dramatic inspiration, whether it be fancy or reality, the dance composer constructs from it his own dramatic sequence and plans whatever musical or verbal accompaniment is necessary for its artistic achievement.

Historical Dance Forms

Dance forms of the past have been a great source of creative inspiration to the dance composer. Primitive ritual themes have enjoyed especial popularity as subject matter for dance. Court dances of the preclassic period, such as the pavane, courante, and saraband, have also been used many times as a basis for modern choreography. Ancient and medieval dances, although perhaps less familiar to most dance students than the above, offer interesting possibilities as motivation for composition, provided the dancers have source material available and are willing to make the effort to investigate the characteristics of the authentic forms. Much excellent research has been done in the field of dance history (see the bibliography). The absence of an adequate method of dance notation in the past, however, has handicapped the efforts of historians to uncover a complete and accurate record of dance movement. The meager factual information available regarding the dance of various periods can be partially supplemented through a study of the cultural background of the people involved and an examination of their less transient art forms. Even with the aid of such information, however, it is unlikely that any modern choreographer can ever create truly authentic historical dance. At best, his composition can be only his own conception of the authentic form. The choreography may approximate the original in external structure, and even to some degree in ideational motivation, but it will always be affected by the fact that the composer is a modern individual living in a modern world.

Occasionally the dance composer may wish to borrow the general style of a period dance as a means of expressing a modern idea. For example, the formal, precisely measured, mincing quality associated with the traditional minuet may seem admirably suited to aid in the projection of such choreographic themes as "According to Convention," "With a Delicate Mien," or "Perfectionist." This kind of use of "period" dance forms is not intended to be historically authentic, but it is appropriate so long as the composer makes clear his creative intentions.

Forms Derived from Other Ethnic and National Cultures

When the dance student attempts to create dance forms that are inspired by dances of other ethnic groups and nationalities, such as Japanese or East Indian, he encounters difficulties similar to those he faces in creating historical dance. One's lack of understanding of other racial and national cultures makes an effort to create artistic forms that represent those cultures a doubtful possibility. An American or Scandinavian, under ordinary circumstances, cannot hope to produce art that may be termed authentically Spanish or Chinese, and his attempt to do so will probably engender results that are superficial and often misrepresentative of the genuine art of these cultures. The further removed the dancer's own cultural background from the culture he is endeavoring to imitate, the more limited are his chances of achieving results of artistic authenticity. The choreographer may legitimately present *his impression* of the art of another race or nationality, but unless he is intimately acquainted with their customs and manners, he cannot honestly claim to do more than this.

On the other hand, racial or national groups may always be used as subject material for dance when they are chosen as a means of epitomizing the hopes and struggles of the human race as a whole. The dramatic production of *The Eternal Road,* directed by the famous Max Reinhardt in 1937, was written about the Jews, but it also symbolically represents the travail of all persecuted peoples.

Current Topics

Man cannot help being greatly moved by events of the present. The present is his own particular bit of eternity which he helps to fashion and which in turn, shapes his life; it is active, stimulating, and richly endowed with vital material with which to quicken his artistic impulses. Unfortunately, lack of perspective sometimes makes it difficult for the young or inexperienced composer to recognize contemporary themes that are worthy of art expression. However, the dance student need only sharpen his senses and deepen his thinking. Newspapers are filled with potential compositional stimuli. If thoughtfully considered, the present can become even more stirring and romantic than fanciful episodes and the romantic deeds of former generations. The events surrounding his work, play, social activities, and religion should be infinitely more significant to the composer than, for example, the tribulations of Little Red Riding Hood. The inexperienced composer may need guidance in selecting themes that are appropriate to his level of intellectual and emotional understanding and technical proficiency. Regardless of his choice of subject matter—whether it deals with the future, the present, or the past—it must be material which the student truly understands and about which he has something to say.

Suggested Problems for Compositional Studies

1. Pantomime the meeting of friends at a party. Notice the spatial relationships established and the interplay of forces in response to one or two specifically characterized individuals such as "the gossip" or "the unpopular girl." Perform the movement sequence a second time but now make it dance

pantomime, exaggerating important movements and eliminating unessential ones. Set the movements to a definite rhythmic count. As a third problem, use the same movement sequence, retaining the spatial relationship of people and the dynamic structure, but transform the movement into pure dance with no attempt at characterization or representation of a specific scene.

2. a. Individually, pantomime the action sequence of catching, dribbling, pivoting, and throwing a basketball. Include contrast of level in the movement pattern. Do the entire pattern in slow motion; then do it as pure movement without the imaginary basketball. Add percussive movement and change of tempo to some part of the pattern for interest. In groups of three, choose one of the three movement patterns and perform it in unison. Now perform it to a slow tango rhythm with tango quality; then relate the same movements to a fast jazz rhythm or to any other dance rhythm that suggests a definite movement style.

   b. In couples, with one individual as a forward and the other as a guard, reconstruct in pantomime the activity of these two players in a basketball game. Include as much variety as possible in floor pattern, change of level, and so forth. Make a definite pattern that can be repeated. As in the above problem, do the pattern in slow motion; then discard the idea of basketball and perform the activity sequence as pure movement, adding sharp, quick movement where they are needed for interest. Use the movement sequence, changing the movement dynamics and focus slightly if necessary, to express the idea of (1) companionship, (2) worship, or (3) lamentation.

3. If percussion instruments, homemade or otherwise, are available for all of the students in a class, work in groups of five or six to compose a short orchestration. (See page 162 for a discussion of percussion orchestration.) Select two of the most interesting orchestrations as stimuli for dance studies to be composed by all of the other groups. Be sure that each orchestral group has an opportunity to compose a dance study to one of the other orchestrations. Try to capture the quality of the instruments in the movement response. Work either with the established rhythm or consciously against it.

4. In groups of four to seven, evolve a movement pattern that is self-accompanied. Do not use words but merely vocal sounds that are directly related to the movements. Move and see what sounds result from the movement, or try certain sounds such as *m-m-m-m, che, omp-pa, e-e-e, plop, o-o-o-o* or *ska-da* and see what kind of movements they suggest. Be sensitive to point of origin of the sound in the body and to its dynamic quality.

5. The stimulus is to be a group of sharply contrasting colors, mounted individually on neutral backgrounds. In groups of convenient size, choose a color as a stimulus for movement. The color may suggest certain moods, or certain activities and objects associated with that color, such as surging water or darting flames. If the dance studies are to represent the students' response to color alone, musical accompaniment should not be introduced until after the dance study has been completed (or if at all) because the music is certain to influence the dancers' own response.

6. The stimulus consists of large swatches of cloth, such as burlap, chiffon, taffeta, wide-ribbed corduroy, slipper satin, and velvet, in colors as neutral as possible. Choose one texture and develop a movement study appropriate in quality and style to that texture. Work principally from the tactile sensation received from handling the material, not only by feeling its surface, but also by noticing how it moves and falls. Associations connected with the use of the material may enter into one's response but should not be the primary source of motivation for dance movement.

7. Place on the blackboard a list of words such as "power," "celebration," "suspicion," "frenzy," "welcome," that are evocative of different types of human activity. In groups of two to five, select a word and try to convey its meaning choreographically. Keep in mind principles of compositional form in developing the dance study.

8. Select some situation of conflict which exists among people that you know or have heard about, such as an unfriendly competition between two individuals for the friendship, admiration, or affection of a third person or group of people. Resolve the situation in some fashion and present it through the medium of dance movement. Avoid the use of literal pantomime as much as possible.

9. Choose a Greek myth such as *Perseus and Medusa,* or any other legend or fairy tale that suggests movement possibilities, and present it by means of dance pantomime in either a serious or a comic vein. Do not perform it merely as a dramatic skit, but translate the dramatic action into dance movement.

10. Study the characteristics of several of the preclassic dance forms such as the pavane, galliard, or allemande. Select one of these dance forms and present it in one of two ways: (1) with as much authenticity as possible, as a court dance of a given period; or (2) as a modernized version of the original form, retaining the rhythmic structure and general quality and style, but imbuing it with contemporary meaning. If the dancers work with a musical score, the structural organization of the music should be observed and followed wherever possible, so that the music and dance forms will not be in co. flict. Otherwise the dance study should be performed with out music, or with music composed to fit the movement.

11. Using the topography of the United States as the ideational source, compose a suite of three dance studies: (1) representing the rolling, wooded hills of the East, (2) representing the limitless horizontal expanse of the plains of the Middle West; (3) representing the piercing ruggedness of the mountains of the Far West. Endeavor to convey the feelings and tensions aroused by these different landscapes rather than attempting a literal representation of the topographical scene. Well-chosen pictures can substitute to some extent for actual experience with the different types of landscapes.

FIGURE 1. *Repetition of Body Design*

FIGURE 2. *Transition in Terms of Movement Design*

FIGURE 3. *Action in Straight Lines*

FIGURE 4. *Movement in Curves*

FIGURE 5. *Focus on Two Points*

FIGURE 6. *Movement in Large Range*

FIGURE 7A. *Duet Pattern Using Complementary Movement*

FIGURE 7B. *Duet Pattern Using Complementary Movement*

FIGURE 8A. *Stage Set for Dance*

FIGURE 8B. *Stage Set for Dance*

FIGURE 9A. *Stage Set Designed by David Weiss for "Blood Wedding"*

FIGURE 9B. *Stage Set for Dance*

Chapter 8

Dance as Art Expression

The ultimate goal in choreography is to create dances that objectify thoughts, feelings, or mental images. To lead the students to a point at which they are able to do this should be the dance educator's prime objective. As indicated in the preceding chapter, every student comes to the teacher endowed with natural source materials for creative expression. It is up to the teacher to help students recognize these sources and to provide them with the necessary opportunities to create. Until the desire to express is the impelling force governing choreography, however, dance movement cannot justly be claimed as art. Compositions that owe their existence to other motivating causes are merely exploratory devices for increasing technical knowledge of construction and an understanding of the potentialities of movement as an art medium.

When the dancer finally attempts to use movement as a means of art expression, the teacher's guiding role must be subordinated. Young artists need to be permitted to try their wings unfettered by any extraneous limitations. Only in this way do they ultimately develop imagination and ingenuity in gathering ideas and creating forms that are their own. Choreographers can fashion art images only as they comprehend them in terms of their total life experiences. The exact method of creative procedure must be an individual one.

Even such a question as "How long should I make my dance?" cannot be answered directly by the teacher. The only kind of reply to such a query can be,

> Your choreography should be long enough to satisfy completely the needs of your dance idea. You must use movement economically so that it does not become overrepetitious and tiresome, but you must also develop your material. If your idea is not suficiently important that there are a number of things that you wish to say about it with movement, then perhaps you had better choose another subject. The dance should be long enough to contain all that you wish to express. When you have done that adequately, the dance should be finished.

Nor can the choreographer be advised as to the form his composition should take. If the student, through experimental studies, has been made aware of the necessity for structural organization in dance, and if he has been taught how to achieve it, the instructor can do no more. The final choice of the choreographic pattern must rest with the choreographer and should be determined primarily by his necessity for adequate expression.

The Idea And Its Development

Before the dancer begins to compose, he must consider whether or not his idea is a suitable one. Is it danceable? Does it lend itself well to movement expression? This, also, is a question that must be answered individually. A subject that one person may feel is ideally expressed through a graphic medium, may seem to another essentially suited to movement. And what may appear to the instructor to be an idea completely unadaptable to dance may occasionally, in the hands of the student, result in highly satisfactory choreographic expression. Each medium provides the means for communicating certain concepts that cannot be uttered as completely or as well in any other medium. The choreographer should ask himself not only "Is my dance idea one that is readily communicable in terms of movement?" but also "Do I have something to say that is worthy of art expression?" and "Is the subject one that is within my experience so that I can dance it intelligently and comprehensively?" Furthermore, as Margaret H'Doubler has said, "greatness in art is dependent not only upon the personal power and richness of the creative artist but also upon the richness of experience being communicated."[1] If the choreogrpaher's idea can satisfy these requirements, then he has chosen his subject wisely.

Students are often inclined to fall into the trap of using over and over the same approach to choreography, such as setting dance movement to popular music. Students are comfortable when they stay within the realm of the familiar instead of daring to challenge themselves to try new ways of moving and choreographing. Although solving movement problems through dance studies does help force students to discover new movement and compositional possibilities, when it comes to the creation of dances the teacher may eventually need to encourage students to expand their choreographic horizons by assigning them, over a period of time, to create, for example:

1) a dance related to a short piece of formally structured classical music

2) a dance that portrays a dramatic story

3) an abstract dance dealing with the inventive use of a specific style or quality of movement

[1] Margaret H'Doubler, *Dance: A Creative Art Experience*, p.54.

4) a choreographic representation of a personality type

5) a dance expression of a selected mood or feeling

6) a presentation of comedy, either based upon a humorous situation or upon a humorous treatment of movement itself.

Mature choreographers eventually select approaches that they find to be the most appropriate to their expressive needs, but until that time arrives, students ought to try as many different ways of choreographing as possible.

Music as Choreographic Inspiration

Using music as inspiration for dance has always been a favorite approach to composition, especially among young choreographers. Because music has such direct appeal to the emotions and can be so rhythmically compelling, it is often tempting to use the music mindlessly, without awareness of a need to give purpose to the choreography. Dance and music can work in partnership to reinforce a chosen mood, to establish a specific ethnic or historical style, or to suggest programmatic meaning. Unique rhythms and specific structural forms integral to the music can also be used as important motivation for choreography. Whether a choreographer intends literally to imitate in movement the melody and structured design of his music, as in Ruth St. Denis's dance visualizations, or instead to create movement patterns that complement the established musical structure, as in the works of Doris Humphrey, it is essential for a choreographer to understand the music in terms of its rhythmic structure, phrasing, and specific musical form in order to be able to work with it intelligently. Further discussion of the use of music will be presented later in Chapter 10.

Dramatic Dance—Tragedy, Comedy, Fantasy

The richer the cultural background of the dancer, the more experience and understanding he will be able to bring to bear upon his art expression. If the dancer is working in a dramatic idiom or in the realm of comedy or fantasy, he will need to appreciate its essential qualities. A study of the classics of drama and poetry may help to disclose some of the inherent characteristics of serious drama. He will discover that tragedy implies a conflict of forces and a collapse of something of value—a fallen grandeur that is logical in development and final in denouement; or a losing struggle against invincible forces, never a passive acceptance. Tragedy is universal rather than personal in its implications. It should produce a feeling of pathos, not bathos. *The Moor's Pavane* by

José Limón and Kurt Jooss' *Green Table* are two excellent examples of serious dramatic choreography.

In composing tragic dances, there is a recurrent tendency among young dancers to be overdramatic—to depend on outbursts of profuse emotionalism rather than presenting a logical dramatic sequence and distilling significant movement to project the tragic state. Conscious understatement and abstraction, in many instances, will correct this tendency and give the composition subtlety, dignity, and inner strength.

Although in literature a writer can successfully develop complex stories containing plots and subplots, in dance the choreographer is most successful when the dramatic story-line is simple and uncluttered. Dramatic meaning depends upon movement alone. It is especially important to identify the moment of dramatic climax through focus, momentary suspension of movement, or some other choreographic means rather than allowing it to be glossed over, because the denouement of a drama hinges upon that event.

Comic action, in contrast to serious drama, is ordinarily illogical; it derives its effectiveness from elements of surprise and deviation from the norm. In creating humorous choreography, dancers may use many of the same principles that are observable in dramatic theater. Exaggeration, caricature, extremes of contrast, or sudden deflation after a tremendous buildup are all well known comic devices. Proper timing is especially important. Comic action, generally speaking, must move quickly in order to be effective, although the use of dramatic pauses that have humorous implications should not be overlooked. In some instances, however, the humor of a situation is increased when the audience is permitted to forsee the a predicament of which, to all appearances, the dancer or actor is unaware.

Comedy in dance does not necessarily depend upon a humorous situation; it may be established by a humorous treatment of the medium. Abstract movement can provide a basis for comedy when it is sufficiently removed from normal behavior. The dynamics of certain movements can be given a comic twist, or the timing or the range of the movement can be distorted to create a ludicrous effect. Any type of comedy other than slapstick, however, in order to be artistically effective, needs to be kept within the bounds of subtlety and nuance.

Extreme distortion of movement may also be used to produce weird, unearthly, grotesque, or whimsical choreography. When such is the case, dance moves into the realm of fantasy. Fantasy of quite another sort as typified in romantic ballet, may be produced by using delicate movements and steps of elevation that appear to defy gravity. Either the character of the movement itself or the highly imaginative nature of the dance idea may provide a basis for creation of dances of fantasy.

Dances of Characterization

A dance of characterization might be defined as a dance in which the choreographer through his choice of movement attempts to portray either a specific personality or a general type of individual with whom an audience can identify. Martha Graham's Jocasta in *Night Journey* is an excellent example of a portrayal of a specific character. Although a story-line is present, the story itself is incidental—a mere motivation or justification for the emotional turmoil and consequent movement responses of the principal character. In Graham's *Seraphic Dialog,* three women are used to portray various facets of the personality of Joan of Arc. On the other hand, in *Every Soul's a Circus,* Graham portrays, not a specific woman, but rather all women who are silly and vain. Likewise, Mary Wigman's *Witch Dance* is a personification, not of a specific witch, but of witchery.

Dances of mood, such as Graham's *Lamentation,* do not attempt to portray either specific or universal figures but rather human movement motivated by particular states of feeling. Dances of mood as well as of characterization require of the choreographer an acute awareness of human movement responses to life situations as observed in himself and others. The choreographer does not imitate reality but distills, reshapes, abstracts, and clarifies the movement forms, molding them into art expression that has universal meanings.

Abstract Dance Forms

Abstract or non-literal dances neither tell a story nor portray a character. In such dances the choreographer is dealing with movement for its own sake, exploring its many possibilities for variation in terms of space, shape, direction, rhythm, dynamics, and so forth with all their infinite combinations. Although mood may be sensed in the final product, such mood is not usually the motivating impetus for the dance.

Various dance artists, such as Merce Cunningham, Alwin Nikolais, and in some instances, George Balanchine, have chosen this approach, all with totally different artistic purposes and choreographic results. Merce, through his use of movement choices determined mostly through chance, has endeavored to force himself and his dancers to discover new movement forms and rhythmic and spatial relationships, thus freeing themselves from established movement cliches. Nikolais depersonalized his dancers through costumes that often conceal or distort the human form, and the use of properties that can extend human movement, and by adding sound and light to create an effect that he called "total theater." Balanchine, although his works are often inspired by music, created visual masterpieces that force attention upon beauty of body line and subtle changes in spatial relationships of his dancers. In some instances, abstract dances may be built upon traditional movement resources such as ethnic dances or social dances from given historical periods. In other instances the movement is invented by the choreographer to create a specific effect that the artist has in mind—be it visual design or expression of dynamic energy or a lingering sense of mood. Without exterior motivation, such as a story-line, the choreographer must seek his stimulus within the movement itself. To do this, creators of abstract dance often rely upon movement improvisation to reveal possibilities they might not conceive of otherwise. Having a specific movement goal in mind helps a composer to give his work a sense of unity of form and artistic purpose. Without exterior guidelines such as musical structure or dramatic story-line, it is easy for young choreographers to become self-indulgent in the use of movement, stringing unrelated movements together in unending sequences with little regard for choreographic form. Discipline is required to keep oneself focused upon chosen choreographic objectives, using movement selectively and economically to attain ones ultimate goals.

The Choreographic Development

In developing compositional form, a fundamental consideration is its freshness and originality. Although the dance idea itself may not be new, it may be accorded new significance and choreographic value if it is expressed with ingenuity. Forms of expression that have been overused but are nonetheless new to the novice choreographer may contribute to his own growth, but if art is to be deemed worthwhile in terms of general culture, it must add something in artistic content, form, or style to the general storehouse of human experience.

It is important for the choreographer to remain true to his art medium. Although visual design is important and moments of active stillness can be a legitimate part of choreography, a composer should also remember, for instance, that dance is not primarily a pictorial art and that static picture-making cannot substitute for expressive movement. Likewise, literal pantomime and individual characterization should be left to the dramatic idiom. The purpose of dance is not to represent characters realistically but to express universal qualities, feelings, and experiences typified by these personalities.

The choreographer should give thoughtful regard to the compositional needs for unity, variety, contrast, repetition, sequence, transition, balance, proportion, climax, and harmony. If during the dance-making process these structural elements are considered in relation to the content of the dance, the likelihood of arriving at a suitable and aesthetically pleasing movement form is thereby increased.

The choreographer also needs to endeavor to keep in mind the technical limitations of his performers. Simple movements, well executed, are artistically more effective than difficult movements poorly done or movements that obtrude because of their spectacular performance. Unless the choreographic concept is communicated, the movement itself fails to be dance in terms of art expression.

Throughout the choreographic process it is important to share with the dancers the choreographic intent of the movement. The more completely the performers understand this intent the better they will be able to convey it to an audience. Projection of idea is not something to be added to the dance at the last minute, as icing on a cake; from the beginning, it must be an integral part of the creative experience.

The Staging

In planning a dance, the choreographer needs also to be cognizant of the location of strong space areas on the stage. To a play director such knowledge is elementary, but most dancers are only subconsciously aware of it. The center portion of the stage is a region of dominance because it is the center of focus. Downstage center is probably the strongest of all stage space. Downstage areas, because they are closer to the audience, are stronger than upstage areas; this principle is particularly true of the sides because the sight lines often cut into the upstage portions of these areas. Action that progresses downstage is potentially more dynamic than that which recedes from the audience, and movement that carries one toward stage center is more emphatic than that which proceeds in the opposite direction. In addition, some theorists claim that movement which progresses from audience left to right is stronger than that which proceeds in the opposite direction. They base their claim on the fact that in Western culture it is customary to read from left to right and they think that the oppposite motion "feels" contrary to custom. Such subtle differentiations may seem a bit far-fetched but they might be worthy of consideration.

Stage settings, like costumes and musical accompaniment, are most appropriate from the dancer's point of view when they are simple and unobtrusive. For indoor staging a curtain of velour, outing flannel, or some other soft but heavy material in a neutral hue—such as grayed-blue, gray, beige, or black—provides a very suitable backround for dance. A setting of this type, in addition to being pleasing to the eye, possesses the advantage of adaptability. Its abstract simplicity permits the members of the audience to imagine whatever specific setting they may feel to be appropriate for each dance that is presented. If a material of neutral tone can be delicately splatter-painted in several colors, the texture of the drapery can be greatly enriched and its responsiveness to colored lights increased. It is important to keep the color of the back drape in mind when dances are being costumed to allow for sufficient contrast for interest and visibility.

For an outdoor effect, a plain undraped blue cyclorama is a practical solution that establishes an impression of boundless space. A variety of impressions can be achieved in the use of such a cyclorama by sometimes lighting the curtain strongly at the top or at the bottom or by streaking strong shafts of light diagonally across it. The principle disadvantage in the use of a cyclorama of this sort is that it provides no center opening from which the dancers can make entrances. Whenever possible, the choreographer should ascertain what entrances will be available in the stage setting he plans to use before he composes a dance.

Actual outdoor performances introduce a number of additional considerations with reference to staging. Although many people entertain a romantic notion regarding the suitability of outdoor settings for dance performances, in actuality, such settings are usually far from ideal. The firmness of the earth's surface offers no give and absorbs most of the spring from movements of elevation, and the ground is often rough and uneven unless a temporary wooden floor can be provided. The movements of the dancers can also become swallowed up in the immensity of their surroundings. When the dances are presented outdoors, their effectiveness is increased if the performing area can be partially enclosed by means of screens, shrubbery, or lighting. Even when the stage is thus limited, the size of the dance group often needs to be augmented in order to appear significant in the expanse of the environment. If the performance is given on a lawn against a setting of trees or shrubbery, the green of the backround will need to be taken into account in the planning of costume colors.

In any setting, simple, suggestive painted or constructed scenery also may be used with artistic integrity. The possibilities of design are limitless. The use of uncovered folding screen frames strung with heavy strands of colored yarn to form pleasing abstract designs when placed in strategic spots on the stage can provide an interesting means of breaking up the space without actually obstructing the audiences' view of the dancers. Strips of colored cloth or ropes that have been painted or sprinkled with glitter can also be hung in attractive space patterns; these give to the stage an effect of increased depth and established intriguing spatial relationships between the stationary perpendiculars and the dancers' movements.

Modern technology has made it possible also to project photographic scenes or abstract images upon a scrim in place of painted scenic environments. Slide projections can be an economic solution to many problems; they can facilitate rapid scene changes and provide environmental illusions that would be impossible to create through other means.

The use of steps, platforms, and ramps as part of a dance setting can provide an interesting means of establishing choreographic accent. In a group dance, attention is automatically drawn to movement performed by an individual who is on a different level, particularly a higher one, from that of the other members of the group. The use of several floor levels intensifies the three-dimensional quality of a dance and increases the effectiveness and visibility of the group choreography. The scope of artistry in a dance composition is often sufficiently increased to justify the fact that platforms are expensive to build and frequently somewhat unwieldy to handle and transport. Padded cloth-covered boxes of various sizes and shapes that can be used together in a variety of ways to form different-shaped structures on and around which to dance are excellent standard equipment for any dance group. The availability of such equipment can inspire some highly desirable scenic variety in a lengthy dance program. Figures 8 and 9 illustrate several different types of stage sets (figures will be found in the insert between pages 118 and 119).

Occasionally, stage properties are needed to help project the meaning of a dance. In such instances, their use is justifiable, provided they do not distract from the movement. If a property can be suggested rather than literally represented, the artistic effect is often increased: A coil of chicken wire manipulated by the dancer to suggest the restraining or protective boundaries that enfold him; oversized empty cardboard pictures, framed and pinned on the curtains to simulate an art gallery; or a string of mothball-sized pearls used to provide the motivating object of a melodrama can stir the imagination of the audience in a way that use of the actual objects could never do. Ordinarily, however, the meaning of a dance that has been well conceived and executed should be discernible without the aid of costumes, scenery, or lighting. In the final analysis, the worth of a dance must be measured primarily in terms of movement expression.

The Title

A completed dance needs a name in order to establish its identity. If the dancer wishes his observer to concentrate on the dance movement, rather than spending his time wondering what the name of the dance has to do with the choreography, he should choose titles that are understandable at first glance. Titles should evidence originality, but a deliberate attempt to be obtuse can be self-defeating. The name of the dance should give the observer the cue that he needs in order to be properly prepared for what he is about to see. On the other hand, a title should not be so specific that it intrudes on the rights of the perceiver; it should be sufficiently general to allow for individual differences in interpretation of the dance movement. The argument may be presented that a good dance needs no title; this is true in one sense. But the dancer must also realize that the intent of the dance is often not revealed until the piece is nearly finished. By that time the early portion of the dance is past and can be interpreted only through the process of memory recall. If a dance work can be seen a number of times, then the observer can assign his own title to it. If the composition is to be seen only once, however, the members of the audience deserve to be given at least some indication of that which is to follow in order that they may set themselves in the proper frame of mind to receive it. If the movement of a dance is sheer nonsense, however, then a nonsense title may be appropriate.

When a dance is dramatically complex, program notes may be necessary. They should be brief; verbose explanations are confusing and usually hard to read. On the other hand, explanations that are too sketchy will fail to accomplish their purpose. The wording of program notes must be clear, concise, and graphic.

Critical Evaluation

When the choreographer's efforts are finally presented onstage, the compositional results might be judged by some of the following criteria:

1. Was the idea worthwhile and was it danceable?
2. Did the choreography contain elements of freshness and originality?
3. Did the choreography continually maintain the viewer's interest, or did it become predictable?
4. If there was a story-line involved, was it clearly delineated in an easy-to-follow sequence of events?
5. If the movement itself was the idea, was it well chosen to command interest, make a statement, and/or elicit aesthetic pleasure?
6. Was the idea adequately yet economically presented through the dance movement?
7. Was the movement style clearly established and consistently maintained?

8. Did the dance have a beginning, middle, and ending, or if not, did it evolve with a structure and sense of continuity?

9. Was the choreography pleasing in terms of its spatial plan and rhythmic and dynamic interest?

10. Was the general dance structure satisfactory according to aesthetic principles of form?

11. Was the choreography technically well executed and suitable to the dancers' capabilities?

12. Were the number of dancers appropriate to the choreography as well as to the performing area?

13. Was the title suitable and helpful?

14. Was the music or sound appropriate to the dance idea, movement quality, and style?

15. Were the costumes supportive of the dance movement and appropriate to the dance idea? Did they enhance the appearance of the dancers?

16. Did the lighting and staging provide the right atmosphere and support for the choreography?

Many of the above questions need to be addressed long before a dance is completed. Too oftern students wait too long before asking an outside eye to critique their choreographic efforts. When one is immersed in the creative process, it is difficult to view one's results objectively. Students need to be encouraged to seek helpful criticism of their choreography in plenty of time to make changes, if necessary, without having to throw away quantities of material over which they have soulfully belabored.

Students often respond most favorably to criticism of their works when they are encouraged to participate in the critical process themselves. Asking a student to verbalize his own evaluation of his choreography first may direct his thoughts toward acceptance of ideas for possible changes. A student should never be made to feel obligated to make changes with which he is not in agreement, but a wise student will at least consider with an open mind the choreographic suggestions that are proffered to him by others.

No teacher has ever created an artist through the process of instruction; he merely stimulates the untapped resources that lie within the dancer's being and assists him in technical details. Motivation, advice, and encouragement can all be offered the student choreographer by the teacher, but the final proof of artistry rests with the choreographer alone.

Chapter 9

Preparing a Dance Production:

Program Planning, Auditions,

Rehearsals, and Performance

In most situations a dance teacher is faced, sooner or later, with the responsibility of supervising the presentation of a dance program. The program may be given the form of a dance demonstration in which certain movement techniques or principles of movement and composition are explained and illustrated to the observer; or the program may be presented as theater or concert dance, comprised entirely of finished dances designed to be enjoyed as art expression.

In some instances a combination of the two types of presentation may be desirable. Choice of the kind of program to be given should be governed by the special needs of each particular school or community. If members of the community who are to be in the audience need help in understanding dance, or if the dance students themselves need experience in working with and presenting exploratory dance forms, a demonstration may be in order. If, on the other hand, both the dance group and the audience have an adequate background of experience and understanding of contemporary dance, a demonstration may seem superfluous. More often than not, however, the level of sophistication of the participants and observers cannot be so homogeneously defined. A combination demonstration-concert can be sometimes used as a means of satisfying the needs of both groups.

Dance Demonstrations

Lecture-demonstrations are generally of two types. One type consists of an informal presentation of the dance material. The choreographic substance is not created in advance of the presentation. The audience, instead of viewing a series of completed dance studies, is permitted to watch the creative process in an actual learning situation. The performers are presented with creative problems which they are expected to solve while they are being observed. Such a method necessitates considerable experience on the part of the directing teacher because it is essential to know how to motivate the demonstration group both quickly and effectively. Unless the participants are a selected group, the measure of success resulting from such a procedure is sometimes unpredictable. A superior teacher, however, can almost always obtain worthwhile results provided there is at least an average group of performers. This type of demonstration is interesting to an audience because the creative process itself is fascinating to watch; in addition, it is valuable as a means of transforming dance as creative activity from mere abstract theory in the minds of laymen to understandable reality. On the other hand, the degree of complexity of the compositional problems presented must necessarily be limited by the time element involved.

Compositional results must be achieved quickly if the audience is not to become bored. On the other hand, a minimum of time must be allowed for dancers to experiment, sense kinesthetically, evaluate, and select their ultimate movement solutions. If time permits, the dancers themselves can elaborate on a creative problem in their individual presentations of it. But the wise director will select problems that can be easily understood, solved individually or in small groups in a minimum amount of time, and presented without loss of spontaneity. By these criteria, large group compositions or complex dance structures are ruled out. When there is need for a demonstration to include such forms, the dance director should organize his presentation on a different basis. Some examples of compositional problems small enough in scope to be used for informal demonstration purposes are

- the transformation of a movement pattern from a stationary to a locomotor base;
- the individual interpretation of a given rhythmic pattern of one or two measures, or of a given linear design;
- the creation of simple movement themes out of specified elements of movement;
- the improvisation of variations on a given movement theme;
- the improvised expression of a simple idea through dance movement.

A second kind of demonstration is one in which dance studies are prepared in advance of the program. This method permits the composing group to work with increased selectivity, because it allows ample time for experimentation. Studies of all degrees of complexity may be included, provided the students are capable of coping with them and provided the audience is capable of grasping their significance. However, relative simplicity of both idea and movement technique is usually desirable, from the standpoint of audience comprehension, in any type of demonstration. Not only can moderately simple technique be perceived by the observer with greater clarity than can elaborate movement forms, but it can also be performed with increased conviction by most student dancers. Movement, to be effective, must be kept alive and spontaneous. The fact that a dance study is not a dance is no argument for allowing the movement to be mechanical. Regardless of whether the composition is a dance or a study, the dancer must be encouraged to concentrate on the kinesthetic sensation produced by the movement if it is to have any projective value for the audience.

Scope of Material

It is often a great temptation to try to include every important principle pertaining to dance movement in an hour-long demonstration. When too many ideas are introduced in a single program, the audience is likely to depart feeling both confused and overwhelmed. In most instances it is advisable to select only a few of what are considered to be major issues concerning dance and to concentrate on them. Or, if a series of demonstrations is to be given, each demonstration might be devoted to a different phase of dance, such as the use of rhythm, space, movement technique, or various kinds of accompaniment for dance. By such a plan each topic can be explored and developed fully, yet variety can be achieved within each topic by purposely creating studies that will contrast with each other.

Organization

A dance demonstration may be organized in such a manner that each dance element under discussion is presented by means of a study especially composed for that purpose. Below are examples of five relatively short demonstrations that are organized on this basis.

Demonstration of Dance Technique
1. Fundamentals of body movement
   a. rotation, flexion, and extension
   b. lateral movement
   c. arm patterns—lyrical, stylized, grotesque
   d. three studies of dramatic content using techniques previously demonstrated

2. Fundamental means of locomotion
   a. eight basic steps
   b. variations on a simple step pattern
3. fall study

Demonstration of a Rhythmic Approach to Dance

1. Basic rhythms, 3/4, 4/4, 5/4
2. Resultant rhythm
3. Study in accents
4. Three interpretations of the same rhythmic pattern
5. The effect of tempo on movement, twice as fast and twice as slow
6. Canon form

Demonstration of a Spatial Approach to Dance

1. Studies of design in space
   a. directions
   b. focus
      (1) Focus on one point
      (2) Focus on two points
   c. symmetrical design
   d. curved line
   e. straight line
   f. range or dimension
   g. three linear designs

Demonstration Illustrating Structural Organization in Dance

1. Unison movement
2. Successional movement
3. Round
4. Antiphonal movement
5. Rhapsodic movement
6. A B A form
7. Rondo
8. Ground bass
9. Theme and variations

Demonstration Illustrating the Use of Different Types of

Accompaniment for Dance

1. Percussion
   a. drums
   b. gongs
   c. drums and temple blocks-self-accompaniment by the dancers
2. Voice
   a. speaking voice preceding the dance
   b. speaking voice—self-accompaniment by the dancers
   c. singing voice
3. Musical instruments
   a. flute
   b. cello
   c. piano

The programming of these demonstrations as given here is merely an announcement of the titles of the dance studies that are being presented. The printed program in each case would need to be augmented by oral explanations of the studies or by program notes, in order for the audience to reap the full benefits of such demonstrations.

It is also possible to use a previously completed dance form for the object of analysis. The dance can be broken down into its component parts and excerpts from it can be presented to illustrate the use of specific elements of dance movement; that is, the specific movement themes that are significant to the meaning of the dance can be separated from the composition as a whole and presented for special examination. Sometimes an explanation of the derivation of the themes will add to the appreciative powers of the audience in understanding how a dance is composed. Sometimes, also, it may be advantageous to present the composition in its entirety first; then break it down for critical analysis; and finally to present it again in its completed form. In this way the observer is able to enjoy in the second performance many of the nuances of movement he was unable to perceive at first. Such a procedure might also be called a deductive method of presentation.

Another demonstration possibility is that of carrying a fairly complex dance through the various stages of its development. Starting with nothing but the idea, the demonstration group gradually evolves the form of the dance by introducing separately various compositional elements. For example, the dancers might first walk through the floor pattern; then repeat the floor pattern moving in accordance with the rhythmic pattern where it deviates from the steady beat; then add the specific step combinations employed in the dance, and so forth. How the composition is to be built up for the audience will depend to a large extent on how the composer went about developing his composition in the first place. Sometimes the presentation may be designed to disclose how one movement sequence was chosen as an outgrowth of the previous movements. The demonstration is simply a reconstruction of the creative process. This procedure represents the inductive method.

Still another type of organization is essentially like a theme and variations, in which a single basic dance structure is presented a number of times but the pattern is given a different kind of compositional emphasis with each repetition. For example, a relatively simple movement pattern might be used to illustrate the contrasting compositional results that may be obtained by stressing rhythmic interest in one instance, by varying the movement range in a second repetition of the pattern, by changing the dynamic quality of the movement, and so forth. Or the movement sequence might be presented first in literal pantomime; second, as pantomimic dance; and finally, as abstract dance.

There are doubtless many other successful ways of organizing and presenting dance demonstrations, each method having its own individual values. Whatever plan is used, if it is to fulfill its purpose, the demonstration must be arranged so that it will function smoothly; so that it will follow a logical sequence of development for the sake of audience comprehension; and so that it will be both varied and entertaining as well as instructional.

Presentation

As stated previously, in any type of dance demonstration there is usually a need for some sort of accompanying verbal explanation of the studies being presented. Such explanation may be given by the directing teacher or by the students themselves if they have been sufficiently trained to express their ideas clearly. Program notes have also been used to convey helpful explanatory information. For a demonstration illustrating accumulative meter, for example, the notes for the program might appear as follows:

Accumulative meter

A study based on a sequence of measures in which the number of beats in each measure is increased or decreased according to a definite scheme. The pattern of beats per measure used in this movement study is 1,2,3,4,5,5,4,3,2,1.

Written descriptions if used alone are often too sketchy to be adequate in themselves or too involved to be readable in a theater situation. An informal talk has the added advantage of establishing a feeling of rapport between the dancers and the members of the audience. However, the speaker should bear in mind that the audience is not primarily interested in a lecture but has come to see dance. Explanations should include only the essentials necessary to an understanding of dance studies; they must be intelligently conceived and concisely presented. Another scheme for presenting verbal explanations, which can be highly successful if skillfully done, it is for the performers to discuss elements of movement on stage among themselves (following a prepared script), demonstrating in dance the ideas they have chosen to discuss. Such an arrangement can create a pleasing illusion of complete spontaneity if the dancers speak their lines and move with dramatic conviction.

A method of presenting demonstration material that permits the audience to participate, by analyzing, selecting, evaluating, or providing accompaniment for the movement, can also be a helpful means of increasing the observer's interest in and response to the demonstration.

Demonstration/Concerts

The practice of including a short lecture demonstration as the opening section of a dance concert offers several advantages. First, it provides a compromise solution to the ever-present problem of how to handle audiences in which the level of understanding varies. Second, the demonstration helps to disclose a means of viewing the concert dances and thereby increases audience appreciation and pleasure. Ideally, dance should require no explanation; but as is true of any art, the more one understands of the technique and principles that govern its creation, the greater is one's capacity for artistic enjoyment. The demonstration shows the audience what to look for in a dance program. By the introduction of different elements of dance at each succeeding demonstration/concert, the level of audience appreciation can be expanded gradually to that of a connoisseur. Or, by demonstrating movement excerpts from a dance that is to be presented following the demonstration, audiences can be prepared to watch the choreography with increased understanding and enjoyment.

It is important for the success of the program that such preliminary demonstration sections be presented in a form that is not painfully and obviously educational. And, although explanations must be couched in simple terms, one should guard against any tendency to talk down to an audience. In the arrangement of a program, the demonstration section and concert numbers need to be clearly separated from each other, because their functions are not identical. The audience needs to understand that the lecture-demonstration is not a dance and be adequately prepared to see the presentation without special costumes and lighting effects. However, if clearly planned and executed, and intelligently programmed, a demonstration can be as fully enjoyable as any other part of the dance program.

Dance Concerts

In the presentation of a program of concert dances, the initial step consists of selecting the ideas to be choreographed. If the concert is to be the students' program, composed and performed by them, the dance ideas should also be theirs. The teacher can make suggestions and recommendations but he must also be sure that the dance ideas undertaken are within the scope of student interest, experience, and technical ability.

Selection of Program Material

Regardless of who is presenting or participating in a concert, it is of paramount importance that the balance of the program as a whole be considered at the outset. After the dances have been completed and one discovers, for example, that the program leans too weightily on the side of enigmatic abstraction or on depressing dramatic forms, it is usually too late to do much about it. Although themes of social significance have been a basis for much excellent choreography, an audience does not attend a dance concert solely to receive sociological messages. On the other hand, a dance program consisting principally of fantasy and froth is likely to leave some audiences feeling intellectually and emotionally unsatisfied. Movement that is ugly according to classical standards may frequently be justified and enjoyed on the grounds of its expressive value. Nevertheless, the dancer will do well to remember that movement considered beautiful in its own right is a universal source of aesthetic satisfaction. In "speaking" to the members of an audience the dancer should not lose sight of an equivalent need to charm them. Choreography of a highly esoteric nature often limits its appeal to those intellectuals who have been initiated into the "inner circle" of aesthetic understanding. Such dances, however, do have a legitimate place in theater productions if they have been artistically conceived and projected. The dancer must compose his dances in accordance with his own expressive needs, and not necessarily in accordance with the tastes of his audience. In selecting and arranging a program of dances to be viewed and enjoyed by the general public, however, audience interest also needs to be considered.

Audiences crave variety. Variety in the programming of dances therefore can be a primary asset in successfully appealing to an audience, just as in a musical concert public interest is heightened by the inclusion of works by different composers that incorporate a variety of themes, musical structures, and styles. In this respect the dancer who presents a solo concert suffers a slight disadvantage. Because every individual has a characteristic style that pervades every dance he creates, the soloist will need to rely on the choice of ideas and the structural patterning of them, and on the costuming and accompaniment as means of achieving variety. A program that includes the works of a number of choreographers has the advantage of containing a variety of compositional styles. The need for humor to balance profundity and tragedy was recognized by the early Greeks, who customarily followed a trilogy of tragedies with a comic or satirical play. The Japanese have traditionally presented humorous Kyogen playlets as interludes between serious Noh dramas. Even Shakespeare introduced into his profoundest tragedies characters, such as Falstaff, for comic relief. Theoretically, a well-balanced program will include both the comic and the serious, the real and the fantastic, the lyric and the dramatic, the abstract and the pantomimic.

If one purpose of a production is to please an audience, then the varied tastes and levels of experience of that audience need to be considered. This is not to imply that one stoops to satisfy the lowest level of taste and understanding. But little is to be gained by giving a program so far beyond the reach of the majority present that no communication is possible. It is important for audiences to be exposed to new experiences and challenged by works that puzzle them. On the other hand, audiences are likely to be more receptive to strangeness if, on the same program, they are also given the security of seeing works that they know how to enjoy. Otherwise they either secretly brand themselves as hopelessly stupid or openly condemn the choreography and leave, never to return.

Although Far Eastern audiences are accustomed to watching theater events literally for hours on end, Western audiences are not. A good program length lies somewhere between an hour and half and two hours. After two hours of attention, audience enthusiasm begins to plummet in geometric ratio to the length of the overtime. No amount of good performance can sustain it. Psychologically, a program is a good length when it leaves members of an audience satisfied but still in a receptive frame of mind—wishing they might see more.

It is wise to make a dance demonstration somewhat shorter than a program of finished dances because a demonstration is primarily an educative experience. The observer has more difficulty in concentrating for long periods of time on educational material than on material designed principally to appeal to his aesthetic sense or to entertain him.

A satisfactory time length for a dance demonstration ordinarily will range from a half hour to an hour, depending on the demands of the particular situation. Dance concerts, on the other hand, can sustain interest satisfactorily for an hour and a half or longer, provided they are well presented.

Dance educators are often tempted to extend a program beyond an ideal length to allow more student works to be seen or more students to participate; in doing so the entire program suffers. Sometimes an overextended program is arrived at inadvertently through miscalculations of timing. Dances that were thought to be ten minutes long are really fifteen, or the choreographer discovers that it requires more time to develop his dance idea than he had originally intended. Usually, however, dances will be improved by a tightening of the choreographic material. Unlimited use of time often leads to self-indulgence rather than increased artistry or even clarified meaning. Before any program gets too far under way, it is wise to time the music of pieces for which precomposed music has been selected and to set tentative time limits for other uncompleted compositions. After adding the total time for all if these dances plus anticipated time needed for costume, lighting, and scenery changes, as well as intermissions, one can decide whether or not one or two dances should be omitted. Such decisions made early are apt to be less painful than if made at the last minute after all the dances have been completed.

Program Arrangement

Once the dances for a program have been chosen, the matter of arranging their sequence needs to be undertaken immediately. Doing so enables one to determine whether or not there are satisfactory opening and closing numbers among the dances. If not, there may still be time to make one. Knowing the order of the program before the dances are finished also enables one to discover awkward costume changes in time to make some shifts in casting or adjustments in the choreography. Dances with difficult scene changes may need to be placed just before or after an intermission. The elimination of long waits between numbers is crucial to the success of any program. It is important for the success of the concert as a whole, and also for the individual dances, that the chronological arrangement of the numbers be planned with care. Excellent dances can suffer a loss of effectiveness through poor placement.

Dances that need to be chosen with special care are those that open and close the various sections of a program. The opening dance ought to be one that can be understood and enjoyed immediately; it should not require great concentration on the part of the audience, which is usually still in the process of settling down to the evening's entertainment. The number may sometimes be composed as a dance of greeting whereby the dancers introduce themselves to the audience; or it may be employed as a kind of choreographic overture in which the movement themes for succeeding numbers are introduced and interwoven. Usually a group dance is preferable to a solo or duet as a program opener because of the potential strength that may be achieved through the use of more people.

Dances that precede intermissions are also important; these should measure relatively high in popular appeal in order to make sure that the audience will be in a good mood to return for more. The effectiveness of these dances, also, is ordinarily increased by the use of group choreography. A dance that follows an intermission is, in a minor sense, like an opening dance; it again must prepare the audience's mood for the part of the program to follow. Usually, it is advisable to present weighty, intellectually significant numbers, which require concentrated attention, by at least the middle of the program before the audience becomes tired.

The last two dance numbers hold the position of climax; hence, they need to be selected with exceeding care. Both compositions should represent the best of the dancers' technical and choreographic powers. In addition, the last dance must be considered from the standpoint of its role in closing the program. This dance establishes the final impression and the mood with which the audience is left. As a rule, it is desirable to end the program in some relatively pleasant vein. Psychologically, the audience should be permitted to leave the concert in a positive frame of mind. A concluding number should also be a group dance, if possible, in order that it may have added interest and numerical strength. A group dance that is lively and colorfully costumed usually makes an ideal concert finale.

Program chronology also needs to be considered from the standpoint of the interaction of adjacent dances. An audience enjoys variety, but the contrast of mood should not be shocking. It is often dangerous, for example, to have a comedy immediately precede a serious dramatic number. Usually a wise procedure is to place dances of somewhat neutral mood between the extremes. Dances of similar style, mood, or quality should also, in most cases, be separated for the sake of variety. Occasionally, however, short dances of like nature may be grouped as a unit. One needs to exercise care in recognizing problems and making the necessary adjustments.

Another aspect of program arrangement that the instructor must bear in mind is that of planning the juxtaposition of dances in terms of the number of performers involved. Contrast of solos or duets with large group compositions is usually desirable for the sake of program variety.

Although not to be taken as absolute, the following suggested checklist for arranging the order of dances for a program from the standpoint of choreographic content is given below:

- for an opener, select a dance that is light, pleasant, and easily understood, making no demands on audience concentration;
- place long, serious, or thought-provoking dances fairly early in the program before the audience begins to tire;
- try to arrange the order or dances in a way that will achieve a sense of variety or contrast;
- avoid placing a hilarious comedy immediately before a deeply serious dance;
- be sure that the dance immediately preceding an intermission is sufficiently intriguing and popular with the audience to make people want to return;
- if a program has only one intermission the portion following the intermission should be slightly shorter than that which preceded it;
- the dance following the intermission should be one that will recapture audience attention;
- remember that the closing number is the one viewers will take home with them—it should be a group dance worthy of its place of honor as a finale.

Contrast in costuming and settings is almost as important to the success of a dance production as contrast in the choreography. Once the program of dances has been selected, the choreographers, the costumer, and the scene designer need to examine it together—first, in terms of its total content, and secondly, in terms of the juxtaposition of dances. Is there an overbalance in the use of undisguised tights and leotards? Is there an overuse of a given color or color group? Is backlighting against a cyclorama, for example, becoming a cliché to the destruction of its dramatic value? Is there a need for increased use of levels and three-dimensional settings to relieve monotony in staging? Have two dances with similar settings or costumes in the same color been inadvertently placed together on the program? Again, an early discovery of such problems can permit time for program rearrangements, for the dance composer to remodel his choreography to encompass new scenic possibilities, or for the scenic designers or the costumer to submit alternative lighting effects or color schemes to the choreographer.

Regardless of how good a dance concert is, it suffers if there are many long waits between numbers. The necessity for lightning costume or set changes should be eliminated wherever possible. If the original casting of the dances is done with some concern for these mechanical problems of costuming, many of the difficulties can be foreseen and avoided. Intelligent program arrangement can usually obviate many of the awkward waits that might result from costume changes.

The current trend, especially among professionals, toward presenting only three or four lengthy works separated by intermissions, eliminates some of the problems created by juxtapositions of short dances. The need remains, however, for contrast as well as unity within the substructure of long compositions, for contrast between the dance pieces themselves, and for psychological and dynamic building of the total program.

Because so many different factors must be taken into consideration an ideally arranged program is rarely achieved. In the case of conflict of necessities, decisions must be based on the comparative importance of the factors involved. When the program has been tentatively arranged it should be viewed in its entirety in terms of aesthetic principles of form relative to the situation in which it is being given.

Auditions

When the dance ideas have been crystallized, it is usually desirable to hold auditions before casting the parts. No matter how certain one may be that an individual is exactly right for a role, an audition for the part often discloses many surprises. The person mentally chosen may prove to have no feeling for the part, and other talented performers, previously overlooked, may be revealed to the choreographer through the audition.

Preparation for the audition requires careful advance planning. The choreographer may wish to teach a movement sequence that contains some of the technical challenges and movement qualities intrinsic to the dance. The sequence should not be so long that it is difficult to remember; otherwise the auditioners will be concentrating upon recalling the movement rather than upon dancing the part. The movement must be carefully analyzed technically and rhythmically so that time is not wasted in confusion. For some dances the choreographer may prefer to present an improvisational problem for the dancers. While this approach may sound easier than setting a pattern, it actually requires a great deal of thought and planning on the part of the choreographer to give the essential motivation for the dancers to respond intelligently.

In selecting the dancers it is also wise to choose one or two people to act as understudies. Not only is this experience valuable for the understudy, but it protects the choreographer in case of emergencies and provides an incentive to members of the cast to work diligently in the face of possible replacements.

Rehearsals and Performance

Once the cast has been set, the next task is to schedule rehearsals. The number of rehearsals per week depends a great deal upon the length and complexity of the work and proximity of its performance date. Usually a minimum of two rehearsals per week is required. The rehearsals need to be spaced so that too much time does not elapse between them in which the dancers can forget what they have learned, yet sufficiently separated to permit the choreographer time and perspective to plan for the next session. In order to profit from the choreographic momentum that normally develops during a rehearsal, the rehearsal time, whenever possible, should be at least an hour and a half in length.

If rehearsals are to be successful, they must be planned to use everybody's time to best advantage. Nothing is more demoralizing to members of a cast than to feel that their time is being squandered. When the choreographer is concentrating on the movement of one or two dancers the others should be given something to practice. One must guard against the tendency to overrehearse portions of the dance that are composed first, thereby neglecting the climax and concluding phases.

Some composers prefer to create every detail of the choreography themselves. When this method is used, however, it is important to clarify to the dancers the choreographic intent of the movement. Other composers like to share the creative process with their dancers, thus permitting the dancers to discover movements that feel and look right on their own bodies. However, even when this method is used, the choreographer must always come prepared with adequate motivation for this creative discovery, with a full knowledge of what effect he is striving for, and with suggestions for movement possibilities.

While creating the dance, the composer also needs to envision as clearly as possible the costumes, lighting, and total setting for the choreography. The sets and costumes should be completed at the first possible moment (usually as soon as it is certain that the dance will actually materialize). Meanwhile makeshift costumes and sets resembling the final product will need to be improvised for rehearsals because the dancer's movement is bound to be affected by them. The envisioned costumes may impose restrictions upon some of the dance movement or at other times magnify their effectiveness. These discoveries need to be made when the choreography is still in its formative stage so that advantage may be taken of the costume possibilities. A three-dimensional stage set with ramps, boxes, or levels, has no function unless its space potential is fully used in choreography. No amount of imagining on the part of the director or the dancers can substitute for actual experimentation on the sets themselves. An early look at the stage space, an awareness of the placement of entrances and exits, a knowledge of the availability and placement of curtains, legs, scrims, and cyclorama, and an understanding of lighting possibilities and limitations, can save much last-minute frustration and disappointment. The more clearly the choreographer can visualize his total dance concept and the possibilities for his end product before he begins to compose and the more adequately he prepares himself for his rehearsals, the greater are the chances that his work will succeed in having clarity of form and expression.

The rehearsal director is responsible for seeing that the dancers are committed to attend rehearsals regularly and on time; that they are totally concentrated during the rehearsal sessions; and that they maintain a positive working attitude, which is open to constructive criticism and adaptable to choreographic changes. When a member of a cast, after repeated correction, cannot meet these requirements, a replacement may be in order.

In any learning situation it is well known that positive reinforcement is more effective than constant negative criticism in encouraging students to do their best. The rehearsal director must demand the best that students are able to give to their performances, but should also endeavor to refrain from foisting their personal frustrations onto members of the cast. Successful rehearsals are the result of teamwork and mutual respect on the parts of the dancers, rehearsal director, and choreographer.

Dress rehearsals are extremely important as a means of accustoming the dancers to the effect of their costumes relative to the movement, and to the special problems created by their environment. The more at home the dancers can be made to feel in their performance situation the more their minds will be free to concentrate on the projection of the dance ideas. Staging, lighting, properties, accompaniment cues, and the mechanics of smooth entrances and exits need to be worked out well in advance.

Preliminary Showings

As an experienced choreographer knows, the objective eye of a good dance critic or group of critics can be very helpful in evaluating a work-in-progress. With inexperienced choreographers the need for periodic impartial criticism from a choreographic advisor or an informed audience is particularly important. Often young choreographers are too close to their own works to be able to view them objectively. They see what they want to see and not what is actually present; they become enamored of their own movement and fail to economize and select. If allowed to proceed on their own, students usually wait until a work is nearly completed before asking for criticism. By this time the form is solidified and little more than minor changes can be made without destroying the total fabric of the choreography. For this reason the first formal preliminary showing of choreography-in-progress should be scheduled about a third to halfway through the rehearsals before the production date. If certain dances are to be chosen for actual production from the total group of works-in-progress there should be adequate time allowed between this preliminary showing and the selection date to enable the choreographers to act upon the criticisms received. No choreographers, of course, should feel obligated to make changes to suit his critics, but he must also be prepared to accept the consequences of his decisions.

Selecting dances to be used on a program and eliminating others is always painful. Student committees find it difficult to be objective when their friends are involved as choreographers or performers. If available, it is often advantageous to appoint a jury of experts not directly involved with the concert to make the selection, thus minimizing subjective judgments and personal prejudices that can create problems. Although students are bound to be disappointed if their pieces are eliminated from a program, the experience can also be educationally valuable if they can understand the reasons for such decisions. The truism that we learn from our failures more than from our successes is applicable if the teacher takes the time and effort to help the student to evaluate objectively the strengths and weaknesses of his own choreography.

Sometimes flaws in program planning are difficult to foresee except under conditions of actual performance. The presentation of a preliminary informal guest program often can be of help in uncovering minor faults that need to be rectified. A program of this type is of particular value when the members of the audience can be persuaded to serve as critics. Such a performance also provides incentive for completing the dance far enough in advance of the public presentation for the dancers to grow into their parts. In productions performed by beginning dancers, however, it is important to bear in mind that dances completed far ahead of schedule or given repeated performances can occasionally suffer from a loss of spontaneity. One of the most difficult problems with which a dancer is faced is that of keeping a dance alive when repeating it on a series of programs.

Once rehearsals are over and it is time to "put the show on the road," the teacher's role is to make the performance experience as pleasurable as possible for the students. Time for criticism and correction has passed. As previously stated, a production that has been carefully planned and well rehearsed will minimize last-minute apprehensions and enable the dancers to concentrate on their roles without unnecessary worry or distractions. Especially with amateur performers, mistakes are bound to occur, but now is the time to focus on the joy of performance and the pleasure of sharing the creative experience with members of an audience.

Directing a program of theatrical dimensions can entail tremendous responsibilities. In its highly professional form, a dance concert demands not only considerable technical ability and artistic judgment on the parts of the dancers and choreographers, but also the talents of experienced musicians, designers, dressmakers, electricians, and business and publicity directors. The ultimate success of such productions depends on the degree of mutual understanding and cooperation that is obtained among all of the directors and participants.

Much genuinely artistic dance, however, can be created out of simple techniques that are within range of general student ability and that employ simple costumes and settings within the scope of the school situation. The artistic value of a dance program is not based on the lavishness of its production, but on the artistic sensitivity with which it has been conceived and produced.

Chapter 10

Music for Choreography

Selecting the right music for choreography is almost as difficult as selecting the right steps for the dance. At various times a choreographer will make a dance with a previously composed piece of music in mind and with the steps and the length of the piece built around the music. In this instance, of course, the choice of music is not a problem. But often a dance may start as a short study without music and it isn't until the dance is under way or nearing completion that the choreographer begins to think about a score for the piece. Some choreographers, in fact, prefer to work without the constraints of music. But if the dance is highly structured and the steps are carefully counted, it may be difficult or impossible to find the perfect piece of music for the dance. Modern aleatoric or abstract music sometimes can be useful in these situations because it may convey the right atmosphere for the dance without imposing too severe rhythmic or structural restrictions on the choreography.

Collaborating with a Composer

Ideally, it is desirable to work with a composer who has experience in writing for dance and who can provide the choreographer with music that is truly appropriate for the piece, and even more ideally, can provide the music well enough in advance of the performance that the choreographer has sufficient time to rehearse the dancers to the music and make any changes in choreography or music that are necessary. This ideal situation, of course, rarely occurs, and even when it does, it brings other problems along with it. Will the music be performed live? If so, will the musicians need microphones? When will they rehearse? Will they need to be paid? Will the choreographer have a tape of the music that is of sufficient quality that the dance may be performed at a later date without needing live musicians?

Given these caveats, a satisfying collaboration between choreographer and composer is usually dependent on good communication. If the choreographer has some fluency in the language of music and a familiarity with traditional musical forms, he will have a much simpler time explaining what the movement needs in terms of musical support.

Likewise, if the composer has done some dancing or at least attended dance concerts, the collaboration will go that much more smoothly.

However, if there is little previous experience in collaboration or a lack of a common language then a little extra preparation is in order. The choreographer can assist the process considerably by knowing in advance (1) the length of the piece, (2) the number of sections, (3) the number of dancers in each section, (4) the movement qualities, the tempos, and rhythmic feel of the sections, and (5) the areas of dynamic significance. Equally important, though often elusive, is a clear description by the choreographer of any emotional and imagistic nuances that are associated with the piece. Whatever metaphors, poetic references, or visual ideas (photographs, paintings, filmic descriptions) can be presented to the composer will greatly assist in translating the movement ideas into musical actualities.

Accompaniment Derived from the Dance Movement

The following discussion of the relation of musical accompaniment to dance is intended primarily to assist the inexperienced choreographer and the inexperienced music composer in reaching mutual understanding. The material is presented also with the aim of providing the dancer with musical terminology which may facilitate communication with his music. In considering the composition of music for dance, it should be remembered that music, like all art, is in a continuous state of development, corresponding to changes in the general culture. Furthermore, theory concerning music as dance accompaniment is also continually developing and changing.

Beginning dancers usually need the support of music that parallels the movement quality in a fairly literal fashion. Later, however, when the dancers and the musician have become relatively expert in performing and working together, they can strive to create forms of art that are complementary rather than reiterative.

Movement Tension

Generally speaking, current forms of choreography reveal a greater range of bodily tension than was formerly exhibited in either classical or romantic dance. Although classical ballet involved a great deal of actual strength and bodily control, the aim, especially in women's dancing, was often to conceal rather than display the muscular tension. The dancer of the romantic era, on the other hand, admittedly sought a flowing, lyric style of movement that was considered natural. In contemporary dance strong tension in movement frequently is deemed necessary for expressive purposes. The musical composer is called upon to find means of reflecting in the accompaniment the qualities of muscular tension inherent in the dance. The use of dissonance or harmonic tension, of rhythmic tension, and of strong dynamic attack are among the possible methods of creating musically an impression of strong tension.

Dissonant chords refer to those harmonies that create in the mind of the listener a feeling of opposition and unrest and a need for resolution. The individual tones of a chord pull against one another in the same way that one set of muscles pulls against another. The resulting musical quality is readily associable with physical tension. The following measures illustrate dissonance or harmonic tension.

The degree of tension produced by a dissonant chord can be increased by intensifying the sound of the chord. It must be noted, however, that harmonies considered to be chords of dissonance or strong tension during one era of musical expression are not always considered to be so in later periods.

Rhythmic tensions in the accompaniment can be effectively created by several different procedures. One method is to establish accents on normally unaccented beats, thereby producing syncopation. In any rhythm there is normally an accent, known as the primary metrical accent, on the first beat of each measure. When the number of beats in a measure exceeds three, secondary metrical accents are felt as a result of the need for further rhythmic organization. Examples are given below of the occurrence of primary and secondary metrical accents.

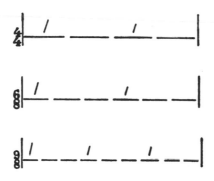

Accents that do not conform to these normal metrical accents can be established in two ways. The musician can arbitrarily play any normally unaccented beat with increased force, thereby causing it to be accented.

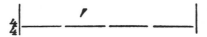

The impression of irregularity and syncopation is increased, however, when the metrical accent is firmly established first before the introduction of irregular accents, as illustrated in the following example:

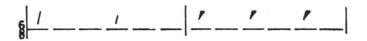

Again irregular accents can be established by creating a rhythmic pattern in which long note values occur on normally unaccented beats or portions of beats. The following patterns are rhythms of this kind.

An effect of rhythmic tension is also produced in meters such as 5/4 and 7/4, which contain an odd number of beats, when the secondary accents are stressed, thereby creating an irregular grouping of beats.

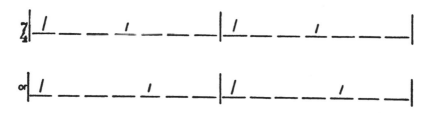

The use of rhythmic counterpoint is still another means of producing rhythmic tension. Rhythmic counterpoint refers to the simultaneous presentation of two or more contrasting rhythms that are related to the same underlying beat. Musically, the rhythmic counterpoint can be established by creating a rhythm in the treble clef opposed to that in the bass.

Strong dynamic attack simply refers to the degree of force employed by the musician in playing the accompaniment. Harmonic and rhythmic tension can be nullified by a limp or indecisive touch on the part of the accompanist. This is not necessarily to imply that the musician should always play with force or volume, but rather that his approach should always be sure, positive, and strong.

Harmonic and rhythmic tension and dynamic attack function as expressive means of emphasizing points of emotional stress and dramatic climax. An overuse of any of these elements in the musical accompaniment, however, tends to lessen the power of their impact, owing to the lack of sufficient contrast.

Harmonic consonance is inherently related to movement in which strong tension is not evident: consecutive thirds and sixths lend themselves well to lyric movement, as is demonstrated in the following musical fragment.

On the other hand, excessive use of consonance is inclined to give the music a sentimental flavor, which is frequently unsuitable to the character of modern dance. Dissonance that has been subjected to dynamic modification also can be appropriately incorporated into lyrical accompaniment. Its presence often adds the harmonic interest and variety that is requisite to good musical composition. The following two measures illustrate dissonance designed for lyrical accompaniment.

Movement Qualities

Swinging.   Each movement quality requires a particularized type of musical treatment which the composer of choreographic music should understand. For example, the accompanist should know that organic structure of swinging movement is ternary (based on three beats); that the characteristic tendency of the swing to return on itself makes it ideally suited to moderate or slow 6/8 meter that has a definite feeling of accent on the first and fourth beats. The first three counts of the meter thus are used for the initial swing, the last three for the return. If each beat in 2/4 meter is divided into triplets, its form and functions become similar to those of a normally accented 6/8. Moderately fast 3/4 rhythms are sometimes usable also for swinging accompaniment but not all 3/4 or 6/8 music has a feeling of swing. Any meter with a ternary organization can be used as a suitable basic scheme on which to invent rhythmic variations that will support the swinging movement. The use of a grace note run preceding the first and fourth beats (in 6/8 meter) will give an increased emphasis to the beginning of the swing where the strongest force is exerted. Sometimes the musician may choose to withhold the sound of the accompaniment on the normally accented beats, thereby transferring to the dancer all responsibility for establishing the accent. Swinging movement is relatively easy to accompany, but the accompanist must guard against the tendency to be monotonous and trite, relying upon singsong melodies and rhythms such as a recurrent

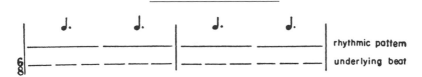

The challenge to the accompanist lies in finding rhythms and harmonies that are fresh and that enliven the choreography. A brief example of suitable accompaniment for swinging movement is given below.

Pulsating. Either 3/8 or 2/4 meter can be used to accompany pulsating movement. Pulsation performed in the ternary 3/8 rhythm results in an easy, partially relaxed type of movement—a miniature swing. Accompaniment for 3/8 pulsating movement might be written as follows:

A characteristic feature of both ternary pulsation and a naturally timed swing is the fact that there is a momentary suspension of movement during the third beat of the tripart rhythm. When pulsating movement is given a binary or two-part rhythm this suspension or rest period is of necessity omitted, thus increasing the bodily tension. In the accompaniment, each beat of the 2/4 meter is generally divided into two equal parts that correspond to the downward phase of the movement and its returning upward inflection. Thus there are two pulsations for each measure of 2/4 meter. The example given below illustrates this type of piano accompaniment.

Pulsating movement sometimes creates a mildly hypnotic effect when it is continued for any length of time; it also functions occasionally as an anticipatory device for the more dynamic phases of a dance. In either instance the accompanying music for pulsation should not be too strongly accented. Harmonies and dynamics should have little variation, and the pitch should be generally low and limited in range. The melody may resolve itself into a simple alternation of two or three tones.

Vibratory.   When pulsating movement is performed with extreme rapidity, it becomes vibration. Accompaniment for vibratory movement can be satisfactorily composed through the use of a four- or five-note passage, ascending and descending on a chromatic or whole-tone scale line, played very rapidly and high in pitch, and with a tension of the movement indicated further by dissonant chords punctuating the rhythmic pulse. The following measure illustrates this type of accompaniment for vibratory movement.

Other musical devices may prove to be equally successful. However, a tremolo, although consistent with the movement quality, is not good as dance accompaniment, since it permits the dancer to depend upon this imitative vibratory aspect of the music as a substitute for the movement itself.

Sustained. Sustained movement has its natural counterpart in legato music. A single melodic line, played by both hands (preferably two octaves apart) mirrors the simplicity that is generally characteristic of sustained movement. Whole-tone progressions, both harmonic and melodic; consecutive intervals of the same size, which preserve the constancy of the movement quality; and division of beats into two or three even parts, which establishes an effect of flowing continuity, are types of musical treatment that help to emphasize characteristics intrinsic to sustained movement quality. The three musical examples presented below illustrate the use of

1. A simple melodic line played by both hands

2. Whole-tone progressions

3. Consecutive intervals in accompanying sustained movement

Strict adherence to all of these suggestions throughout a composition would doubtless result in monotony. Variety can be achieved by alternate stressing of some of these musical devices. Staccato music can also be used to accompany sustained movement, provided the tensions in the harmonic structure are designed to support the movement quality. Musicians should avoid the use of many wide skips in the melodic line; of strong metrical accents unless they coincide with the beginnings of movement phrases; and of sudden changes in dynamics—all of which punctuate the flowing quality of the movement.

Percussive.   Both large explosive action and short staccato movement call for accompaniment that is played with a sharp energetic attack. Intervals of seconds, fourths, fifths, and sevenths; chords built in fourths or fifths rather than thirds; unrelated chord and interval progressions; and rests used in the rhythmic scheme, all contribute to achieving musical effect appropriate to percussive movement. An illustration of this type of musical accompaniment for staccato movement appears below.

For powerful explosive movement strong musical dynamics is necessary. A low bass and a wide range in tone also help to give increased strength and weight to the total impression, as shown by the example below.

Collapsing.   For collapsing movement a descending passage of several notes played in a rapid succession or glissando is an obvious but serviceable device to emphasize the successional character of the movement form. A briefly intimated, downward melodic inflection (two or three notes) followed perhaps by an accented chord in a lower pitch is another conceivable form of accompaniment. The melodic line need not necessarily progress in a downward direction; an inversion of the normally anticipated direction may prove to be interesting. Single chords that contrast in pitch or harmonic texture with the rest of the music may also be used effectively. If the collapsing movement is intended to be humorous, the effect of comedy can often be increased by accenting the movement with a chord or sound that is musically incongruous with the rest of the accompaniment.

Range of Movement

If the choreography employs large, expansive movement, the feeling of spaciousness may be expressed musically through the use of octaves and open chords and a wide range of the keyboard. Consecutive augmented chords produce an excellent effect of large range, as the following example will demonstrate.

Conversely, small range and diminutive movement may be supported successfully by the use of close harmonies and a narrow range in the melodic line. Minor seconds and diminished fifths are contributary to such an end. A brief example of such accompaniment for small-range movement is presented below. Small, delicate movement calls for musical accompaniment in which there is relatively little harmonic tension. If the character of the movement is strongly contractive, on the other hand,

the harmonic tensions of the music should be designed to create an impression of actively pulling in.

Rhythm

Rhythmically, the music must harmonize with the rhythmic action of the dance, but it does not have to follow the dance movement identically. Interchange of accent between the dancer and the accompanist often adds interest to the total effect. The dynamic quality of movement is frequently augmented by the appropriate use of intervals of silence in the accompaniment. Such moments of silence cause the dancer to move with increased force in order to fill the void. The audience, similarly, responds to the unaccompanied movement with added empathic intensity. Accompaniment that establishes a rhythmic counterpoint to the dance movement also is likely to cause the dancer to intensify his movement in order to hold his own against the accompaniment, provided the counterpoint is not carried to the extreme of being distracting. Sometimes the rhythmic interest may be concentrated in the dance movement while the accompaniment provides a simple, slow-moving rhythmic background for contrast. In dances of rhythmic complexity, it often becomes advisable to establish the rhythmic pattern of the dance movement first before deviating from it in the accompaniment. The less experienced the dancers, the more closely the musician will need to follow the exact rhythmic pattern of the dancer. With advanced performers the musician can allow his rhythmic ingenuity increased scope, thereby making possible results that are in most cases proportionately more stimulating to both dancer and observer.

If the composer is not kinesthetically sensitive, the choreographer may need to point out differences in qualities of movement. It may be necessary for him to explain the existence and recurrence of movement themes. Spatial qualities must also be noted. Such information, which may seem very obvious to the choreographer, may be just as obscure to the musician as the structural details of music are to an unenlightened dancer. Finally, the choreographer and composer should be in complete accord regarding the character of the dance idea.

Generally speaking, the composer should be careful not to let the score for the dance become too full. Such sound is apt to seem self-sufficient, making the dance movement superfluous. If music is too "notey," the dancer's movements are likely to be swallowed up in the intricate rhythms of the accompaniment.

Choreographic accompaniment should be relatively flexible in structure and, for most purposes, simple and unpretentious in style. Only for decorative movement is a decorative style of accompaniment appropriately employed. Most movement styles—formal, romantic, abstract, impressionistic, and so forth—have their prototypes in musical styles which, if used as accompaniment, can heighten the effectiveness of the dance.

If the choreography has already been completed and is awaiting a score, the composer has both an easier and harder task: easier because the form and flow of the piece is clearly evident; harder because now the composer needs to shape his structural instincts to fit someone else's sense of form. The most important consideration is that the score does not slavishly imitate the movement. The music should have an independent life of its own, which runs parallel to yet supports the choreography. Sections of counterpoint between the music and the dance should be balanced with sections of unison. The score needs to allow the dance to be seen fully on its own terms and thus not be a distraction with a contrary intention. Yet the music must also not be mere wallpaper, and thus so incidental as to add nothing to the piece.

If the choice is made to work with live music and one is working with a limited budget, an option is to check with a music department to see if any composition major is interested in trying his hand at composing for dance. In this instance, one should make sure the composer has more than adequate time to prepare and rehearse the score since inexperience will probably mean several revisions before both choreographer and composer are satisfied. Also, one should try to have the piece recorded well in advance so that there is both a work tape for rehearsals and a master for future performances. Recording live music is a highly technical skill and requires good equipment, an understanding of selection and placement of microphones, and the accumulation of past experience so that the recording session is completed with a minimum number of takes.

One should try to be flexible. On occasion, the composer may want to insert or delete a measure or two of music to give the piece more continuity. One should be prepared to allow this to happen if it does not seriously jeopardize the choreographic concept. At other times the choreographer may need to add a few measures to extend some important action. It is sometimes helpful to listen to the music that other composers such as Stravinsky and Copland have made for dances, try to understand why it is so effective, and then apply that understanding to one's own needs as a choreographer.

Creating One's Own Score

Another musical option open to the choreographer is to create one's own sound score. It can be an immensely satisfying effort. It can also be very time-consuming and take energy and hours away from the choreographic process. However, with that reservation in mind, the choreographer may try making a score expressly designed for the dance. Some of the raw materials may be conventional instruments used in unconventional ways; pedestrian and ordinary street sounds; supermarket or cafeteria sounds; excerpts from television or radio shows; music from homemade instruments; spoken pieces from poetry, prose, or speech fragments; or tape manipulations of ordinary sounds. All of these can be the basis for provocative scores.

In creating a percussion score for dance, success will be more readily achieved if one adheres to certain basic principles of composition in developing the accompaniment. For example, the orchestration should have unity. The attainment of orchestral unity can be greatly enhanced by the following means: First, one should endeavor to select instruments for the percussion orchestra that are capable of blending in tone and timbre. One cannot always predict in advance how the various instrumental qualities will blend. The best test is for the composer to stand a little apart from the orchestral sound and to listen with a critical ear to the total impression. Second, a simple basic rhythm and tonal effect, such as drum beat, can be established and continued as a constant factor throughout the composition. A thread of unity is thus provided that binds together the varying rhythms and tones of the rest of the orchestration.

The percussion accompaniment must also have clarity. When an orchestral composition becomes cluttered with too many simultaneous rhythmic intricacies or tonal variations, clarity is lost. These defects may be avoided to some extent by allowing some of the instruments to enter successionally and to be heard alternately. Climax may be established by a gradual augmentation of the rhythmic and dynamic texture of the orchestral accompaniment.

Working collaboratively with a composer or creating one's own score is a challenging and often gratifying experience. More typically, however, the choreographer ends up using prerecorded music, and in this instance, there is a different set of considerations.

Accompaniment Derived from Existing Musical Forms

If the dance is a solo, duet, or trio, one should be careful not to overwhelm the dancers by selecting a large orchestral piece of music. Generally, one should avoid using music that is so associated with a ballet or movie that the audience already has preconceptions about the kind of dance that should go with it. There are, of course, exceptions to this rule, one of which is using very familiar music as commentary, satire, or for its comic value.

Music that has a strong rhythmic underpinning and yet is still legato in its melodic structure will allow the choreographer to go in either direction in choosing movement qualities. Stravinsky is a good example of a composer who created music that often was both lyrical and highly rhythmic.

Popular music is tricky to work with. No matter how much the music means to the choreographer, if it is popular it probably has considerable meaning to many in the audience. Thus, the choreographer's vision of the music may not be that of the audience. In addition, the music may soon no longer be popular and in this manner, date the piece faster than the choreographer might wish. Twyla Tharp's Deuce Coupe (1973) to music by the Beach Boys quickly became nostalgic by virtue of the fact that the music is no longer current. It is already reminiscent of another era.

Especially with young, inexperienced choreographers who have had slight exposure to a range of music literature, there is a predilection to choose popular music with which they are familiar as inspiration for their dances. While occasionally this may work, often the chosen music itself may have slight artistic merit, which immediately impedes the creation of imaginative choreography. The choice of mediocre music almost certainly guarantees mediocre choreography. Sometimes the dance teacher or music advisor can suggest alternative accompaniment that possesses qualities supportive of the student's initial movement ideas. However, students often reject such suggestions and must learn by their own failures. Possible ways to avoid these situations are (1) to begin as early as possible to expose students to a variety of danceable music literature, (2) to show them examples of successful choreography that has involved the use of classical music; and (3) to assign problems in composition class in which the students must choreograph to traditional musical forms.

Electronic music has considerable appeal to many choreographers. The unusual timbre of the sounds and the spatial quality that is possible with synthesizers and echo devices can make the theater seem larger than it actually is. Also, the very unfamiliarity of such music helps to suspend the audience's disbelief and allows the choreographer to work with very abstract and unusual movement forms if that is his choice.

Electronic music can also be grating, abrasive, and cause aural fatigue in much the same fashion that too many lighting effects can exhaust concertgoers and diminish their concentration during the course of a performance. In programming a concert, it is usually desirable to intersperse dances that use electronic music with dances that use more conventional musical forms.

Editing, splicing or otherwise rearranging a piece of recorded music to suit one's purposes is not the way to win the affections of the person who wrote the music or of the musicians who are familiar with the piece. However, often the composer is no longer alive, or lives in some distant land like Berlin, or the Bronx, or Barstow, so that it may be difficult to contact him regarding liberties that need to be taken with the music. It is best, of course, to leave the music as it is, but if one must edit at all, one should try to do so in a way that is not offensive to the spirit of the piece. For example, doubling a section or repeating the whole piece, if it is too short, is not as damaging to the composer's intention as is arbitrarily splicing out bits of the music which don't suit the choreographer's purpose. If one absolutely must remove these passages, one should try to preserve the integrity of the music by removing only specific sections, for instance, the adagio from one Vivaldi concerto leaving the allegro and presto sections intact. One should try to leave in openings and finales. If one has questions regarding editorial decisions, it is usually wise to consult a composer or musician for his opinion. As a final test, one should put himself in the composer's shoes. What parts of your dance would you be willing to remove and still feel that the integrity of the choreography had been maintained?

Joining several pieces of music together to make a collage has its own set of virtues and difficulties. Collages permit a choreographer to make a rapid and often dramatic shifts in texture and movement quality. They can also permit the simultaneous overlay of different "voices" or moods to create a kind of counterpoint. But putting together a collage usually requires spicing techniques and/or skill in operating a mixer so that sound fades in and out and is overlaid with sensitivity and smoothness. One must be aware of the aesthetic choices involved in juxtaposing one piece of music with another. In addition, music collages as well as pictorial collages run the danger of being too busy and imposing a nervous, somewhat frenetic quality on a dance which may or may not be the choreographer's intention. So in making a collage, one must choose with care both the music/sound and the places where they will be spliced or faded together.

One other consideration in working with prerecorded music is that its use may be in violation of copyright laws. If there is any question about this, it may be wise to contact the local office of such music publishing companies as ASCAP or BMI for a correct interpretation of how the laws apply.

Technical Concerns

When editing or slicing recordings it is advisable to find someone who has done it and who can give "hands on" training in the various procedures. Or, one may take a recording to a professional studio with careful and complete instructions as to what changes and editing need to be done. This can be expensive, so it is recommended that one learn to splice and save production budget monies for such necessities as costumes. Splicing is useful not only in making the music the right length for the dance, but in adding leader to master tapes, creating silences where necessary, and in some instances, removing pops and the sound of record scratches.

After the music has been recorded, it is important that it be played back properly. If the quality of sound that comes out of the speakers during the performance is inferior, it will distract from the dance no matter how eloquent the music is. With the advent of compact discs many of the problems of obtaining clean sound have disappeared. But if the only recording available is an LP, there may be the hazards of surface noise and scratches imbedded in the vinyl. There are few exercises of concentration more difficult than trying to view a dance and not hear that pop from a tape of a cracked record as it comes around again and again and again.

There are ways to avoid some of these sonic curses. The music can be selected in advance and a fresh copy of the recording can be obtained. If the music has to be ordered from a record company, it may take from two to six weeks to arrive, so one must plan accordingly.

Once the new disc is in hand, it should be recorded in stereo on the best machine available, using the highest quality tape one can afford. It is important to avoid reusing tape that has already had something recorded on it, and to avoid recording on both sides of a master tape. After the initial tape has been made, a second copy should be immediately recorded which can be used in case of loss or damage to the master. It also might be well to consider recording a cassette copy to be used as a work tape.

One should make sure the master tape has sufficient leader at both the beginning and the end and that it is stored "tails out." This is a procedure whereby the tape is played through and then not rewound until just before it is to be played again. This process helps to avoid "print through," an annoying characteristic of tape whereby the sound on one part of the tape is transferred magnetically to the next layer and is often heard as a faint ghost or preecho of the music before it actually begins. Also, storing tape after it has been fast-forwarded or fast-reversed tends to store it under tension and increases the possibility of both "print through" and tape stretching.

One should keep the master tape in a relatively cool and dry place away from such magnetic fields as electronic motors, hi-fi speakers, or amplifiers. Storing it in an aluminum film can will help to preserve the tape should it accidentally pass near a magnetic field or be left in direct sunlight.

In most cases the tape should be recorded at 7 1/2 inches per second in a quarter-track stereo. One should check with the stage manager of the theater in which the piece will be performed to make sure that this format is compatible with whatever playback machinery is on hand.

The next concern is the sound test. After all the pains that presumably have been taken to assure that the master tape is of the highest quality, it would be a shame not to see to it that the final sound coming out of the speakers is the right volume level and the right balance of bass and treble.

First one must decide whether to play back the music in mono or stereo. A stereo image usually has greater presence than mono. But in those theaters that are exceptionally wide, the audience sitting on the sides may hear only the left or right channel as the case may be. Mono playback assures that everyone hears the entire sound, though with some loss of transparency.

Next, the volume level should be set by standing in several areas of the theater. Try to find a compromised setting if there is a wide disparity in levels. An audience will absorb a certain amount of sound unless the theater seats are padded on the underside so as to simulate the acoustic properties of a full house. It is important to make sure there is a monitor system off stage so that the dancers can hear the music clearly. Volume levels should also be set for these speakers at this time.

One should determine whether the treble and bass are properly set so that the sound is neither too boomy or too tinny. It is quite possible that these tone controls will have to be repositioned for each piece along with the volume levels. Knowing that the apparent volume of sound can change with dancers on a lit stage, one should try to recheck the sound levels during dress rehearsals.

One final consideration: the dancers may have been rehearsing with a work tape on a cassette machine that has a speed quite different from that of the theater tape recorder. It is important to make sure that all choreographers or directors have enough time to check the tempos of the accompaniment during the run-throughs so that there are no unfortunate surprises on opening night.

If all goes well and the sound system doesn't fail (back-up systems are an added expense but a good precautionary measure), then the music should appear to be transparent to the dance. Without drawing undue attention to itself, the accompaniment will work to reveal the inner logic of the choreography and give added presence to the dancers.

Basic Music Resources

Baroque

Bach, J. S.
Brandenburg Concerti
Sonatas and Partitas for
Violin
Suites for Unaccompanied
Cello

Scarlatti, D.
Keyboard Sonatas
Vivaldi, A.
Four Seasons

Classical

Beethoven, L. V.
Bagatelles
Late String Quartets

Mozart, W. A.
Concerto #14 for Piano
and Orchestra K. 449
Concerto #23 for Piano
and Orchestra
Sinfonia Concertante
K. 364

Romantic

Brahms, J.
Intermezzi
Chopin, F.
Mazurka in Ami Op. 17
no. 4
Various Waltzes,
Impromptus, and
Nocturnes

Mussorgsky
Pictures at an Exhibition

Impressionism

Debussy, C.
Ondine
Images
Syrinx

Ravel, M.
Piano Concerto in G Major
Pavane pour une Infante de
Funte
Gaspard de la Nuit

Twentieth Century

Schoenberg, A.
  Suite for Klavier, op. 25
  Verkarte Nacht
  Pierrot Lunaire
Stravinsky, I.
  Suite #1 for Small
    Orchestra
  3 Pieces for Clarinet
  Petrouchka
  Firebird Suite
  Le Sacre du Printemps
Webern, A.
  #4 from Six Pieces for
    Orchestra, op. 6 Col.
    ML 5616
Bartok, B.
  Mikrokosmos
  Music for Strings,
    Percussion, and Celesta
Prokofiev, S.
  Prelude, op. 12 #7
  Lieutenant Kijé Suite
Hindemith, P.
  Kleine Kammermusik,
    op. 24 #2
Messiaen, O.
  Merles Noir
  Quartet for the End of
    Time
Villa-Lobos, H.
  Prelude #4 for Guitar
  Bachianas Brasileiras, #5
  Music for Piano
Copland, A.
  Dance Panels
  Appalachian Spring
  Rodeo
Barber, S.
  Summer Music
  Adagio for Strings

Hovanhess, A.
  On Enchanted
    Ground
Bernstein, L.
  Sonata for Clarinet and
    Piano
  Candide Overture
Britten, B.
  Nocturnal, op. 70
Poulenc, F.
  Sonata for Oboe and Piano
  Pierlot and Ferrier
    (Nonesuch 71033)
  Sonata for Clarinet and
    Piano
Berg, A.
  Lyric Suite
  Four Pieces for Clarinet
  Piano
Boulex, P.
  Marteau Sans Maître
  Pli Selon Pli
Carter, E.
  Double Concerto
  Sonata for Flute, Oboe,
    Cello, and Harpsichord
deFalla, M.
  El Amor Brujo
  Three Cornered Hat:
    Dances
Gershwin, G.
  American in Paris
  Rhapsody in Blue
Ginastera, A.
  Concerto for Harp and
    Orchestra
  Creole Dance Suite
Lecuona, E.
  Piano Music

Twentieth Century (continued)

Milhaud, D.
  LeCarnaval d'Aix
  Saudades do Brasil
Mompou, F.
  Suite Compostelana
Nazareth, E.
  Piano Music

Orff, C.
  Carmina Burana
Vaughn, Williams R.
  *Fantasia on a Theme of
  Thomas Tallis*
  Lark Ascending
Weill, K.
  Three Penny Opera

Twentieth Century Experimental

Ives, C.
  *The Housatonic and
  Stockbridge from 3 Places
  in New England
  (DGG2530 048)*
  Calcium Light Night
Cowell, H.
  Ostinato Pianissimo
Partch, H.
  Daphne of the Dunes
  Delusion of the Fury
Cage, J.
  *Indeterminacy (Folkways
  FT 3704)*
  *Sonatas and Interludes for
  Prepared Piano*
Crumb, G.
  Voice of the Whale
  Ancient Voices of Children
  Black Angels

Berio, L.
  Sequenza V for Trombone
  Omaggio a Joyce
  Sequenza VII
  Sinfonia
Harrison, L.
  *Suite for Violin, Piano, and
  Small Orchestra
  (CRI SD114)*
  Pacifika Rondo
  Suite for Percussion
Nancarrow, C.
  Studies for Player Piano
Henri, P.
  *Variations for a Door and a
  Sigh (Limelight LS 860 59)*
Stockhausen, K.
  Telemusik
Subotnick, M.
  Touch
  A Sky of Cloudless Sulpher
Antheil, G.
  Ballet Mechanique

Minimalism

Adams, J.
  Shaker Loops
  Harmonielehre
  Negative Love

Glass, P.
  Facades

Minimalism (continued)

Reich, S.
Come Out
Drumming
Music for 18 Musicians
Octet

Riley, T.
In C
Rainbow in Curved Air

Jazz

Anthony Davis
Chick Corea
Miles Davis
Weather Report
Eberhard Weber
Jean-Luc Ponty
John Surman
Jan Garbarek
Ralph Towner
Pat Metheney

Carla Bley
World Saxophone Quartet
Wayne Horvitz
Lesiter Bowie
Egberto Grismonti
Art Lande
Thelonius Monk
Andy Narrell
Bobby McFerrin

New Wave

Laurie Anderson
Jean-Michel Jarre
Brian Eno
Peter Gabriel

Jon Hassell
Scott Johnson
Henry Kaiser

Chapter 11

Designing the Costumes

Costuming and staging for dance during the seventies and eighties have often appeared to be greatly deemphasized, in part because of the influence of minimalism in the arts, but also because production budgets, in general, are notoriously small and choreographers cannot afford the expense of specifically designed costumes and sets. Often stage sets are simply patterns of colored lights or slides projected upon a backdrop, and costumes are basic leotards and tights or selections of everyday clothing.

There are, however, occasions when specific costuming is highly desirable or even necessary as in the case of historical dances or for dances presented in formal concert situations. Dancers need to know how to design and make their own costumes because most theater costumers do not understand the unique needs of the dancer as opposed to the actor, and choreographers in schools and colleges can seldom afford to hire such people anyway.

Although costumes for dance have undergone many transformations over the years, the criteria for good costume design remain unaltered. A dance costume can never be considered as an isolated object d'art; its success is measured in terms of its support of the dance idea and dance movement as well as in terms of its effect upon the appearance of the wearer and its relationship to the performance environment. Any costume design involves a consideration of at least three factors: the shape of the costume and the lines within it; the color or colors of the costume; and the texture, weight, and motion of the fabric.

Costume Shape and Line

Anyone who has ever seen illustrations of historical costumes in silhouette cannot fail to recognize the tremendous importance of costume shape or outline in defining a particular historical period. Society's attitude toward the human body is reflected in costume. Through the ages, especially among societies that encourage affectation, or upon occasions when the wearer seeks to move the viewers to states of shock, mystery, or amusement, the shape of the natural human figure tends to be con-

171

cealed or distorted by the costume silhouette. In producing theater costumes for a given historical period or ethnic group, the designer needs to examine the lines of the authentic costumes as determined by the typical lines of the neck, waist, sleeves, skirt, and so forth. While the costumer for realistic theater attempts to copy the original with little or no modification, the costume designer for dance attempts rather to convey the feeling of the period or culture from which the dance is derived. Because dance itself is an abstraction of reality, the costumes should be designed to suggest rather than to represent literally the dance characters. Selecting those costume characteristics that are especially typical of the people or era being portrayed and also supportive of the dance mood and movement, the costume designer for dance emphasizes these features while minimizing or eliminating others. To convey a late medieval or early Renaissance atmosphere, one designer selected from the traditional women's fifteenth century costumes the high waistline, the collared V-neckline, the generous train, and tall conical hat, and applied them to a basic unitard. No one missed the long skirt of the traditional costume. The real essentials were present and the movement of bodies and feet of the dancers were more clearly revealed than the authentic dress would have permitted. Sometimes, however, it is important to retain the movement-restricting features of a "period" costume because those very movement restraints may be an essential characteristic of the movement of people of that era. The disproportionately tall hats of the ladies of late medieval time could not help but limit head movements and affect general carriage. In the same way, the concealing hooped skirts of the court ladies of Marie Antoinette's day left their mark upon court dances.

When costume shape is greatly exaggerated, the effect becomes humorous. Huge leg-of-mutton sleeves or exaggerated bustles provoke amusement. Any element of surprise, such as a modest turn-of-the-century bathing costume that becomes a risqué bikini when viewed from the rear, invokes laughter.

A costume shape and line can do more than place a dance within a given era or ethnic group, or establish it as a humorous or serious piece. Line has many subtle implications. Experiments have shown that patterns of lines affect observers psychologically in a rather consistent fashion either for psychological reasons or as a result of experience and association. Straight lines appear strong while most curves seem gentle; horizontal lines seem quiescent (though they may also suggest speed); verticals suggest poise and equanimity; diagonals appear active and unresolved. Sharp angles are dynamic, restless, exciting; curved patterns are flowing. Furthermore, symmetrical designs present an effect of stability, formality, dignity, and tradition; asymmetrical designs are free, informal, and unpredictable. These are effects that the choreographer needs to bear in mind not only in designing the movement and floor patterns of his choreography, but also in planning the stage sets and costumes for the dancers.

Generally speaking, ornamentation should be simple and so arranged that it is in keeping with the design of the costume as a whole. Overelaborate costuming places the emphasis on the dancer's clothing instead of on his movement. Glittery materials such as lamé or sequins, which attract the eye to themselves, ordinarily should be used sparingly. Stylized motifs, appropriate to the dance idea, can sometimes be applied to dance costumes to help carry out a choreographic theme.

Costume Color

Color, like music, seems to have a direct appeal to the emotions. The effect of color upon the viewer is four-fold. From a physiological standpoint, colors can be classified as warm or cool. Color pigments at the red end of the spectrum—reds, oranges, and yellows—absorb the short length, rapidly vibrating violet rays while reflecting their own longer-length light rays. Rapidly vibrating light waves create heat, so reds, oranges, and yellows are sensed as warm colors. The opposite is true at the violet end of the spectrum, so violets, blues, and blue-greens are cool colors. These temperature differences can actually be measured.

Again, physiologically, when one looks at colors, certain ones appear to advance toward the viewer while others recede. This phenomenon is more than mere illusion; it is the result of the refracted wave lengths of different colors. Reds, oranges, yellows, yellow-greens, and white are the so-called advancing colors, while blue-greens, blues, violets, and blacks are all receding. This is why traffic signs are painted red or yellow rather than violet or blue. In dance, when the costumer, set designer, or lighting director wishes to give a feeling of cavernous expanse or distance, he chooses violets, blues, blue-greens or blacks, not only because they are associated with the expansiveness or distant haze as seen in nature, but also because these colors appear to recede from our vision. Opposingly, reds, yellows, oranges, and yellow-greens are colors of immediacy, demanding attention from the audience because of their advancing qualities.

Psychologically, also, the viewer is affected by color, a human reaction that is common knowledge among people working with the emotionally disturbed. Colors at the red end of the spectrum (reds, oranges, yellows, and yellow-greens) tend to excite, while blue-greens, blues, and violets except in their brightest intensities, can calm, soothe, or even depress. Brightness of color increases its stimulating qualities. Grays and blacks are somber in effect. Color-tints (colors diluted with white) and color-shades (colors diluted with black), or color intensities that have been muted by addition of their color complements, have proportionately lessened excitement and emotional impact in direct ratio to loss, brightness, or intensity.

Beyond these universal reactions to color for which there are scientific explanations, there are also individual responses based upon personal experiences and cultural conditioning. Cultural mores of most occidental societies designate white for marriage as a symbol of purity, purple (originally crimson) for royalty, and black for mourning. Among some Far Eastern cultures, red is associated with weddings and yellow is a symbol of the emperor. The colors seen in nature cause us to associate blue with water and sky, green with forests or spring growth, white with snow, and so forth. Colors have certain meanings under certain conditions and the color symbolism changes according to circumstance. Each individual, depending upon his experience, has his own particular patterns of association. It becomes obvious, then, that from the standpoint of association, no two people will react to color in exactly the same way. Yet, within a given culture, there are enough shared experiences with color to guide the costume and stage designer for dance in selecting colors that will best convey the mood and meaning of the dance.

Particularly in serious dances, the designer may not want to appear obvious in the use of color symbolism at the risk of becoming banal. To avoid this pitfall one might select off-shades of the true colors, shades that would suggest rather than shout to the audience the concepts held in mind. On one occasion, for a dance of patriotic significance, it seemed appropriate to incorporate red, white, and blue into the costuming. Such a color scheme, unmodified, would have made the costume look like bunting from a Fourth of July grandstand. Instead, the costume designer used red and a rich cream-beige with soft gray-blue. The effect was subtly suggestive of a patriotic mood, but it was artistically abstracted. On the other hand, a designer may deliberately choose completely unexpected colors for the sets or costumes to create an effect of fantasy or theatrical abstraction. But the total color impression must harmonize with the intended dance idea or else the designer and the choreographer will find themselves working at cross-purposes.

Certain color combinations are more pleasing to the eye than others. However, exact combinations that seem particularly satisfying vary from period to period and culture to culture and are influenced to a large extent by what the eye or ear has become accustomed. Analogous color schemes—that is, a sequence of colors that are immediately adjacent on a color wheel (yellow-green, yellow, yellow-orange, and orange; or violet, blue-violet, blue, and blue-green)—give both a sense of unity and variety to the color organization. Use of different tints, shades, and other variations of the same color accomplishes the same result, but with increased subtlety, giving depth to the visual impression.

Complementary colors such as red and green, yellow and violet, or orange and blue—pigments that appear on opposite sides of the color wheel and possess opposing physical properties—may appear too obvious in their color contrasts when used full-strength. They are also difficult to light, because the light that brings out one color tends to kill the other. A given color and the two hues on either side of its complement, such as red, blue-green, and yellow-green, known as "split complements," while still somewhat difficult to light, are more subtle in their color contrast than a choice of true complements. Unusual colors are apt to be more interesting than pure primary or secondary colors and make for increased variety when used in combination.

If more than one color is used in a costume or a group of costumes, it is usually wise to make the proportion of colors uneven so that one color appears to dominate. Dominance of color can be regulated by adjusting either the amount of the given color or its intensity relative to the others. In designing a group of costumes, a single color can be applied in large or small amounts to the different costumes as a means of tying them together; or a neutral color such as gray, tan, white, or black can be incorporated in all the costumes to provide the unifying thread. Especially when bright colors are used, a large amount of neutral color is needed to produce the necessary balance.

When looking for the right combination of colors for a dance, a collection of swatches of various tints and shades of every color, such as are to be found in paint catalogs, can be useful. By playing with these swatches, new color harmonies can be discovered. Colors that appear to clash at close range may prove exciting when viewed from a distance and under theater lights. Color combinations found in store window dressings, paintings, or magazine illustrations may also suggest effective possibilities. The next problem, which is not always easy, is then to find the chosen colors in the appropriate costume fabrics.

After this has been done, these fabrics need to be tested under theater lights because different fabrics of the same color may change in appearance under artificial lighting as a result of differences in fabric texture. Some colors are easier to light than others. Yellows, especially, can be difficult to light. Pale creams and off-whites are usually more successfully lighted than dead-white, and also have a richer appearance.

Costume Texture and Fabric

Another aspect of costume fabric with which the designer must be concerned is the texture of the material, which includes not only its surface appearance but also the way in which the fabric hangs or moves on the wearer. The surface texture of the material may be dull, shiny, rough, smooth, or velvety; the material itself may be transparent or opaque. In its hang and movement, costume fabric can drape gracefully on the body, stand stiffly away from it, cling to itself, fall heavily to the ground and swirl around energetically, or float lazily in the air. All of these characteristics may have their appropriate uses in costuming dances.

Materials that drape most beautifully are silk, rayon, acrylic, and wool jerseys. Nylon tricot and other lingerie fabrics are very useful since they are wide, inexpensive, and come in various weights, colors, and degrees of shininess; they also dye well and seldom ravel or run. Silk, rayon, or nylon jerseys can be heavy or diaphanous, depending upon the weight of the material. On the other hand, wool jerseys are heavy, and skirts of this material move beautifully in response to body turns. Heavy fabrics always move with greater speed and centrifugal force than light-weight materials.

Crepes of all kinds drape beautifully. Acetate lining fabrics are lightweight, relatively inexpensive, and come in a variety of colors; however, they drape only moderately well and are usually dye resistant. Polyester broadcloth is somewhat stiffer than crepe and lacks its rich surface texture. One should keep in mind that polyester materials are difficult to dye. Unbleached muslin is one of the most economical of fabrics; it comes in several widths and weights and can be easily dyed in almost any soft color. Lightweight muslin contains a lot of sizing and may lack body after washing. Sheets, especially king-size, if not too old and worn, are good for making costumes. The wide material is particularly advantageous for circle skirts. Denim is good when a sturdy fabric is needed. It comes in many different plain colors as well as in stripes and prints. Because of its shiny surface, satin is flashy on stage and is only appropriate for certain situations or types of dances. Crepe-backed satin, which is relatively inexpensive, has the appearance of satin but has an added advantage of moving softly, like crepe.

Taffetas are probably among the best fabrics to use when stiffness and formality are desired, though it is possible to heavy-starch or spray with "magic sizing" other kinds of material, or to line them with pellon. Taffeta is relatively inexpensive and comes in a great variety of colors; however, it loses body with washing and cleaning and tends to crack when folded. Taffeta also makes a rustling sound in movement, which may or may not be a desirable added dividend.

Heavy cotton flannel looks rich in texture under the lights, but it does have a tendency to cling to itself. Velvet, of course, is beautiful, though expensive. Velveteen and corduroy, especially ribless corduroy, resemble velvet under lights and are far less expensive. Small touches of velvet, brocade, satin or other rich materials added to a costume made of inexpensive fabrics can often create an illusion of total elegance. One should never combine real and fake velvet or real and fake fur, however, since the deception is immediately discernable.

Printed materials can be cut out and appliqued on plain materials to resemble embroidery. Fabrics to be used for appliqueing on tights and leotards, however, must have the same stretch capabilities as the tights and leotards themselves. Old leotards that can be cut up and used for this purpose provide the most ideal material. Nylon stretch tubing used for maternity clothes can be purchased in black and white; the white tubing can be dyed. Other non-bonded jerseys are also usable. Leotard fabrics, especially milliskin, and patterns for making leotards and tights can be obtained from fabric wholesale companies.

Lightweight materials are tulles, organdies, organzas, nets, georgettes, and chiffons. Net and organdies have a starchy, brittle quality. Organzas, which have a delicate luster, and nylon chiffons drape somewhat more softly than tulles and organdies but still contain a certain amount of resilience. Silk chiffons and rayon georgettes, on the other hand, hang softly. Silk chiffons are much more expensive than nylon chiffons, but the difference in fabric quality may be worth the difference in cost.

A small printed pattern on the costume fabric can give the material a rich textured appearance even though the print itself is not large enough to carry as such to the audience. If a printed pattern is intended to be seen in a theater situation, then it must be extremely large. In selecting such a print it is wise to test it by looking at the bolt of material from the distance of the length of the store. It is often surprising how the appearance of a print can change at such a distance. Even trimmings, such as bands of sequins, need to be seen from the back of a large auditorium.

Not all costume materials are found in dress fabric departments. Drapery and curtain materials and upholstery trim have been known to solve many a costume problem. Although drapery fabrics are expensive, they are so wide that it is usually unnecessary to purchase much yardage. Costume houses carry fabrics also, but many of their materials are designed for commercial dance events and are usually too flashy for the needs of the modern dancer. Too much glitter onstage can be distracting.

Creating the Design

The costume designer need not be limited to using conventional patterns that are available in commercial costume and pattern books. One can experiment, creating newspaper or muslin patterns of one's own devising until a design that is completely appropriate to the style of movement of the dance is found.

In designing costumes for a specific dance, there are many factors to be considered. First, and most important, is the dance concept itself. Does it belong to a particular historical period or ethnic culture? Is it a comedy or a serious dance? Is it programmatic and fairly literal in concept or is it partially or completely abstract?

Where is the movement interest focused? Is it in the feet, the arms, the legs, the hips, or in the body shapes? If footwork is important, then the feet must not be hidden by a floor-length skirt. Large leg movement requires the freedom of action that can be provided by a flared or a split skirt or by the total absence of a skirt. If a pelvic movement is intended to show, the costume will need to be fitted closely around the hips, though it can flair below the hipline, a style characteristic of Spanish Flamenco costumes. Arm movement that must be seen with clarity normally requires the use of a simple, fitted sleeve or no sleeve at all. Leotards and tights usually provide the best costuming for dances in which body line, shape, and motion are paramount.

The movement quality of the dance is another factor that influences costume design. Most affected is probably the choice of costume fabric as discussed heretofore. The general shape and flow of the costume can also play a supportive role in underlining the movement quality. Strong, percussive movement, if clothed in anything other than leotard and tights, demands the use of stiff or weighty fabrics with lines that are strong, direct, and usually straight or angular. Lyrical movement quality, on the other hand, is best augmented by lines that curve and fabrics that flow, swirl, or float, possibly a flared skirt and belled sleeve. Staccato movement that is light and brittle suggests the use of starchy, lightweight fabrics and acute angles.

Closely allied to the movement quality of a dance is its general mood. Because people are so emotionally affected by color, the importance of selecting costume colors that will support the dance feeling or mood cannot be overestimated. No other costume element can do as much to emphasize or destroy a given mood as color itself.

A further consideration in the costume design must be the body structure of the dancers who are to be the wearers. Onstage, a dancer looks taller and larger than he appears normally. Added height is usually not undesirable, but added corpulence is quite another matter. Bodies that need to look thinner than they are can be made so by the avoidance of all horizontal lines, particularly those that tend to cut the body in half, and by the use of vertical lines whenever possible. Costumes with dark side panels running the length of the torso or costumes sprayed or dip-dyed to be dark along one or both sides can be very slenderizing. Costumes that fit too tightly tend to emphasize overweight proportions of the body.

Most good costume designs have a focal point or center of interest. One must be sure to place the color accents or decorative motifs where one wants the eye to go. When a single body area is disproportionately large, it is wise to design a costume to draw the eyes elsewhere or to use lines to give an impression of increased breadth to some other part of the body. The use of receding colors and grayish hues can also make the undesirable aspects of a figure less obvious to the eye.

Empire waistlines can be attractive on slender, small-bosomed figures if the material is sheer enough to allow the body silhouette to show through or if the costume is slightly fitted to the waist, but they can be disaster on a buxom or full-busted figure. On the other hand, a drop waistline that permits the flair of skirt to begin on the hips rather than at the waist can lengthen and slenderize a body that is short-waisted or slightly heavy in the middle, but can be devastating to a "hippy" person. The same basic principles in the use of vertical and horizontal lines can be applied to men's costumes. For men who have overly thin legs, wool tights are more flattering than nylon tights because the thickness of the wool gives added girth to the leg. The same corrective effect can be obtained by wearing a pair of flesh colored tights under the nylon tights of a costume. Whenever possible, dark colors should be assigned to dancers with large figures, light colors to diminutive figures.

The background against which the dancers are to perform will be another determining factor in costume design, particularly in the choice of costume colors. Although it has been said that light colors of low intensity show off body movement more effectively than bright or dark colors, even more important is the degree of color and value contrast between the dancers' costumes and the curtains, cyclorama, or other scenic background. While the effect of a cyclorama can be changed by lights, there is not much that one can do to transform a black curtain. For the most satisfactory effect, the costume and staging should be planned together so that one can be made to enhance the other and the total effect of design and color harmony can be unified.

Colors of strong intensity are fatiguing to the eye. For large groups or long dances it may be wise to soften or gray the intensities slightly or to dilute the effect of the strong colors with the use of a large proportion of blacks, grays, whites, or other neutral colors. Pure hues and strong intensities work best in folk dance costumes and dances for children. In group dances where it is intended for the dancers to be related, a unifying color or color harmony can be used to tie the dancers together. If a basic color is not used, a common design can serve to unify the group.

For a dance of several sections, the use of basic costume throughout the dance to which different accessories can be applied not only helps to tie all the parts together but may sometimes provide a means of economizing on costume costs when finances are limited. By way of illustration, one costume specifically designed for a suite of court dances was adapted to the contrasting qualities of the various sections of the suite through the use of different costume accessories—a single glove to suggest the formality of a sarabande, later removed, and a sheer flowered overskirt added to harmonize with the playful music of a badinerie.

Dominant figures in a dance need to be costumed so that they will stand out against the group either by means of the color that attracts the eye or by contrast in costume design. It is also important to remember that a costume design eminently suitable for a solo figure may have lines that are too overpowering or too decorative when applied to a large group. Large groups require rather simple, uncluttered costumes. Ideally, the costume designer should also be acquainted with the other dances, costumes, and sets to be used on the program so that the designs can be planned to contrast with each other in color and general style.

The choreographer should endeavor to formulate the costume needs as soon as possible. However, it is usually a dangerous practice to make the costumes before the dance movement has actually been determined because a dance may change many times in the process of creation. The exception, of course, is a dance in which the costume itself is intended to help determine the movement, in which case the making of at least a sample costume is needed in advance of the choreography.

Before planning a set of costumes, the designer, whether it is the choreographer or someone else appointed to this role, should carefully observe the dance with particular recognition of costume needs. Notes should be made of the movement qualities, focus of movement interest, range of movement required, important movement accents that need to be reinforced, dance mood, floor pattern and general spatial design, groupings of dancers, solo figures, and any special deviations from the "ideal" dancer's figure that may present costuming problems.

If the costume designer is someone other than the choreographer, the two will then need to meet so that the designer can learn the choreographer's intent (which does not always agree with what the designer observed in movement) and there can be a exchange of ideas. Usually the costumes must be well under way before the choreography is completed, in which case the designer will need to know the general plan for completion of the dance.

Once the costume ideas have begun to take shape on the drawing board, it is necessary to reflect upon the fact that the final product will be three-dimensional and must be interesting or attractive in appearance from all sides. Adequate consideration must also be given to the ease with which the dancers can get in and out of their costumes in the allowed program time. As a final test of the costume designs one should ask:

1) Do the costumes totally support the dance concept and its resulting movement?

2) Do the lines and colors of the costumes make the dancers' bodies as attractive as possible in terms of their varied structures while remaining appropriate to the choreographic idea?

3) Do the costumes permit the movement to convey the dance idea rather than becoming a substitute for the movement?

4) Do the costumes remain sufficiently simple so that they do not intrude upon the audience's attention?

5) Do the costumes allow the dancer total freedom to move without restriction?

6) Do the costumes contribute to the total unity of the theater piece?

7) Does the effect justify the cost in terms of time, money, and its contribution to the whole?

Most school budgets for costumes are not very generous. However, materials need not be expensive to create a pleasing result. Dyed bleached and unbleached muslins for example can be extremely effective under lights. A slightly uneven dye job will often add richness to the total aspect of the costume. A little creative ingenuity on the part of the costumer can do much to keep the costume expenses within budget.

Building a Basic Wardrobe

One way of reducing costume costs is to build a basic wardrobe that can be adapted to many uses. Blouses, skirts, sets of simple dresses in various lengths and colors, slacks, turtleneck T-shirts, and old white sport shirts that can be dyed are the kinds of articles that can be modified and used over and over again. But perhaps the most versatile of all are leotards and tights because of their complete simplicity. Sets of leotards in different colors and styles with matching or neutral tights can not only be used repeatedly without change for many kinds of dances, but their appearance can also be transformed by the use of dyes, paints, appliques, and scissors. The addition of accessories such as overskirts, belts, sashes, and sleeves can also do much to transform costumes already on hand.

A simple uniform costume of attractive design is serviceable also for the presentation of movement techniques and compositional studies for demonstration purposes. Dance costumes designed for this latter purpose should be such that they will be appropriate for a variety of qualities and styles of movement. Leotards and tights with which long or short skirts can be used interchangeably are often of practical value. Boy's or men's costumes for use in demonstrations need also to be of simple design, usually consisting of leotards or plain-colored T-shirts and slacks or tights, either matching the costumes of the girls in color or contrasting with them.

Hair Styling and Makeup

The dancer's visual appearance on stage includes not only the costume, but hairstyle and makeup as well. Dressing the hair in a way that is appropriate to the dance is every bit as important as the costuming. Period pieces should at least have a suggestion of the hairstyling of the period whenever possible. Long hair, of course, is much more versatile for these purposes than short hair. The complexity of the styling is another important consideration, keeping in mind the amount of time the dancer will have between dances to dress the hair. Wigs are always a possibility, but these are expensive to rent and one may not wish to be so totally realistic in the representation of period dress.

Usually a simple, unobtrusive hairstyle is best. If a group of dancers is dressed alike, a uniform hair styling adds to the uniformity of the effect. In lyrical dances, wearing long hair down so that the hair movement adds to the flowing quality of the dance may be desirable. But in all cases, one must be sure that the hair can be controlled so that it does not fall in the face at inappropriate moments. If hair is worn up, it must be properly secured so that it will withstand any violent movement of the head or action of the body.

Makeup can be as simple as the mere exaggeration of makeup normally worn in daily life or so complex that it literally becomes an extension of the costume itself. For many dances, especially those performed in small, intimate theater settings, simple makeup is sufficient. In general, the purpose of makeup is to make the dancer as attractive as possible to the audience and to reinforce, when necessary, the features and coloring of the dancer that tend to disappear with distance or fade under colored lights. When dance performances are held in large auditoriums or theaters such as those often found on high school or university campuses, enhancement and exaggeration of everyday makeup becomes increasingly important. Following are some suggestions for application of theatrical makeup for situations in which its use is appropriate.

A smooth foundation base is first applied to the face and neck, blending it down below the neckline of the costume or leotard. This foundation base can be either in the form of grease paint or liquid foundation cream. Liquid cream is usually easier and less messy to apply than grease paint, and because of its greaseless nature is apt to be less damaging to costumes. For women, except those with very dark coloring, the foundation color should be a shade or two darker than the person's natural skin color. A standard color used by all the dancers helps to give them a look of uniformity. For men, the basc makeup, if used, should be a couple of shades darker than the makeup used by women.

Before the rest of the facial makeup is applied, one may wish to consider the need to remedy facial defects by placing darker or lighter makeup on the critical areas. A face that is too square can be made to appear less so by subtly darkening the foundation makeup around the outside corners of the jawbone. A broad face can be narrowed by bringing the dark makeup around the outer edges of the cheeks. A small nose can be made to look more prominent by blending a line of light makeup down the center of the nose, and a long nose can be shortened by slightly darkening the makeup at the tip of the nose. The same can be done for a chin that is too long.

Color on the cheeks is usually applied on the cheekbone slightly outside the center of the cheek and blended outward in all directions. If the face is too narrow, the color is applied slightly farther outside the normal placement and if broad, slightly inside. Men usually do not use cheek coloring.

The eyes are of special importance. For large theater performance, the eyes need to be given clear definition and sometimes enlargement. The amount of eye makeup depends to a great extent on the amount of distance between the performers and the audience and the amount of artificial lighting to be used. The closer the audience, the less makeup is needed. Makeup should create an illusion but should never call attention to itself.

Some dancers prefer to begin with eye makeup by covering the lid and area beneath the eyebrow with a thin coat of clown white to which eye shadow is then applied. The color of eye shadow will depend to a large degree upon the dancer's hair and eye coloring. Each individual should experiment to discover the color that is most effective. It is important to examine the eyes carefully to see what improvements can be made through illusion. When the eyes are large and widely spaced, eye shadow can be applied over the entire eyelid and continued out horizontally slightly beyond the outer corners of the eye. If the eyes are close together, very little if any shadow should be used on the inside portion of the eyelid but should be begun about the middle of the eyelid and extend horizontally well beyond the outer corners of the eyes. If eyes are deep set, leaving the lids uncolored and concentrating the color at the crease above the eye, blending it upward and outward, will bring the eyes forward. When false eyelashes are used, some people prefer to add false eyelashes next; others add the eyeliner and then the lashes.

Large, widely spaced eyes can simply be outlined as they are, but eyes that are too small or too close together need special treatment. To enlarge the eye one can draw the outline of the eye slightly above the edge of the upper eyelid and below the edge of the lower lid, whitening the space between this line and the edge of the lid. For all eyes, it is flattering to leave the upper and lower lines open at the outside corners of the eyes (rather than bringing them together), extending them slightly and placing a line of clown white between them. If the eyes are close together, the outline of the lower lid should not be drawn from the inside corner of the eye, but only from the middle of the eye outward.

Eyebrows, neatly shaped, may need to be further delineated with eyebrow pencil, using light, feathery strokes along the upper edges. Eyelashes can be treated with mascara, for intimate theater spaces, or with false eyelashes. Most people use false eyelashes on the upper lids only, but some may wish to apply them to the lower lids as well. For small eyes, the lashes can be placed slightly outside the natural lash line as is done with eyeliner. In all instances, the lashes should be shaped to flatter the eye and look as natural as possible from a distance. Eye makeup for men is less complicated than for women, consisting mostly of outlining the eye with eyeliner.

The mouth is the final consideration. A warm, rich color that blends with the rest of the makeup is advisable. Too light a color will fade under lights. Most men prefer to use a brownish lipstick. Thin lips need to be filled out slightly and all lips attractively shaped. Full lips can be effectively treated by using a slightly darker lipstick around the outer edges than that used to paint the rest of the lips. The lips should be neatly outlined with a lipstick brush, or if preferred, very lightly outlined with an eyebrow pencil.

When the makeup is completed, the performer may wish to powder it lightly to keep the makeup from smudging and rubbing off on costumes, though some people prefer to keep the glossy look. Powder, which should be at least as dark as the foundation cream, is best applied with a brush, stroking gently in all directions, using as little powder as possible.

Makeup is very much an individual matter. No rules apply to everyone. The only true test for each performer is to examine, critically, the result of his efforts, standing at some distance from the mirror to see that the final effect is to his liking. Experimentation is the only real means of arriving at a successful formula.

Conclusion

The type of dance program being presented and the kind of environment in which dancers are to appear will determine to a large extent the degree of simplicity or elaborateness of costuming, hair styling, and makeup that is appropriate to the occasion. In all instances it is important to remember that movement, not costuming, is the essence of dance. Costuming does not have to be elaborate or expensive. Amazingly effective costuming can be achieved with the aid of a little creative imagination, good taste, and ingenuity.

Chapter 12

Constructing the Costumes

Most dancers who are not experts in the art of dressmaking are terrified at the thought of constructing their own costumes. After one has learned some of the secrets, however, costume-making is not actually as difficult as it is time-consuming. While the costumemaker can take some short-cuts, there is really no quick way to make costumes. For this reason it is important to start costume construction at the earliest possible moment so that the dancers can become accustomed to wearing the costumes and the designer can make changes where necessary before the actual performance.

Modifying the Basic Leotard and Tights

Probably the easiest way to change the appearance of leotards and tights is to dye them. Fortunately, the stretch materials from which most of these articles are made are highly receptive to home dyes. This extreme receptivity, however, can also create problems. An article dipped in a strong dyebath will absorb the full strength of the color almost immediately and nothing short of the use of color remover will make it light again. For this reason it is prudent to start with a dye bath of no greater intensity than one wishes to obtain by repeated dippings. By immersing a sample of the material or a small portion of the garment where it will not show, one can test the effect of the dye before dipping the total article. Dye-absorbent materials are also likely to streak unless they are kept totally immersed and constantly moving in the dye bath. Further instructions for successful dyeing of materials will be discussed later in the chapter.

Decorative designs of various sorts can be applied to leotards or tights by the processes of painting or appliqueing. In either case the garment will need to be stretched as it would be on the human body while the design is being applied. Since either process is usually quite time-consuming, the acquisition of a discarded mannequin from a local department store to be used as a body substitute can be of great assistance.

It is sometimes a problem to find the kind of textile paints that will provide the desired results for a given situation. One must first decide if one wishes to make the design indelible, to stand up under several washings or drycleanings, or if a design that can later be removed from the garments after the production is over is preferable. Prang textile paints will hold up under numerous washings and drycleanings. Flow-Master inks, also permanent, can be applied with a paint brush to stretched fabric surfaces. This procedure creates an indistinct outline which can be sharpened, if desired, by the use of a Flow-Master felt-tipped pen around the edges.

Some felt-tipped pens are waterproof; others are not. Temporary effects can be achieved by using Whitman's Flow-tip watercolor felt pens that can be purchased in at least eight different colors. These inks will wash out of leotards without leaving any permanent aftereffects. Pens made under other trade names would probably work in similar fashions but each type should be carefully tested for the particular desired results. Needless to say, since inks are similar to dyes, it is possible to create dark designs on light backgrounds, but not vice versa. The same rules that govern the application of one color over another in dyeing (to be discussed later on page 196) apply also to the use of inks.

Small designs can be created by using stencils and household enamel spray paints, which are permanent, washable, and come in a variety of high intensity colors. Since the enamel dye readily penetrates the fabric, care must be taken when applying the paint to protect the dancer's skin and underclothes with plastic sheeting or something similar if a mannequin is not available. Enamel paints, while excellent for making small designs, are not satisfactory for large ones since they stiffen the fabric. Analine dyes and tempera paints are two other possible substances that can be used for creating designs, but analine dyes will wash out and tempera tends to flake off the costume when the wearer begins to move.

As indicated previously, if designs of any size are to be appliqued upon the leotard or tights, the material used for the applique must have the same stretch quality as the leotard fabric itself and must be sewn onto the garment when it is stretched to the shape of the wearer; otherwise the applique will be quickly ripped loose by the dancer's movements. The smaller the applique, the less stretchability required. If the fabric frays easily, the edges of the applique will need to be turned under. Tightly woven materials can be pinked. In any case the applique should be basted in place on the model, then machine-sewn with a loose zigzag stitch, rather than a straight stitch, to prevent the thread from breaking when the garment is stretched again. Non-stretch trims that have been glued onto a leotard are apt to loosen and fall off because of the elasticity of the base fabric. Braid and tape can be used to decorate a leotard or tights, but they must be wide enough to be seen by the audience, and again, fastened in place using the same techniques as have been described for attaching other appliques.

In some instances, when one wishes to divide parts of a leotard and tights into several colors, leotards of different hues can be cut apart in exactly the same way and the pieces exchanged. Leotards so treated may, in some cases, need to be one size larger than normally worn to provide the extra material that will be required for the seams. The seams will need to be sewn with a light zigzag stitch. If a zigzag machine is unavailable, the material must be fully stretched during the process of straight sewing, or the seams sewn with elastic thread. All seams should be double-stitched.

Another way to change the appearance of a leotard is to alter the neckline or backline in some fashion or to cut out certain areas in the body of the leotard or, for that matter, the tights. Because of the nature of the stretch material, the shape of the opening may tend to become distorted when the leotard is cut. Cut-outs should be drawn with chalk while the dancer is wearing the garment to make sure the spacing and size are appropriate. These openings can be secured by filling in the cut-out areas with pieces of flesh-colored net that cannot be seen from the audience. Most stretch fabrics also have a tendency to run when edges are left raw. To prevent running, the edge of the stretch material can be seared with a match flame which melts the fiber, or, if desired, the edges can be turned under with a small, but loose, running stitch, or zigzagged.

If a figure pattern for leotards is appropriate, there are generally available numerous unbonded print jerseys from which leotards can be made. Such jerseys, however, lack the degree of stretch found in most commercial leotard fabrics, so that more material will be needed than is used in a regular leotard. Two-way stretch swim suit material is another excellent resource that should not be overlooked. It is desirable to cut the leotard slightly too large and then fit it to the dancer's body, making sure that the dancer can get in and out of the leotard once it has been fitted.

A leotard provides an ideal bodice for costumes that need to be smooth-fitting and flattering to the torso. Overskirts can be worn, or skirts can be sewn directly onto the leotard. Collars, cuffs, or belts can be added; belled or circular sleeves can be added to the elbow or the leotard sleeves can be removed and other sleeves substituted. The straps of a sleeveless leotard can be removed and flesh-colored elastic substituted to create a strapless effect. One of the simplest and most flattering lyrical costumes combines this so-called strapless bodice with a two-layered double-circle skirt of silk chiffon (four circles in all) attached to the leotard slightly below the natural waistline at the top of the pelvic bones. A touch of braid or sequins added to the leotard completes the costume.

Pattern Making, Cutting, Fitting, and Sewing

In preparing a pattern for any dance costume one must know the movement needs of the dance for which the costume has been designed. Most commercial costume patterns are designed more for Halloween parties and masquerades than to meet a choreographer's needs. However, the acquisition of a few ordinary commercial patterns for women's bodices, sleeves, men's trousers, and so forth, that have been tested for their good-fitting qualities can save the costumer hours of time. Because paper patterns are fragile, it is usually wise to reproduce in muslin or lightweight pellon those standard pattern pieces that will be used over and over again; they should be as carefully marked as the original pattern pieces, including an indication of the pattern size.

Patterns can be adjusted to accommodate different sizes by making slight additions or subtractions along every seam as well as vertically in the center front and back. Some dressmakers prefer to make the addition or subtraction vertically about two inches in from the side seams. The pattern should be fitted to the dancer before cutting the costume material. It is inadvisable to change a pattern more than an inch in measurement to adapt it to a dancer's body; however, the measurements of most dancers within a group will not vary more than one or two sizes. In situations where the same dancers are going to be fitted for costumes repeatedly, a bodice pattern for each dancer can be made out of good muslin and kept on file. Costumes that are likely to be worn by a number of different dancers should be made with hems that can be adjusted and seams that can be refitted if necessary.

Side seams can be made five-eighths of an inch to an inch wide, with the realization, of course, that large seams add bulk to the figure. However, in order to prevent pulling, firmly woven fabrics may need to be clipped, particularly over the bustline, if seams are wide, in which case the capability for future refitting to larger figures is diminished. Deep hems are impossible to make on circular skirts without spoiling the hang of the costumes.

The costume designer should not be timid about devising costume patterns of his own. Fortunately, newspaper is plentiful and cheap so that one can cut, shape, recut, patch, and reshape to one's heart's content until finally achieving the effect desired. Because of the stiffness of newspaper it is generally advisable to transfer the resulting pattern to a piece of muslin that can be draped on the body as the costume material is intended to do, so that minor adjustments can be made in the pattern before cutting the final costumes. Experience will eventually teach the costumer how to attain the results envisioned without much trial and error. But if all else fails, one can engage a creative dressmaker to devise a pattern from the designer's sketch and the costumer can carry on from there.

Most dance skirts can be made without commercial patterns. The appearance of the skirt will differ greatly according to the way it is cut. A straight skirt is made on the straight of the material with darts taken at the waistline and little, if any, flair on the sides. Such skirts are usually left open along one or both seams to allow room for the dance movement. Straight skirts can also be made of narrow, overlapping, but free-hanging strips or panels of material that separate when the dancer moves, revealing the legs in motion. Gathered "folk" skirts are usually more flattering to the body if the pieces to be gathered are also slightly gored to avoid too much thickness at the waist.

There are two principal types of flared skirts: the circular skirt and the gored skirt. A circular skirt is easier to make than a gored skirt. The desired amount of fullness will determine how it is made. If only a slight flair is needed, a half circle may be sufficient for the entire skirt. If the skirt should hang fairly straight in the front, but still needs to present an effect of fullness, one can make a skirt by using a quarter circle in the front and a half circle in back. Again, depending upon the amount of fullness required, a generous circular skirt can be made of one complete circle, one and a half circles (a half circle in front and a full circle in back), or two complete circles. The greater the number of half-circle pieces that are used to make a skirt the smaller the half-circle should be that is cut out at the top of each piece to fit around the waist. For a single complete circle skirt a radius equal to $1/6$ of the waist measure will produce a waist circle of the correct size. When in doubt, it is wiser to cut the half-circle too small than to find it has been cut too large so that the skirt will need to be gathered onto the bodice. Circular skirts are attractive to look at and move very well, but they do have a tendency to hang unevenly after the costume has been finished. The looser the weave of the material the longer the costume will need to be left hanging before hem-

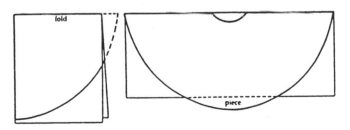

Diagram 11. *Circular Skirt*

ming (if hemming is needed) and the more frequently the hemline will need to be restraightened.

Gored skirts, though more complicated to make, have less tendency to sag than circular skirts. If one is chiefly concerned with saving material and the skirts are short enough so that the gores can be cut crossways on the material, one can place the gores so that they alternate with each other—that is, the wide end of one gore is placed on one selvage, and the wide end of the next gore is placed on the opposite selvage. By such means very little material is wasted. This procedure could be disastrous, however, if the material had a nap. In such cases all of the pieces of a costume pattern would have to be laid in the same direction relative to the nap or the pieces would show color differences under lights.

Unfortunately the most economical way of laying out a gored skirt pattern is not the most effective if one wants the bottom of the skirt to flow gracefully away from the body rather than to hang straight down when the dancer is in repose. If each gore is cut so that the true bias of the material is directly in the center of the gore (Diagram 13) then this center part will flair outward in contrast to the seams which always hang straight down. The improvement in the skirt line may be worth the added expenditure for material. High-waisted skirts, especially, should be cut in gores on the bias so that the costume can be slenderized at the waistline and then swing out.

When an expensive fabric lacks sufficient body to give a skirt the desired effect of fullness, the difficulty can often be remedied by making a full underskirt of nylon net, which is relatively inexpensive. The flair of a skirt can also be increased by sewing horse-hair braid around the bottom. One pleasing skirt variation can be achieved by overlaying a skirt of filmy material upon a basic skirt of heavy fabric.

The length of the skirt will depend upon the movement and the style of the choreography. Skirt lengths for a set of costumes should be

Diagram 12. *Gored Skirt Laid Crosswise on Material*

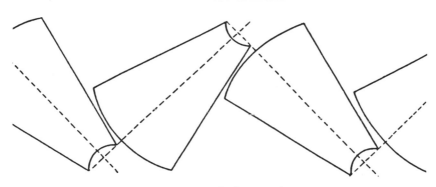

Diagram 13. *Gored Skirt Laid on Bias*

cut approximately the same distance from the floor, but short-legged dancers may need to have their skirts cut just slightly longer than long-legged dancers.

Although a low-cut neckline may at first appear to create a dilemma in terms of keeping the costume in place, the problem is not unsolvable. The narrow V-line down the center of a bodice, which is often very flattering, can be held together with flesh-colored net. A square-necked, low-cut bodice that appears to leave the top of the sleeve completely unsupported on the shoulders may again be achieved by filling in the entire neck front and back with flesh-colored net to which the sleeve tops can be attached.

Long tight sleeves attached to a bodice must always be given special consideration to permit the dancer to move her arms freely. Most regular dress bodice patterns, cut on the straight of the material, to which long sleeves are to be attached, will require the insertion of gussets of diamond-shaped pieces into the underarm (Diagram 14A) seam or along the seam of the bodice and sleeve (Diagram 14B). These gussets are not easy to insert smoothly, but are essential to the dancer's freedom of movement. Although it seems incongruous, the higher the armhole is cut the less need there is for a gusset. Small sideseam gussets, or underarm panels beginning at the waist and extending to the armhole, cut from stretch fabric and dyed to match the costume, work nicely to provide elasticity in armhole and bodice. Some designers avoid the problem altogether by attaching the sleeves to the bodice only at the top, cutting them out at the bottom seam to create an interesting design (Diagram 14C). Puffed sleeves can be completely detached from the bodice, gathered onto the arm by elastic at the top and bottom. Various other shaped sleeve "suggestions" can also be attached to the arms rather than to the costume itself. Bodices with raglan sleeves usually create no movement problems. With fabrics that stretch or drape softly, bodices cut on the true bias with bat-winged sleeves have sufficient give to permit the dancer to move with complete freedom (Diagram 14D).

Men, in particular, need to have freedom of movement for their arms. When making men's tight-fitting jackets or jerkins with long, tight-fitting sleeves, the sleeves need to be completely free of the jacket.

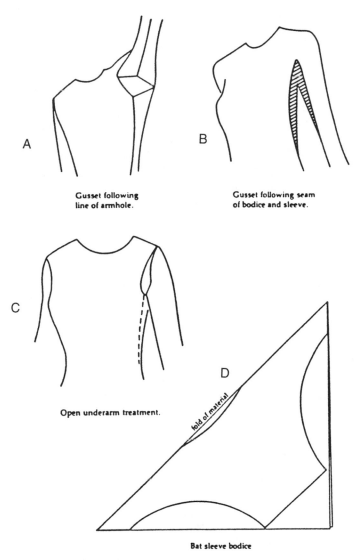

A

Gusset following
line of armhole.

B

Gusset following seam
of bodice and sleeve.

C

Open underarm treatment.

D

fold of material

Bat sleeve bodice

Diagram 14. *Sleeve Treatments*

The jacket can be made sleeveless (Diagram 15A) and the sleeves attached to a short-sleeved T-shirt. A 3- or 4-inch band of the sleeve and jacket fabric should be sewn around the armhole of the T-shirt when the sleeve is attached to keep the T-shirt material from showing when the arms are raised (Diagram 15B). Such an arrangement not only frees the arms for movement, but also permits the jacket or jerkin to remain smoothly on the body at all times. This same device could be applied to some women's costumes. When regular men's shirts are used as costume tops they will look neater if they are fitted down the sides and held in place with elastic, extending under the crotch and attached to the shirt tails.

Men's trousers need to be cut and fitted high in the crotch to permit leg movement. Inner seams should be sewn first and the outer seams fitted to the bodies of the dancers. Seams should be double-stitched with a zigzag stitch and bound with sturdy binding for added safety. Surplus ski pants or navy pants can be successfully refitted for use as dance costumes. White cotton surplus navy pants are relatively inexpensive and can be dyed to almost any color. Bonded jersey is an excellent fabric for making men's pants. Whatever material is used, it should be heavy to prevent the knees from bagging.

Most dance costumes are not lined, but when they are, to ensure proper fit, the lining material needs to be of the same type of material as the outside in terms of its stretchability and hanging quality. Lining helps to control the shape, strength, and fit of a costume; those that are to be used over and over again especially may need to be lined.

Any washable material, unless it has already been preshrunk, must be washed before cutting. In laying out a pattern on the costume material, the presence or absence of nap is of vital importance. Two-tone materials and materials with nap tend to flatten out more when viewed

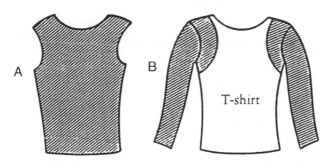

Diagram 15. *Men's Jerkin*

from one direction than from another. It is important to examine the material carefully to discover the direction that will give the greatest richness of texture and color to the fabric. If the costume is to appear all one color then all of the pieces of the pattern must be laid out in the same direction. Materials without nap present no problem and pattern pieces can sometimes be cut crosswise on the fabric to economize on material. Crosscut pieces will hang slightly more stiffly than those cut lengthwise. With careful planning much yardage can be saved when several costumes are to be cut from the same fabric. In order to be flattering to the body, costumes should be fitted neither too tightly nor too loosely. Dress, skirt, and even pants openings are less conspicuous and costumes are smoother fitting and easier to get into when zippers are placed in the back of the garment instead of in front or at the sides. Hidden zippers, made so that no metal is permitted to show, can be used when possible. Such zippers, however, are more fragile than regular zippers and a special sewing machine zipper foot is needed to insert them. A simple way to put in a zipper is to machine baste the seam shut to zipper length. Sew the zipper in on the underside and then unpick the basting.

Some skirts hang best without hemming. Jerseys especially, need no hemming. Chiffon may appear more diaphanous if left unhemmed, although its tendency to ravel may necessitate frequent trimming. The use of pinking shears can help to minimize this problem. When hemming is required, tape should be sewn with a zigzag stitch to the bottom of the material, which is then hemmed by hand; sheer fabrics, such as chiffon, can be hemmed by overcasting with a wide, tight zigzag stitch in matching thread. Many machines today also have a blind hemstitch. In sewing, one should endeavor not to stretch the hem.

Where portions of a costume need to be stiffened, the fabric can be reinforced with press-on pellon, press-on canvas, or other products such as "Stitch-Witchery" before the segment of the costume is cut. These products, however, tend to come loose with washing or drycleaning.

If an effect of massive embroidery is needed for folk or ethnic costumes, one can create the illusion by selecting printed fabrics out of which designs or borders can be cut for appliqueing onto the costumes. Old costume jewelry can also serve to add sparkle and decorativeness to a costume where such an effect is appropriate.

Costume Dyeing

Often, to use inexpensive materials for costumes, such as unbleached muslin, or to obtain the right color combinations in the costumes, it is necessary to dye them. Whenever possible, one should dye the materials before cutting and making the costumes in case of fabric shrinkage. Some fabrics, such as acrylics and polyesters, are extremely dye-resistant, so it is always wise to test-dye a sample of the material before proceeding too far.

It seems unnecessary to state that dark colors cannot be changed into light ones or colors changed into their color complements. The following chart indicates the general effect that certain colored dyes will have upon colored fabrics. The exact result depends upon the intensity and purity of the fabric color relative to the intensity of the dye.

If it is impossible to dye over an old color to achieve a desired effect it may be possible to remove the original color and begin again. One must remember, however, that it is sometimes virtually impossible to remove the color from some commercially dyed fabrics. While liquid dyes are easier to work with than powdered dyes they are hard to find in many colors. No home-dyed fabrics will be as brilliant as those commercially dyed. One can obtain reasonably intense reds, yellows, and oranges, but brilliant purples and royal blues are much more difficult to achieve. A satisfactory royal blue may be obtained by combining cobalt blue dye with a bit of royal blue. For some reason, purple dye is also difficult to dissolve and needs to be strained through a cloth to eliminate undissolved particles. A pleasing violet color of moderate intensity can be obtained by using numerous packages of orchid dye, rather than the powdered purple dye which produces a rather dull, grayed color. All

			Dye			
Fabric Color	**red**	**orange**	**yellow**	**green**	**blue**	**violet**
red		orange-red	orange-red	gray to brown	violet	red-violet
orange	red-orange		yellow-orange	brown	gray to brown	brown
yellow	orange	yellow-orange		yellow-green	green	gray to brown
green	gray to brown	brown	yellow green		blue-green	brown
blue	violet	gray to brown	green	blue-green		blue-violet
violet	red-violet	brown	brown	brown	blue-violet	

Diagram 16. *The Effect of Dyes on Fabrics*

pastel tints can be achieved rather easily. No matter how simple the dye process may appear to be it is always wise to test-dye a sample of material before dyeing the costume. Although one usually aims to obtain an even dye effect where clothing is concerned, it is consoling to the novice to know that fabric unevenly dyed looks richer under stage lights than evenly dyed material. It is also well to remember that color intensities and contrasts of light and dark tend to fade under theater lights so that in dyeing costume fabrics one should aim for colors slightly stronger than one expects to see from the audience.

Tie-dyeing is another process that can add decorative interest to a costume. By pleating or gathering portions of the costume and tying them tightly with heavy cord or string, then dipping the garment in the dye bath, decorative patterns can be made; the dye is unable to reach those portions of material held by the cord. Practice on scrap materials may be needed to determine exactly how to achieve a desired effect. Dye companies have free pamphlets with suggestions of tie-dyeing techniques that may be helpful to the uninitiated.

When one is dyeing large quantities of material and no special problems are involved, such as that of matching a particular color or obtaining an exact intensity, an automatic washer can be used to achieve an efficient and even dye job. But when one is dyeing in small quantities or when one needs to control the exact hue or intensity of a color, the dyeing must be done by hand.

To obtain an even dye result, the material must be thoroughly soaked in hot water and washed free of any soil or fabric sizing. If powdered dye is used, it must be completely dissolved in hot water, preferably in a vessel other than the one to be used for dyeing the fabric. Special care needs to be taken to see that there are no undissolved granules in the bottom of the pan or around the edges of the vessel. If necessary, the dye can be strained through a piece of nylon hose. The dye can then be diluted with water to the desired degree. The hotter the water the more readily the fabric will absorb the dye.

If possible, all of the material, loosely crumpled, should be immersed in the water at the same time in order for it to be subjected to the same concentration of dye. Once the material is placed in the dye bath it must be stirred constantly. A long wooden spoon and a pair of rubber gloves will enable the operator to perform these tasks easily without dyeing or scalding his hands in the process. When fabrics are slow to absorb the dye, their resistance sometimes can be reduced by heating the water on the stove. In so doing, however, it is especially important to keep the fabric in motion since the material nearest the heat will be most receptive to the dye.

When one is attempting to match the color of some fabric, a sample of that fabric should be wet and used as a color guide, since cloth, when wet, is much darker than when it is dry. Or, a small swatch of the material being dyed can be dipped in the dye and then pressed dry to compare with the original color.

When colors are to be mixed, a process of top dyeing one color over another can give the cloth an enriched appearance under lights; this is done by dipping the fabric in another dye bath after it has been dyed once. The material can still be wet, or dry. An especially rich, textured effect can be achieved by twisting or crumpling the material when putting it in the second dye bath to give it a mottled appearance. A similar result can be obtained by unevenly spray-dyeing or spatter-painting one color over another. Scene paint mixed with water and dissolved ground glue is particularly effective since it will stay on the surface of the cloth. A sponge can be useful in applying the surface coat unevenly to add depth to the textural appearance. One way of obtaining a rich brocade effect is to spray gold paint, through open lace, onto the costume material. The lace, now gold, can be saved and used later when needed for a costume.

Once the material has been dyed to the desired hue and intensity it should be removed from the dye bath and thoroughly rinsed in warm water until no further dye bleeds out. When a fabric is wrung out forcibly, the excess dye tends to accumulate in the creases. For a smooth dye job, the excess moisture should be squeezed gently out of the fabric without wringing.

When dyeing muslin, if the material is carefully straightened and stretched when it is hung up to dry, the costume can be cut and made from the unpressed material. The final effect of this slightly crinkly surface under lights will be one of enriched texture.

Costumes that require one color to blend into another should always be dipped in the lighter color first. The portions of the costume that are to receive the other color are then dipped into a second dye bath while the fabric is still wet so that there will be no sharp line of demarcation. The same rules for dyeing one color over another apply to this situation. Costumes dyed in such a fashion cannot be rinsed or washed and must be hung up to dry carefully so that the darker color does not continue to run or bleed onto the lighter one.

Spray-dyes can be used for materials that cannot be immersed in water. "Fab-spray" or florist spray paints are commercial products that work well for this purpose. To soften or change the tone of a fabric one can dust the surface with a spray lacquer such as Krylon that will not make the fabric too stiff.

Making Masks and Headdresses

Some dances require the use of masks and headdresses. When masks are used, the most important thing to remember is that the dancer must be able to see and to breathe. Half-masks, such as those used for masquerade parties, create no problems and can be bought commercially. Most costume houses also carry full-face translucent plastic masks with regular features that give to the face the impersonal look of a mannequin. These plastic masks can also be used as a base upon which to build grotesque or specialized effects with the aid of paper maché, consisting of strips of newspaper coated with flour paste or small pieces of lightweight sticky tape, or strips of muslin dipped in glue, applied in layers to the foundation. Each layer must be thoroughly dried before the next is applied. The drying process can be speeded by placing the object in an oven on low heat. It must be remembered, however, that plastic tends to melt even at moderately hot temperatures. Paper maché can also be applied over modeled clay forms. Prepared paper maché is obtainable in pulp form with glue in it, forming a clay-like substance that can be used for filling out the shape of the mask. A flour paste with paint in it can be used to make the final coat, or a coat of plastic wood can be applied, sanded, and painted.

Some masks, such as animal masks and grotesque faces of numerous sorts, can also be bought commercially, but some of these may obstruct the dancer's vision. When one wishes to blot out the features of the face entirely, a hood can be made of fabric and the face part covered with chiffon or netting which provides a transparent "window" for the dancer, while concealing his face from the audience.

The important thing to remember in making headdresses is that they must fit the head and be sufficiently anchored so that the dancer is not afraid to move. Variously shaped buckram hat forms can be purchased from costume houses; these may or may not provide sufficiently strong and well-fitting bases upon which to structure headdresses, depending, to a degree, upon the height and weight of the headdresses to be fashioned. A very small, lightweight headdress may sometimes be secured with just a headband or combs.

When suitable ready-made forms are unavailable, a basic head form can be made of Celastic, a commercial, plastic-coated, leathery fabric that is cut into strips or shaped and dipped in acetone or a similar solvent, and applied over a clay model of the head. The ensuing Celastic form is then lined with sponge rubber. One can buy from hat or wig supply houses solid wooden head forms that can be used in place of clay head models. Styrofoam head forms are not as satisfactory as wooden ones. The Celastic form, when finished, provides a sturdy base upon which to build most any headdress.

If the Celastic head forms are to fit securely when they are completed, individual head measurements of each headdress wearer must be taken so that the clay head model can be made to the correct size or so that the appropriate size wooden head model can be selected. It is important to spend time to fit the head form carefully. Measurements are taken completely around the head from above the middle of the forehead to the base of the skull and also over the top of the head from ear to ear.

The Celastic or buckram head form can be extended and decorated in innumerable ways depending upon the costumer's personal ingenuity. Many different kinds of wire can be used to form variously shaped frames for further decoration. Piano wire is especially good. Heavy aluminum wire is also useful. Willow reed is lightweight and can be used for the same purposes. Chicken wire can be bent into various forms and covered with paper maché. Headdress shapes can also be made of styrofoam. Spray styrofoam can be made in any shape desired. Special paints are available to color the styrofoam; regular paints will not work for this purpose.

It is possible to create headdress decorations from all sorts of material: crepe paper, netting, nylon chiffon, feathers, or products to be found at costume and novelty houses, milliner supplies, magician's supplies, or window display houses. Large feathers that are sometimes too expensive to purchase can be simulated by wiring and fraying rayon cut in the shape of the feather. A little imagination will reveal many possibilities for creating illusions with very little cost.

Foot Gear

Many modern dances do not call for any special costume treatment for the feet. Bare feet or simple soft-soled ballet slippers may suffice. But there are occasions when ballet slippers are not the answer, yet the costume is not complete without some sort of foot dressing. If many pivot turns are required of dancers, they may need some covering for the balls of the feet to enable them to turn easily. The sandasol, or half-sandal, created by Capezio, provides a sole covering while leaving the heel and toes free to grip the floor. An illusion of a sandal with lacings up the leg can be created by crisscrossing wide, black elastic around the leg and anchoring it under the instep. For folk costumes a high sock or stockings may be worn underneath the lacings. Socks without shoes are slippery on some floors and must be tested for safety before the performance. An effect of a medieval shoe can also be achieved by using long, heavy socks, rolled down at the top and purchased too long so that the ends of the feet can be sewn into upturned, pointed toes, stuffed to maintain their shapes.

Where an effect of a low sandal is desired, yet the dancer needs the freedom and security of bare feet, bands of wide, black elastic encircling the ankle, the instep, and the ball of the foot, and fastened together with an elastic T-strap, can be made to simulate the straps of the sandal. Inexpensive boots can be made out of oil cloth to be worn over ballet slippers. A dart is sewn horizontally across the front of the boot where the ankle bends and the boot is secured under the ball of the foot with elastic.

Costume Organization and Final Check

And, now, assuming the costumes have been finished, the name of the wearer should be fastened inside each costume in a place that is easy to find, such as the back of the neck or a shoulder seam. Adhesive tape can be used in place of name tape in instances where the tape can be attached to the lining or an inner seam. It is important to caution each dancer to double -heck to see that all costume parts are together before each performance. A card for each dancer listing all of his costumes and accessories can be of great assistance.

As soon as the costumes are completed the dancers should try moving in them and the costumer should check to see that they are completely satisfactory, both in movement and under stage lights. Even expert costume designers are not infallible; some last-minute modifications will almost always need to be made. It is psychologically important for the dancer to feel right in the costumes to give the best possible performance. Skirts may have to be shortened or lengthened, waistlines raised or lowered, seams further reinforced, bodices refitted, trimmings altered, or colors redyed. The right costumes will add much to the beauty of a dance, but in the long run it is often the simplest costumes, well-made and fitted, that are the most effective.

Working with a Costumer

Some departments are lucky enough to have a specialist in costuming to design and construct their costumes. If the relationship between choreographer and costumer is to be a happy and productive one, there are several considerations to be borne in mind. Communication and mutual respect are the key. The following suggestions to the choreographer are useful in establishing a good working relationship:

1. Remember the costumer is an artist, too. Respect this person's desire to create and have pride in his work. If changes must be made in a design you have previously approved, don't blame the costumer. Calmly explain what the problem is and ask for suggestions on solving the difficulty. Don't rule out changing something besides the costume.

2. When preparing for a theatrical production, a costumer can read the script, study the author's notes, look at pictures of past productions, and research the period. In dance, often the only source of information is the choreographer. If you aren't clear, concise, and detailed in expressing your concept you cannot expect the costumer to reproduce the vision of the dance as you see it in your mind. This means doing your homework. If possible, show the costumer a sketch or picture that resembles what you want. Clarify the number of dancers, the kind of movement, quality of movement, moods, colors— every detail you can before talking to the costumer.

3. Invite the costumer to rehearsals often and early. However, you must respect his valuable time. Make sure the rehearsal involves those activities the costumer needs to see. Don't stop to work on movement details that don't involve the costumer, but do emphasize movement aspects in which the costume is especially important.

4. Send the dancers for fittings promptly and make sure the dancers come to their appointments on time, properly dressed, and with plenty of time to do what is needed.

5. Keep communications open. Be sure the costumer is aware of changes in choreography or dancers. Look at costumes in progress, not in an attempt to put pressure upon the costumer, but to show your interest and to endeavor to head off problems.

6. Establish a realistic but firm time schedule with the costumer. If meetings, deadlines, or rehearsals must be changed, notify the costumer as soon as you know about the change.

7. Have a dress rehearsal as soon as possible. If the costumes are very complex, don't plan on accomplishing much else in that rehearsal. Let the costumer use the time to work out problems concerning how to wear intricate pieces, manage quick changes, stabilize head pieces, and so forth. Stop rehearsal, if necessary; it can save time, confusion, and frazzled nerves in the long run.

8. If you are resetting a previously choreographed work, don't rule out the possibility of a new costume design. There is usually more than one way to design a piece and just possibly this new insight is what the piece needs. If you feel that only a repeat of the original costumes will do, try to get one of these costumes for the costumer to work from. If this isn't possible, or even if it is, still photographs showing the costume full length from every angle are very helpful. Anytime your mind is made up, don't pretend you want a creative design from the costumer. Tell him exactly what you have in mind. Remember that reproducing costumes is the most boring and unrewarding work the costumer has to do this side of laundry. No artist enjoys being a Xerox machine.

9. Don't demand the impossible of the costumer such as asking that new costumes be made after the last dress rehearsal. Some mistakes must be lived with and learned from.

10. When the production is presented, be sure to express your appreciation, both verbally and in program notes, to the costumer. If the costumes have been well-done, no one will applaud the costumes, only the dancers and choreography they have enhanced. The costumer's only positive feedback may be your thank you.

Chapter 13

Lighting the Dance

When a dance is transferred from a laboratory into the theater where it is to be viewed by an audience, the matter of proper lighting must also be considered. Light is an essential element of dance. Since dance is a visual experience, as well as a kinesthetic one, the first duty of the lighting designer is obvious: to make the dance visible. Appropriate lighting can define a dancer's space, suggest mood, create shadows, enliven colors, focus attention upon a special dancer or important movement, or can itself become a focal point in the dance.

Lighting can create a truly magical atmosphere. However, in the hands of an inexperienced or overenthusiastic designer, lighting that is too dark, too spectacular, or too busy with constant changes can become intrusive and fail in its support of the dance. For that reason it is important for the choreographer and lighting designer to plan the lighting effects together and to allow time enough to experiment and evaluate critically the results of their decisions. In order for a choreographer to plan the lighting for a dance or to communicate effectively with a lighting designer, it is necessary to understand something about stage lighting equipment.

Stage Lighting Instruments

Ellipsoidal Reflector Spotlight

Ellipsoidal reflector spotlights, often referred to as "lekos" or "Klieglites," are undoubtedly the most versatile and widely used type of lighting instruments. They produce a bright, sharply defined beam, with a smooth, flat field. The beam can be patterned by use of metal plates in which designs known as gobos have been cut. These instruments are classified according to lens size; two numbers are given, as in 6×9 (six-by-nine). The first number specifies the lens diameter in inches, the second number the lens focal length. Common lens sizes are 3 1/2, 6, 8, and 10 inches. As the size increases so does the wattage of the lamp employed. As the focal length increases, the angle of spread of the lamp beam decreases. Thus a 6×12 instrument throws a more narrow beam of light than does a 6×9.

In dance lighting, 6×9 lekos are commonly used for side lighting and may be used overhead to produce special pools. The large lekos are used from "ante-pro" positions (that is, from positions on the house side of the proscenium). They are designed for long-throw applications.

Fresnels

Fresnel instruments take their name from the type of lens they employ (that is, a step-lens). The beam of light produced by a Fresnel differs from the leko beam in important respects: The beam does not have a sharp, focused edge and it normally appears brighter in the center, feathering out toward the edges. This feature makes it possible to blend the beams from a number of Fresnels into a smooth wash of light over the entire stage. Also the size of the beam thrown by the instrument can be quickly changed from "spot" to "flood." Fresnels are thus very useful when hung from overhead onstage battens. They are not useful from ante-pro positions because they spill a good deal more light than do lekos. Also, the beam cannot be shaped effectively. Barn-door shutters fitted into the color frame slot can be used to control spill. (Barn-doors are often necessary on Fresnels used on the upstage lights to diminish spill of light onto the cyclorama.)

Floodlight

The floodlight, or "scoop" as it is commonly called, is perhaps the simplest lighting instrument used onstage. It consists simply of an ellipsoidal reflector, a lamp, a yoke and clamp, and color frame brackets. It has no lens and the position of the lamp is not adjustable. It is used most often in dance lighting to produce an even wash on the cyclorama. Scoops range in size from about 10 up to about 16 inches in diameter and lamp wattage ranges from about 250 up to 2,000 watts.

Striplight

The striplight (or border light or "x-ray") consists of a number of lamps housed in a single long, narrow housing. The lamps are physically separated, each having its own reflector, but the lamps are circuited not individually but in groups of three or four. Lamps ganged together are gelled the same; some striplights use standard color media while others make use of glass for general overhead washes or for washing the cyclorama. In some theaters, striplights are mounted in the footlight positions in the far downstage area or apron.

Illuminating the Dance Movement

The most important principle of dance lighting is that it must be designed so that the entire body will be lit as it travels throughout the entire stage area. Further, the dancer should be lit in such a way that the body appears three-dimensional. Both of these considerations are best achieved by extensive use of side lighting coupled with even, general illumination from overhead instruments. Strong side lighting gives the body fullness and causes the dancer to stand out nicely from the background. The highlights and shadows on the trunk and extremities that result from side lighting produce this three-dimensional effect. Lighting that is strongest from the front or from overhead produces a flat, two-dimensional appearance since shadows and highlights are washed out and "molding" of the figure is lost.

The best instrument to use for side lighting is the ellipsoidal. Ideally, as many as three or four ellipsoidals would be hung on boom stands in each of as many as five wings. They would usually be gelled in a variety of colors to allow latitude in color effects, tone, and mood. These instruments should be mounted low, ranging from those mounted very near the floor ("shinbusters") up to about eight feet in height. When instruments are mounted much higher, much of their "punch" is lost and their effectiveness diminished in producing the desired effect. Smaller instruments such as 3-1/2 inch ellipsoidals ("baby lekos") can also be used effectively as side-lighting instruments and are particularly convenient for touring groups. Large instruments such as 8- or 10-inch ellipsoidals are of little use as side-lighting instruments as their light beam is generally much too narrow for onstage use. When boom stands (or light "trees" or "ladders") are not available in sufficient number for mounting the side instruments, the technical director may need to use ingenuity in obtaining suitable devices for mounting the instruments. At schools, it is often possible to find portable volleyball net poles or tetherball poles; the kind made from a pipe, an old tire, and concrete are quite suitable because the base is so heavy that several instruments can be hung on them without danger of their tipping.

Second in importance to side lighting is the overhead wash. The wash is an even illumination of uniform color covering the entire stage area. It is produced by using four or more Fresnel instruments on each overhead electrical batten. Because these instruments nearly always work together, they may be patched into the same dimmer in groups that do not exceed the capacity of the dimmer. The usual practice is to hang two or more separate washes, one in cool gel (normally blue tint), one using warm color (amber or pink), and a third wash might be in a relatively neutral tone such as lavender—or it could even be left ungelled. By using both cool and warm wash together, a quite natural illumination (that is, neutral or "white"), can be achieved.

Borderlights (or striplights, or "x-rays") are also quite satisfactory for producing washes. They are normally colored using glass roundels saturated in color. Blue, red, green, and amber are the usual colors available in striplights and combinations of these colors can be used to produce a wide array of color effects. Some striplights use gels and may thus be made any color desired.

The front-of-house or beam lights are used mainly to add fill to the dancer' 'faces and to provide adequate lighting in the downstage area. Scoops normally are used to wash the cyclorama and are usually gelled in primary blue, red, and green, or secondaries such as amber. Borderlights also can be used for cyclorama washes.

One must always be careful to see that the stage areas in which important dance action is to take place are well lighted. An audience does not enjoy straining through a veil of darkness to see dance movement. Even for the sake of atmosphere a dimly lighted stage is not justifiable if important action is lost thereby. Atmospheric lighting cannot substitute for the projective power of the dance itself. Choreographers are often to blame for poorly lighted choreography because many of them unwittingly allow the floor plans of their dances to carry them back into dimly lit corners or so far downstage that the border striplights are unable to reach them. The greater the distance that the dance must be projected the stronger the lighting must be. In evaluating the effect of the lighting on a dance it is well to do so from the back of the room or auditorium.

Artificial lighting can create dramatic areas of light and shade which will emphasize important phases of the dance action. The use of well-defined overhead spotlighting or of follow spotlights on significant figures in a dance can help to bring them sharply into focus. A spotlight directed on the dancers from the front of the stage can produce striking shadow effects of their movements, which may be desirable for some dances and distracting in others. By shifting the strength of the lighted areas, one can transform space to impart new dramatic meanings and to suggest new localities without the use of elaborate stage sets.

Use of Colored Lights

The proper use of colored lights can help both to establish the mood of a dance and to heighten the effectiveness of the costuming. Certain hues of light will intensify the colors of a costume, whereas others will make them appear washed out or grayed or muddy. The effect of colored lights on colored materials is a complex subject. Because the texture of the material that is being lighted will also influence the color effect, it is not always possible to predict the exact result colored light will have on a costume. The ultimate decision concerning the choice of lights will need to be determined by experimentation on the actual garments. Nevertheless, there are a few basic principles that can guide the choreographer in choosing appropriate lighting for his dances.

According to the physics of light, red is the complement or the opposite of green, and yellow is the complement of blue. When a colored light is used on a costume of complementary hue, the result makes the costume appear gray, brown, or even black. Hence, if the color of the costume is to be enjoyed in its full intensity, red light should not be used on greens, or yellow light on blues, or vice versa. For the same reason, green and even blue lights are inclined to give the flesh tones of the dancer a ghastly appearance. Under green light, pinks and reds turn to gray and black, causing the cheeks to appear hollow and the mouth cavernous. Strong blue lights transform the skin coloring to an unhealthy gray. Unless such effects are appropriate to the dance, green or blue lights should not be used alone; they may be combined, however, with other lights, such as pink or soft yellow, which can be directed to neutralize this disastrous effect on the complexions of the dancers. It may be necessary to resort to the use of neutral white light. Softened white light may be obtained by using an untinted frosted gelatin over the lights, or by combining red and yellow lights. Of the different tints of colored light, pink or amber are probably the dancers' best equipment; both are warm and vibrant. Pink light is satisfactory for almost all costume hues except those containing green. Yellow light generally produces pleasing results on all costume colors, with the exception of blue-greens, blues, and violets. Occasionally, contrasting lights such as violets and greens can be thrown on the dancers from opposite sides of the stage to produce a two-tone effect and create interesting colored shadows. Many striking results have sometimes been achieved quite by accident through the process of trial and error.

The basic "palette" of color media used for general illumination in dance normally includes light blue overhead wash, side lighting, and front-of-house, and either a light pink or amber from these same positions. A third set of light lavender side lights can also be used to add some additional intensity and sparkle. It is generally best to steer clear of greenish-blues and stay with "steel" or daylight blue.

Collaboration Between Choreographer and Lighting Designer

Especially when working together for the first time, a choreographer and lighting designer need to communicate and carefully define expectations and limits. Otherwise, the choreographer may find that his expectations have exceeded the limits of the available lighting equipment, or conversely, that the choreographer's studied and refined dance is being transformed into a "light show" by an overzealous lighting designer. On the other hand, a lighting designer needs to feel that the choreographer's instructions are not so restrictive that he is denied any sense of creative flexibility and accomplishment.

Initial conversations between the two will probably be quite general; mood, dynamics, setting, point of view, and so on might be laid out by the choreographer, who might also wish to provide the lighting designer with a preliminary light plot (drafted top view of the stage) in which major set pieces (if any) are drawn and special lighting requirements are indicated. The choreographer should reveal any costume plans to the lighting designer as they are formulated, especially colors to be used in the costumes. The designer might respond in terms of a general color and intensity scheme and might discuss the possibility of special lighting areas, projections, or other special effects.

Once the choreographer has had sufficient time to sketch out the piece with the dancers, the designer should be called to a rehearsal to see the general form of the work. As rehearsals progress, the designer should continue to attend. The more familiar the designer can become with the choreography, the more successful his design is likely to be. While observing the dance, lighting cues can also be written. Much time can be saved if the lighting designer knows the sequence of the dance and has already written a cue sheet for light changes in at least a descriptive way.

A single lighting designer can design for an entire performance, but it often happens that a number of designers are employed, especially in programs including choreography by various individuals. Such instances require that all designers and choreographers meet and be in agreement on a general lighting plot. It is obviously not possible in a performance to change much more than a few gels between numbers. Slightly more change than this can take place at intermission, but even this time should be limited to refocusing a few instruments without involving extensive gel changes or rehanging instruments. When lighting equipment is somewhat limited, it is necessary that compromises be made and a single, flexible, general lighting plot be developed. This is not as limiting as it sounds; a good palette of gel colors and general washes can allow a good deal of variety. It is also important in the technical rehearsal to assign specific time allotments according to the complexity of each dance so that all dances are given their fair share of available time on stage.

Successful lighting requires time, patience, thoughtful planning, and imagination. It cannot make a good dance, but it can do much to support the choreographic mood and bring the movement into proper focus.

In Conclusion

For teaching dance composition or for planning and supervising dance productions, as for all education, there is no single indisputable method. In order to decide the proper direction to take, the teacher must first evaluate the technical and creative abilities his pupils possess, as well as their apparent limitations. Using this information as a guide, the dance educator can select compositional experiences that will strengthen those areas in which the students are weak and that will broaden their total understanding of the use of movement as an expressive art medium.

It is certainly important to make the student of dance objectively aware of form—of such movement elements as spatial design, rhythmic pattern, and thematic organization. But if the teaching approach to composition is channeled in this direction exclusively, the student may lose sight of the fact that, in the final analysis, artistic form cannot be considered apart from its causative motivation. It is equally important for the student to experience compositional assignments that demand a direct movement response to emotional or ideational stimuli; but without the simultaneous development of a growing awareness of elements of form, the young choreographer may lack the insight to make adequate use of his movement medium. Each new approach to composition will enrich the experience of the student choreographer, given the necessary guidance in evaluating the results.

Performing his compositions for others enables the choreographer to share his creative results and to test his communicative powers. Performances, if they are to fulfill their educative purposes, should not be looked upon merely as forms of readily available student entertainment; neither should they be used by dance educators to satisfy their personal ambitions as choreographers employing student dancers as private company members—rather, teachers might discover the satisfaction that comes from helping students to find their own creative potential. School performances should provide the opportunity for the students to present to others the best of their productive efforts and should result in a deepened understanding and appreciation—for the performers and for members of the audience—of dance as art.

Addendum

Nontraditional Choreography—

An Alternative Approach

to Composition and Production

As theatrically produced dramatic dance seemed to be reaching its zenith, a new generation of dancers began searching for fresh approaches to choreography. For those "postmoderns," as they were called, the motivating idea for their choreography was the creative process itself. Characteristically, such creative experimentation resulted in a variety of unique dance forms that have shared in common mainly the choreographers' expressed desire to move away from established tradition and at times similar modes of exploration.

Improvisation and Chance as a Basis for Choreography

Following Cunningham's lead, many of his disciples have continued to use the concept of chance as the format for their dances. Through various creative means the choreographer arrives at chance determinants that dictate such elements as the number of dancers, the order and timing of their entrances and exits, directions of their movement, specific bodily coordinations and locomotor activities, timing and dynamics of the movements, and so forth. Such chance determinants can create extremely challenging unanticipated situations for the dancers but also reveal movement and choreographic possibilities that the choreographer himself might never have imagined.

Improvisation has also been used increasingly as a means by which choreographic forms have been evolved. By setting specific movement challenges and restrictions the choreographer guides the direction of the improvisation. Such directives might include manipulating basic movement elements—time, direction, shape, dynamics—or the use of action words or props, or assignment of certain pedestrian tasks drawn from everyday life. Or the directives might have to do with interrelationships of people such as in contact improvisation, in which motivation for a dancer's movement results from physical contact with another dancer, or the weight of one dancer's body is supported by another in constantly changing relationships.

Most choreographers choose to use improvisation as a source from which to select successful movement combinations and dancer relationships. They then set the dance structure so that it can be repeated. Others prefer to leave a portion of their compositions unset, allowing the dancers freedom to continue to improvise. This practice can add an element of excitement to each performance as the dancers share the immediacy of the creative process with their audience. However, with several dancers on stage at once, each performing difficult complex movements through space to indeterminate timing, the practice of leaving the total choreography to chance can sometimes lead to unforeseen problems.

Minimalist Choreography

The concept of "minimalism" that has pervaded other arts such as painting and sculpture is also evidenced in postmodern choreography. In spite of the vast pool of highly trained dancers available to them, many postmoderns have deliberately chosen to avoid technically challenging movements in favor of movements that anyone can do. Often professional dancers and non-dancers have been combined in the same pieces (Yvonne Rainer, Steve Paxton). Everyday pedestrian activities such as walking, sitting, dressing, undressing, eating, talking, or moving objects from one place to another have all provided the substance for postmodern choreography (Paxton, Anna Halprin). Not all postmodern dances are technically simple, however. Paralleling the use of negative space in visual arts and moments of silence in modern music, active moments of stillness for some postmodern choreographers have become as important as movement itself. Another manifestation of minimalism has been evidenced in dances that employ a single movement motif that is endlessly repeated with only minor variation.

As a further means of minimizing theatricality, dance costumes have been reduced to everyday street wear. Or, sometimes, the dancers have appeared with no clothing at all. Music or other accompaniment might be eliminated or used sporadically, without seeming particularly essential to the dance. In part, because much modern music has been composed with no real beginning, middle, or ending, dances using this type of music as accompaniment give the viewers a similar sense of nonstructure and usually end by simply fading away.

Minimalist choreographers as well as minimalist and pop-artist painters and sculptors seem to be attempting to sensitize the viewer to everyday images and movements that continually surround our lives. There is an equal validity of everything. They may also be attempting to prove to us that "less is more."

Environmental Dances

As a means of separating themselves from traditional theater with its built-in restrictions created by a proscenium arch, some postmoderns experimented first with choreographing for theater-in-the-round in which viewers are seated on all sides. Others expanded the traditional theater performing area to include the audience with whom the dancer freely interacted (Halprin). Finally, leaving the theater environment altogether, some choreographers have chosen to use buildings designed for other purposes, such as museums, notably the Guggenheim Museum with its interior spiraling galleries (Meredith Monk). Others have climbed walls, used rooftops (Trisha Brown), or have continually shifted their dance environments, moving their audiences with them in the process (Monk). Natural settings such as parks, beaches, and even city streets have also served as performance areas. Each different environment has opened new creative challenges and possibilities for choreographic experimentation.

Multimedia Dances

Quite in contrast to the minimalists, another group of postmoderns have chosen to use different media or sensory experiences simultaneously within a given compositional form (Monk). These multimedia choreographers do not necessarily aim to combine their varied sensory stimuli for the purpose of creating a single effect of "total theater" as in the works of Alwin Nikolais. To the contrary, multimedia choreographers sometimes purposely juxtapose seemingly unrelated sounds, words, dance movements, slide projections, and so forth for the provocative effects such unexpected juxtapositions may produce.

A general rule for postmodern choreography has been that there are no rules. Everyone is free to experiment and to discover new choreographic possibilities. Audiences must be prepared to participate in the creative process (at least vicariously) and to share in the ultimate evaluations of the choreographic results. Young choreographers may wish to try some of these creative ideas for themselves or to develop ideas of their own. Undoubtedly not all creative experimentation is successful, but without it, new forms and directions in choreography may never be found.

Much postmodern choreography has proven to be somewhat ephemeral—produced once and never seen again. Especially as dance environments change and much of the choreographic movement remains unset, there is little chance of capturing such works for posterity, except perhaps on film. For most postmoderns the creative process itself is more important than the product. But that process can be both fulfilling and enriching to the participants and the creative discoveries found therein may provide fertile material for dances of the future.

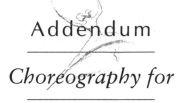

Addendum

Choreography for

Special Movement Styles

and Situations

Ballet, modern dance, jazz, and tap are all different movement styles of the same art form—dance. Generally speaking, the exploration of basic elements of movement and the understanding of aesthetic principles of form discussed earlier in this book provide a sound foundation for all choreography. However, in dealing with composition in each of these areas there may be special considerations for a composition teacher to bear in mind.

Ballet

Of all dance styles, ballet is the one most immersed in tradition. For hundreds of years its role was to entertain the upper classes and nobility. Elaborate scenery, costumes, fine music, and spectacular dancing were combined to titillate the viewers' fancy. In the nineteenth century ballet turned to medieval fairy tales for choreographic inspiration and pointe shoes were added to enable female dancers to appear as weightless sylphs, ethereal creatures of fantasy. Twentieth century ballet inherited these traditions.

Emphasis in most ballet schools has been upon training highly skilled performers. Choreographers have arisen only when individual dancers have had an intense personal desire to create. Such dancers have been rare. Their choreographic training has consisted mainly of observing models provided by the ballets they have seen or in which they have participated.

Although choreography from the past still dominates the repertory of many major ballet companies, increasingly there are choreographers producing pieces that break with tradition. Works of modern dance rebels have also infused ballet choreographers with a new spirit of freedom to invent forms that reflect the contemporary times in which they live. The emergence of many small local ballet companies has made available opportunities for the presentation of such new, experimental choreography. Ballet is no longer exclusively a reflection of aristocratic tastes.

For more than a half a century colleges and universities have provided a home for the training of dance teachers, and, more recently, professional dancers and choreographers. Although curricular emphasis has been largely upon modern dance, increasingly ballet, which can bring to dancers an awareness of line and precise movement, has become an important part of the curriculum. Ballet, as well as modern dance students, are being exposed to classes in dance composition to develop their creative abilities and to encourage those with choreographic talents.

Initially, most ballet students, girls in particular, who have always enjoyed the security of having been told exactly what to do and how to do it, are bewildered and frightened when asked to create dance movements of their own. Even such a simple assignment as composing or improvising to a few bars of music can be extremely intimidating.

Ballet students often lack a conscious understanding of the creative process and therefore are unable to bring anything of "themselves" into the act of composing. For that reason ballet students, even more than modern dance students who tend to be more daring, need to be tenderly nurtured in the early stages of their compositional experience. Through teacher-guided movement explorations these students can gradually be taught to trust in their own inner resources rather than to lean so totally on their former ballet experiences. Ballet students need, first of all, to become familiar with those basic elements of dance (discussed earlier in this book) that are the building blocks for choreography, regardless of movement styles.

Compositional challenges need to be geared to the students' level of creative experience, presented to them in an unthreatening way, while at the same time pressing them to dare a little more. In their ballet technique classes students are constantly pressured to seek perfection. Fear of failure is an ever-present threat. Such students often find it difficult to accept the challenge of risk-taking—of daring to fail. (This, of course, can be true of other students as well.) The concept that one can learn and grow from failure is not immediately appreciated. Eventually, however, the fear that ballet students may have had of creating dance movement will gradually be dispelled as their movement vocabulary is expanded and they become kinesthetically attuned to the very act of movement itself.

The last "security blanket" for some ballet students to relinquish is their pointe shoes. Accustomed as they are to the supportive encasement that these shoes provide, some students feel incapable of performing without them. In the minds of some, dance without pointe shoes is not ballet at all.

The choreographer needs to remember that pointe shoes were designed to enable a ballerina or corps member to present an illusion of lightness—of disembodied denial of gravity—or in the case of some abstract dances, to lengthen the line of the body. For some ballets, pointe shoes are not necessary or even desirable. The choreographer must at once decide what kind of footwear is appropriate to convey his dance idea and then to choreograph his ballet movement accordingly. Ballet dancers need to learn to feel at home, not only in their pointe shoes, but also in soft ballet slippers, cossack boots, heeled shoes, and even (heaven forbid!) in no shoes at all.

With traditional ballet, the formal nature of both its subject matter and the social environment in which it was performed tended to encourage use of symmetry as a choreographic means of reinforcing that formality. What was seen on one side of the stage was mirrored by the other. To some students steeped in that tradition, symmetry is the essence of ballet choreography; thus they tend not to look beyond the obvious in search of other choreographic possibilities. Clearly the age of formal living has long since departed; only in religious ritual does it remain. The choreographic use of informal, asymmetrical patterning can open a myriad of spatial possibilities that can add surprise and charm to a compositional production. Some student choreographers may need a slight nudge to break them away from overuse of symmetry and to encourage them to experience the creative possibilities inherent in the use of asymmetrical design.

Ballet as well as some ethnic dances are forms in which the technical vocabulary for men and women is different. While unisex movement is frequently observed in jazz and modern dance choreography it is seldom seen in ballet. Ballet choreographers are fortunate in having built-in opportunities to achieve exciting compositional effects through a conscious juxtaposition of contrasting movements by the two genders.

Perhaps as a result of having seen technical virtuosity in professional ballets used to heighten the spectacle of a performance, some student choreographers are tempted to show off their own technical prowess by devising choreography that is technically beyond the reach of their dancers. This is invariably a mistake. Not only does this practice subject an audience to the agony of watching dancers fail in their performance but it so embroils the dancers, themselves, in an attempt to master the technical aspects of the movement that they are unable to give it any meaning. It can also lead to physical injuries. Simple movement, imaginatively choreographed, beautifully and expressively performed has a much greater chance of success than choreography that is too technically difficult. A wise choreographer will first determine the strengths and weaknesses of his chosen performers before beginning to choreograph. By using his dancers' strengths he can create a ballet that they will enjoy performing and that will give pleasure to an audience.

All student choreographers would be well to keep their initial compositions short, choosing music that is danceable, suitable to their idea, and short enough so that it need not be cut. The use of a small cast will also help to reduce unnecessary choreographic complications.

Abstract classical ballet has always been admired for its beauty of line and exactness of performance. Creation of beautiful linear designs through interrelationships of dancers' bodies can greatly enhance the visual imagery. The danger arises when static picture-making is allowed to become an end in itself without being an organic part of the total choreography. Visual design is most effective when it can be made to appear and disappear within the ebb and flow of the movement. It is not easy at first for choreographers to achieve such effects but the results can be well worth the effort.

Most ballet choreography is closely tied to its musical accompaniment. It is therefore essential for the choreographer to study carefully the structure of his musical score. He must also listen to his music again and again to memorize the tempos and to appreciate the feeling states and moods that are implicit in its form. An indispensable quality in any choreographer is musicality—an ability to recognize musical phrasing—the metrical and rhythmic structures therein, as well as temporal and dynamic changes as they occur. Such awareness is essential in order to coordinate the choreography and the music. If live music is used the choreographer and music director will need to agree on the exact tempos of the music for optimum performance by the dancers.

Ballet students who choose to choreograph in a strictly classical idiom must have a good eye during rehearsals to detect slight differences in body line and timing among their dancers—differences that are especially noticeable when movement itself is the focus of the choreography. As for the dancers, once the technicalities of performance have been mastered, it is their role to project intended mood or meaning—the motivation for the movement—which presumably has been explained to them by the choreographer.

Some student choreographers prefer to break away from traditions and to try their wings making dances that they feel reflect the life and times of their world of today. Although their ballet training is usually evident in the style of their chosen movement, these choreographers should not hesitate to digress from it when the need arises. In attending an evening of student ballet compositions a viewer may occasionally be pleased to see fresh, imaginatively conceived choreography, and not a tutu in sight.

The abyss that formerly existed between ballet and modern dance once seemed unbridgeable. That gulf has narrowed appreciably. Dancers and choreographers with dual training often move back and forth between the two disciplines with ease and apparent satisfaction.

Jazz Dance

Jazz dance in many ways is the antithesis of ballet. Ballet was created centuries ago as entertainment for the royal courts of Europe. Jazz dance is a dance of today of African-American origin; it was born of the streets. Ballet is the product of a long tradition. Jazz dance has no traditional form. Ballet technique is rigidly codified, requiring years of intensive study for its mastery. Jazz dance is uncodified. Each dancer is free to create his own technique and to improvise; it is a form that anyone can do, but some do it better than others. Ballet appeals to the elite. Jazz dance can be enjoyed by everyone—especially the young people of America for whom jazz music is a part of their heritage. Other than Native American dance, jazz dance and jazz-tap dance are the only dance forms that are uniquely American.

Although from the above discussion it would appear that ballet and jazz dance are at the opposite ends of the spectrum, paradoxically a jazz performer or choreographer needs a strict ballet foundation in order to be truly successful. The jazz center relies on ballet placement, and the ability to transfer from parallel to turned-out opposition and to perform leaps are all needed skills that are obtained directly through classical ballet training.

The basic movement building-blocks of all jazz dance choreography are body isolations; stationary percussive movements; level changes; traveling movement with direction changes; and turns. Overlying all these basic movement blocks is the impelling temporal factor—syncopated rhythm. But as is true of other forms of modern dance the specific techniques of jazz have no set form. Each jazz choreographer/teacher is free to invent his own body isolations, percussion patterns, syncopated rhythms, and so forth, and his students may do the same. Much of the discussion of jazz dance that follows applies to jazz-tap as well.

Jazz dance is a byproduct of jazz music; both are reflections of their African origins. Jazz music is notable for its compelling beat that invariably produces some sort of movement response—nodding heads or tapping feet. For the uninhibited, a dance response is inevitable. As jazz music has evolved and changed over the years from one musical style to another so has the jazz dance that has been inspired by it.

Much jazz music has been originated by groups of musicians who improvise together in jam sessions, as they are called. This has meant that little of this music has ever been written down, though much of it has been recorded. As a consequence jazz choreographers cannot study a musical score as ballet choreographers do; instead they must feel the music. It is possible, by listening carefully, to count the measures, identify the phrases and their repetitions, or even to analyze syncopated rhythms. Such intellectual information can be extremely helpful in setting choreography in relation to the music. But by and large, the jazz dancer depends a great deal upon his own kinesthetically felt response to the music, which is seldom intellectually determined.

Although most jazz music maintains a steady beat, the meter can change, often dissolving into measures of 2's and 3's instead of the expected quarter-time. Other accents can also be added to increase the syncopation. Dancers, too, can create their own syncopated accents through stamps and claps and body slaps. Syncopation is the essence of both jazz music and dance. The rhythmic syncopation created by the music is seldom imitated exactly by the dancers. Rather, the two rhythms created through the dance and the music augment each other in a complementary partnership. Sometimes they seem to be playing games as when the dancers freeze their movement to throw the spotlight on the music or, in turn, sudden silences in the music highlight the syncopated rhythms of the dancing.

When jazz dance was first presented in the theater by such pioneer choreographers as Jack Cole, it was given the form of a simple line dance with all the dancers performing in unison. Interest was achieved through the fascinating movement and syncopated rhythms that characterized Cole's choreography. The dancers' focus was generally on the audience. Since these early days, choreographers who followed have found numerous other ways of arranging their dances in space and time. Here are some of the ways.

Among African cultures, even today, it is traditional for villagers to gather in a circle while the village drummer beats compelling rhythms on his drums. Members from the circle, one at a time, enter the center, improvising dance movement to the drumming, each dancer attempting to outdo the other. The dancers are egged on by the crowd and everyone has a wonderful time. A theatricalized version of the practice can be seen in jazz choreography today. Members of the dance company perform simple background movements to accompany the elaborate improvisations of soloists as they emerge from the group. Improvisation is an integral part of jazz dancing, just as it is of jazz music.

A familiar musical form that also encourages the use of improvisation by both jazz musicians and dancers is the rondo form, sometimes called chorus and verse. In jazz music the chorus is sufficiently set so that it can be repeated, while the different verses that alternate with it are usually improvised by various members of the band. The same basic structure can be followed in dance. A movement motif is choreographed for the chorus and is followed by different improvised sections.

There are many ways that choreographers have found to vary the presentation of jazz dance from the simple line dance of former years. Dancers can be directed to occupy the entire stage space as they do in studio classes and still perform in unison. Or they might be divided into two groups that perform in opposition, the opposite group now mirroring the original. Or two or more groups might perform contrasting movements sometimes with different facings. If the stage becomes too busy with everyone dancing at once, the groups can alternate their performances in conversation fashion. One way of adding choreographic interest is to change the people making up the groups, adding dancers and dropping others in unexpected ways. It keeps the audience on its toes. It is also possible to present a jazz motif as a round with the different groups commencing the pattern one after the other at specified intervals. Inventive choreographers are sure to find other possibilities.

While total unison in jazz choreography tends at times to be overused, it can also produce a very powerful impact. This impact is increasingly effective if such unison can be saved for important moments in a dance.

To choreograph jazz dance, one ideally needs to have a disciplined ballet background, an abundance of experience with a variety of body isolations, percussive movements, stationary and traveling movements, turns, and syncopated rhythms as well as with the dynamically aggressive movement style that typifies jazz dance performance. With these experiences as a basic foundation, jazz dancers are then free to create their own movements and to choreograph in any way they may choose.

Ethnic Dance

Dances that are indigenous to a particular culture are called ethnic dances. They are dances of the people unique to that society, sometimes called folk dances. When ethnic dances are performed entirely for the enjoyment and benefit of the participants or for the sake of religious ritual the choreography is already inherent in the dance. When ethnic dances are performed especially for the entertainment of an audience, however, there may need to be some choreographic changes to make the dances more visually appealing to the viewers. Unless seen from above, a circle, for example, tends to exclude the audience if the circle is maintained for any length of time. While they may be fun and challenging for the participants, line dances, too, can become dull to an audience unless relieved by other configurations. A choreographer may need to change the spatial arrangements of the dancers in order to make the visual imagery interesting to those who have come to watch.

If total authenticity of a performance is not an expectation, a choreographer might wish to combine sections of several dances from the same ethnic area provided the movement qualities and rhythmic structures are compatible. What is important is to remain true to the movement style and characteristic movement patterns that typify the particular culture.

There may be times when the typical features of a given ethnic dance need only be suggested. The original choreography is sufficiently abstracted so that only hints of the traditional steps and formations remain. A good example of such abstraction can be seen in the square dance that occurs in Agnes de Mille's *Rodeo*. There are flashes of the square-dance figures here and there, but no actual square formation, and the number of dancers are fewer than would be needed to perform the dance authentically. Nevertheless, one cannot miss the open, energetic movement that characterizes the dancing of western cowboys and their partners as they glide through the configurations of the dance. No matter what form ethnic dances may take it is of the essence for a choreographer to have intimate knowledge of the authentic ethnic material if the performance is to ring true to its ethnic origins.

The music that accompanies these dances can add to the ethnic flavor provided the music itself is ethnically derived. Every culture has its own unique musical style. The amount of authenticity in the dance will determine, to some extent, the amount of authenticity required of the music.

The same is true of costumes. In most folk cultures there may be slight variations in the traditional dress of the region. In the theater such variations may add interest to the visual picture. On the other hand, for some theater situations it may be preferable to dress the dancers exactly alike to unify the group and to enable them to stand out from other performers in the cast. Much will depend upon how many other people are appearing on the stage at the same time.

Costumes may also be dressed up or dressed down according to the situation. When an effect of spectacle is being sought, ethnic costumes that are perhaps traditionally rather colorless and dull in design may need to be enlivened with the use of brighter colors and decoration. On the other hand, when ethnic dances are abstracted, the choreographer or costume designer may prefer merely to suggest their cultural origins by using just a few significant features of the traditional costume.

Musical Theater

Choreography for musical theater may use any dance style—ballet, modern, jazz, tap—whatever is appropriate to the script. But the choreographer is no longer a free agent to create as he pleases; he is now a member of a team that minimally consists of a general director, musical director, stage designer, costume designer, and himself, the choreographer. The general director is in charge and will make all final decisions, but it is essential for all the team members to work together in close harmony if a unified performance is to be achieved. The choreographer must be included as a member of the team from the outset in order to ascertain the role that the choreography is to play in terms of the total production, as well as to make sure that specific choreographic needs are considered in the initial planning.

There was once a time in the history of musical theater when dancers were used merely to interpret the lyrics, to create spectacle in order to evoke applause or to provide diversion for the audience during scene changes. No more. Ever since the days of *Oklahoma* with Agnes de Mille's famous dream ballet, dancers have been incorporated as an integral part of the theater production. Especially in those rare but fortunate occasions when the roles of general director and choreographer have been joined in one person, as the case in Jerome Robbins' *West Side Story* and *Fiddler on the Roof,* the integration of theatrical elements—music, drama, and dance—has been most beautifully achieved.

In musical theater, dance can have many functions. As Richard Kislan in *Hoofing on Broadway* has summarized so succinctly, dance can be used "to carry a plot, establish atmosphere, embody a theme, replace dialogue, generate comedy, or produce a frankly overwhelming spectacle." Dance can say with brevity that which could require pages of dialogue to convey.

In order to be a fully supportive and contributing team member, the choreographer must carefully study the script and score of the musical. Usually the music for the choreography is already a part of the score and will dictate to a large extent the length and general style of the dancing. In the case of an original or little-known musical, a choreographer might occasionally be able to insert some special music of his own choosing provided that it blends smoothly with the rest of the score. But certainly this would not be permitted when presenting a well-known musical.

Before a choreographer can begin work he will need to discuss with the director what the motivation for each dance is to be and its specific function in terms of the musical as a whole. He will need to know the exact stage space that will be available for the dance; number of dancers in the cast; from where the dancers will be making their entrances and where they are to go at the end of the dance. It is also helpful to know where the actors and singers are to be placed on stage. When a cast is large and the stage is small there may have to be some modifications made in the blocking to enable the dancers to perform effectively. Such considerations are sometimes overlooked in the initial planning and become evident only when all the performers rehearse together for the first time.

From the stage designer the choreographer will need to know what the stage set is to be and any obstacles that might need to be taken into account in planning the choreography. The costume designer and the choreographer also need to work closely together in planning the costumes to make sure that the costumes and shoes will not inhibit the movement of the dancing, or if certain movement restrictions are unavoidable, to keep these limitations in mind in planning the dance movement.

It is essential for the music director and the choreographer to be in complete agreement concerning the tempos for the dance music. Tempos need to be set before the choreography is begun. Accompaniment that is too fast or too slow can be ruinous to a dance performance.

A choreographer may not be able to get all of the answers to his questions at once but that is the reason it is important for all the members of the production team to keep in constant touch with one another. As a member of this team, the choreographer should feel a responsibility to participate in the creative planning and decision-making process, rather than meekly taking orders from the others.

Sometimes videotapes of Broadway productions are available for a choreographer to study if he needs help in envisioning how to set his own dances (please note: professional choreography is usually copyrighted). On the other hand, choreography for a professionally produced show may be totally inappropriate to his particular situation, and seeing the video may actually interfere with his own creative thinking.

When beginning to compose the dances, the choreographer may wish to create all of the dance movement himself. He may, however, prefer to involve his dancers in the creative process by explaining the dance idea and allowing them to improvise with the hope of discovering movement in keeping with his choreographic expectations. In an educational situation the latter approach can be a valuable learning experience for the participants.

In addition to creating the dances, a choreographer may be called upon to design movement for the rest of the cast. Such movement needs to be kept simple. Although in the professional world, many musical theater performers are trained to do everything—sing, dance, and act—in amateur productions, most actors and singers have had little dance training. It is also important to remember that singers cannot face upstage or perform vigorous movement and sing at the same time. A music director of school productions may wish the dancers to join in the choral singing upon occasion to add volume where it is needed. Much of the time, however, it may be preferable to have the dancers mouth the words and leave the actual singing to those best equipped to do so.

In any musical theater production it is critical that a sense of integration be established among its parts. One of the roles of the production team is to ensure that there is a continuous flow from the words of the song to the dance to the stage action and so on. Only when all of the elements are made to work together in harmony to create a single theatrical effect can one hope to achieve a successful musical production.

Selected Readings

Anderson, Jack. *Choreography Observed.* Iowa City, IA: University of Iowa Press, 1987.

Banek, Reinholt and Jon Scoville. *Sound Designs: A Handbook of Musical Instrument Building.* Berkeley, CA: Ten Speed Press, 1980.

Banes, Sally. *Democracy's Body: Judson Dance Theater 1962–1964.* Durham, NC: Duke University Press, 1993.

———. *Terpsichore in Sneakers.* Hanover, NH: University Press of New England, 1987.

Berkson, Robert. *Musical Theatre Choreography.* New York: Watson Gupstill Publishers, 1990.

Blom, Lynne A. and Tanin L. Chaplin. *The Intimate Act of Choreography.* Pittsburgh, PA: University of Pittsburgh Press, 1982.

Cayou, Dolores Kirton. *Modern Jazz Dance.* Palo Alto, CA: Maxfield Publishing Company, 1971.

Cohen, Selma J. *The Modern Dance: Seven Statements of Belief.* Hanover, NH: University Press of New England, 1966.

Dewey, John. *Art As Experience.* New York: Meton, Balch & Company, 1934.

Ellfeldt, Lois. *A Primer for Choreographers.* Palo Alto, CA: The National Press, 1967.

———. *Dance Production Handbook.* Palo Alto, CA: The National Press, 1971.

Harrison, Mary Kent. *How to Dress Dancers: Costuming Techniques for Dance.* Pennington, NJ: Princeton Book Company, Publishers/Dance Horizons, 1979.

Hawkins, Alma. *Creating Through Dance* (Revised Ed.) Pennington, NJ: Princeton Book Company, Publishers/Dance Horizons, 1988.

———. *Moving from Within.* Pennington, NJ: A Capella, 1991.

H'Doubler, Margaret N. *Dance: A Creative Art Experience.* New York: Appleton-Century Crofts, Inc., 1940.

Horst, Louis. *Pre-Classic Dance Forms.* Pennington, NJ: Princeton Book Company, Publishers/Dance Horizons, 1937.

Horst, Louis and Carol Russell. *Modern Dance Forms: In Relation to Other Modern Arts.* Pennington, NJ: Princeton Book Company, Publishers/Dance Horizons, 1961.

Humphrey, Doris. *The Art of Making Dances.* (Reprint Edition.) Pennington, NJ: Princeton Book Company, Publishers/Dance Horizons, 1987.

Kislan, Richard. *Hoofing on Broadway: A History of Show Dancing.* New York: Prentice Hall Press, 1987.

LaPointe-Crump, Janice and Kimberly Stanley. *Discovering Jazz Dance—America's Energy and Soul.* Dubuque, IA: William C. Brown Communications, Inc., 1992.

Minton, Sandra C. *Choreography, A Basic Approach Using Improvisation.* Champaign, IL: Human Kinetics Publishers, Inc., 1986.

Nettl, Paul. *The Story of Dance Music.* New York: Philosophical Library, Inc., 1947.

Payne, Blanche. *History of Costuming from Ancient Egyptians to the Twentieth Century.* New York, Harper and Row, 1965.

Schlaich, Joan and Betty DuPont, editors. *Dance: The Art of Production.* Pennington, NJ: Princeton Book Company, Publishers/Dance Horizons, 1988.

Smith, Jacqueline M. *Dance Composition: A Practical Guide for Teachers.* Pennington, NJ: Princeton Book Company, Publishers/Dance Horizons, 1976.

Steinberg, Cobbett, ed. "Composer/Choreographer: A Symposium by Louis Horst, Norman Dello Joio, Gunther Schuller and Norman Lloyd." From *The Dance Anthology.* New York: New American Library, 1980.

Teck, Katherine. *Ear Training for the Body: A Dancer's Guide to Music.* Pennington, NJ: Princeton Book Company, Publishers/Dance Horizons, forthcoming.

———. *Movement to Music: Musicians in the Dance Studio.* New York: Greenwood Press, 1990.

———. *Music for the Dance: Reflections on a Collaborative Art.* New York: Greenwood Press, 1989.

Turner, Margery J. with Ruth Grauert and Arlene Zallman. *New Dance: Approaches to Nonliteral Choreography.* Pittsburgh, PA: The University of Pittsburgh Press, 1971.

Van Gyn, Geraldine and Donne Van Sant O'Neill. *Jazz Dance.* Champaign, IL: Human Kinetics Publishers, 1987.

Index